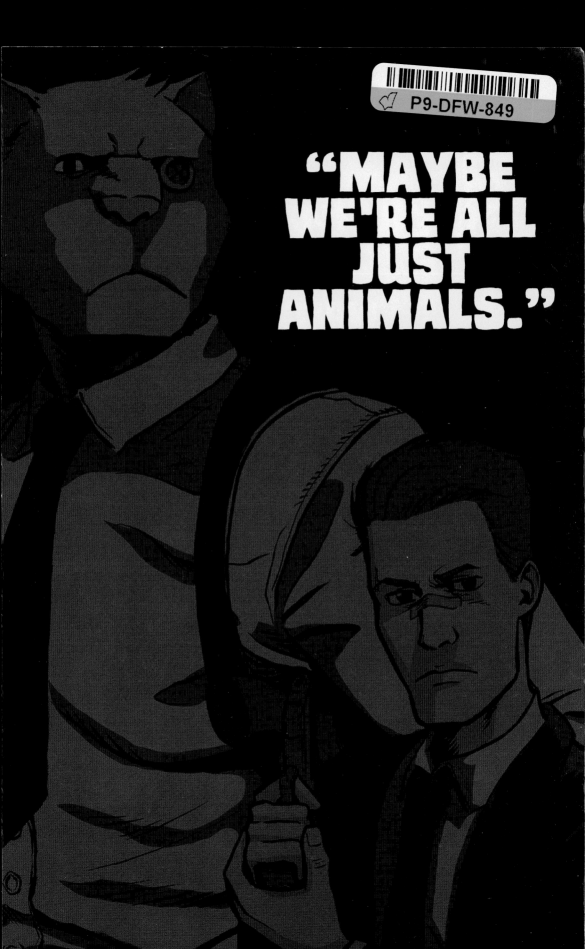

"MAYBE
WE'RE ALL
JUST
ANIMALS."

Spencer & Locke 1

WRITTEN BY
DAVID PEPOSE

ART BY
JORGE SANTIAGO, JR.

COLORS BY
JASEN SMITH

LETTERS BY
COLIN BELL

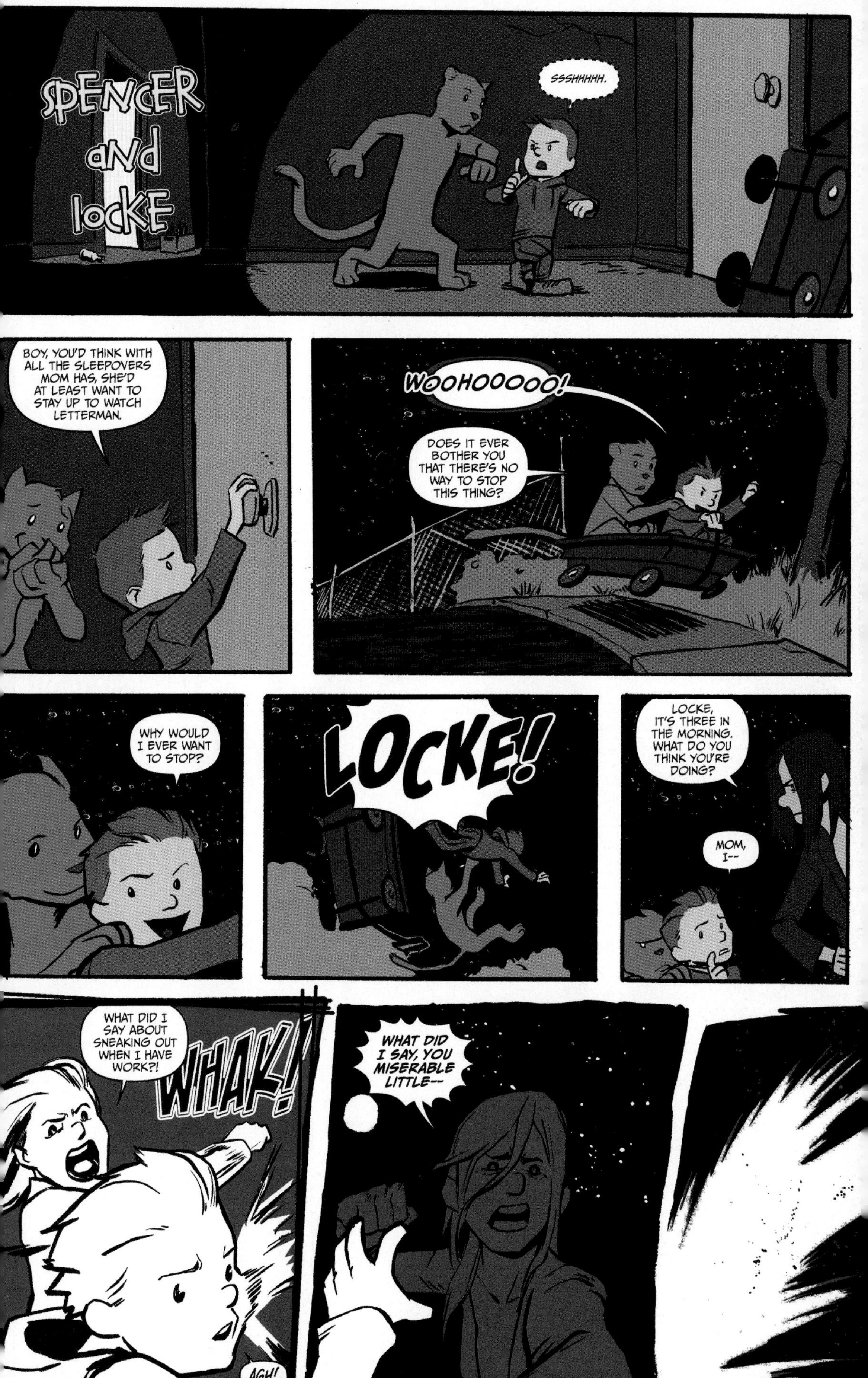

SPENCER and LOCKE
SSSHHHHH.
BOY, YOU'D THINK WITH ALL THE SLEEPOVERS MOM HAS, SHE'D AT LEAST WANT TO STAY UP TO WATCH LETTERMAN.
WOOHOOOOO!
DOES IT EVER BOTHER YOU THAT THERE'S NO WAY TO STOP THIS THING?
WHY WOULD I EVER WANT TO STOP?
LOCKE!
LOCKE, IT'S THREE IN THE MORNING. WHAT DO YOU THINK YOU'RE DOING?
MOM, I--
WHAT DID I SAY ABOUT SNEAKING OUT WHEN I HAVE WORK?!
WHAK!
AGH!
WHAT DID I SAY, YOU MISERABLE LITTLE--

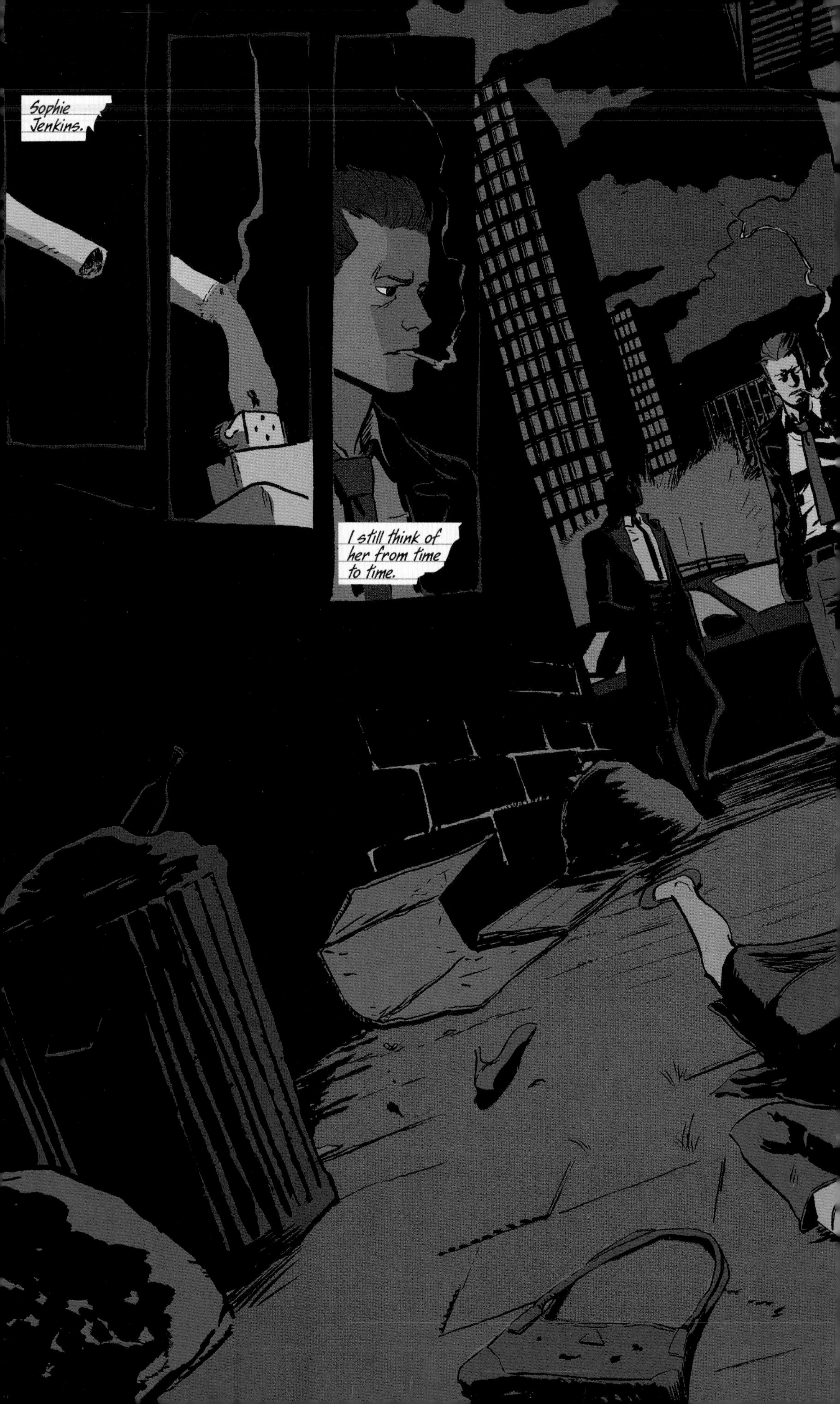
Sophie Jenkins.
I still think of her from time to time.

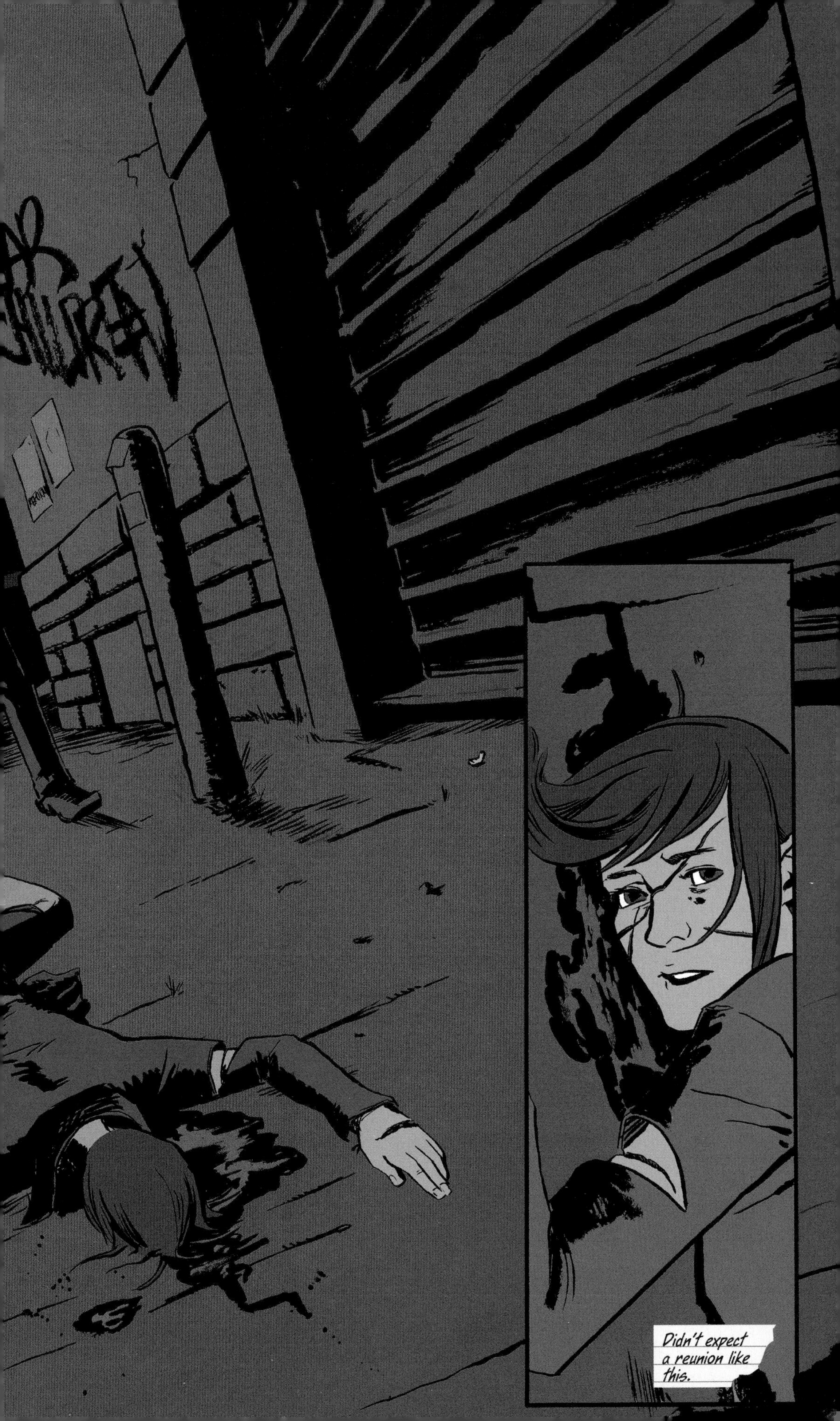
Didn't expect a reunion like this.

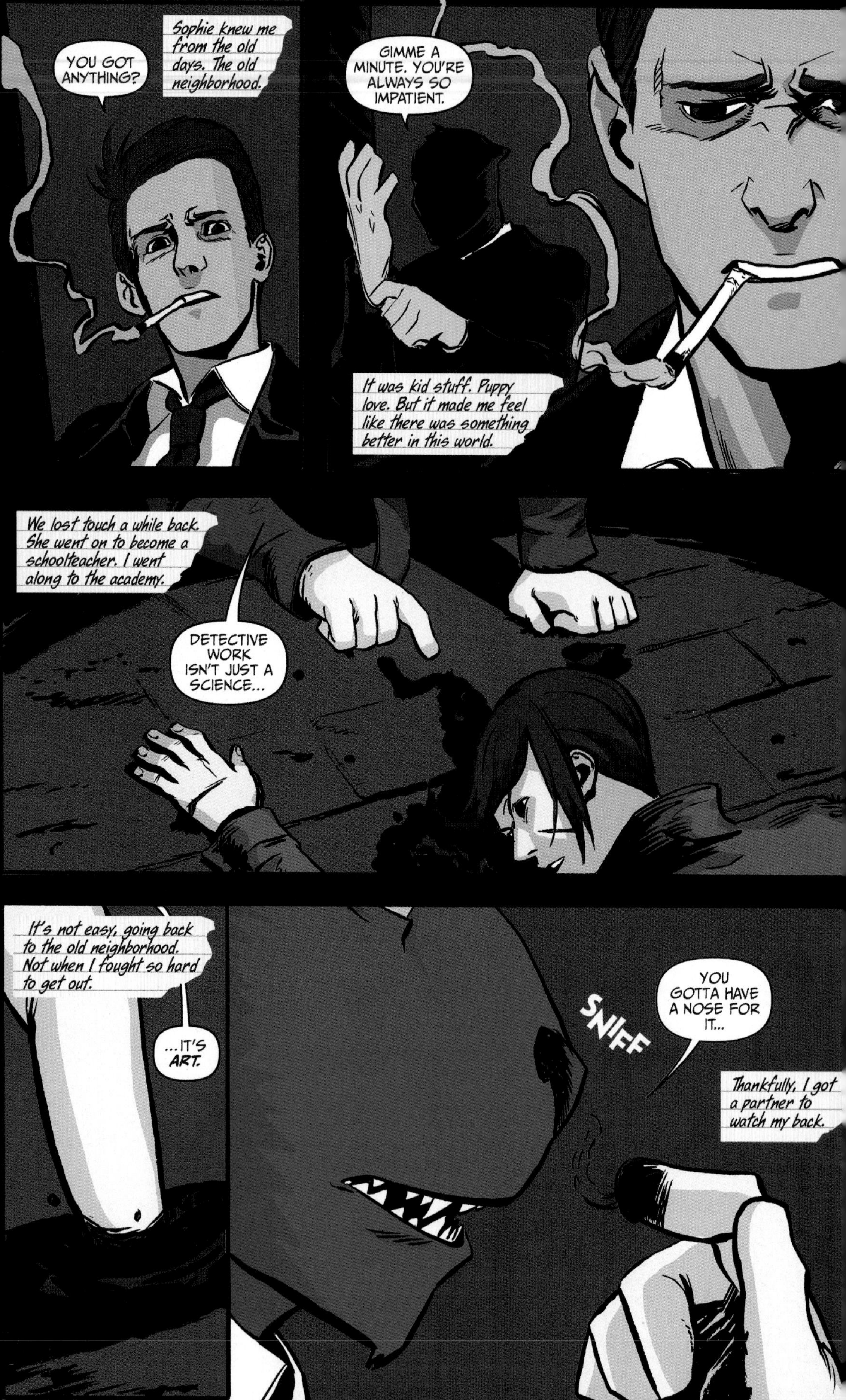
YOU GOT ANYTHING?
Sophie knew me from the old days. The old neighborhood.
GIMME A MINUTE. YOU'RE ALWAYS SO IMPATIENT.
It was kid stuff. Puppy love. But it made me feel like there was something better in this world.
We lost touch a while back. She went on to become a schoolteacher. I went along to the academy.
DETECTIVE WORK ISN'T JUST A SCIENCE...
It's not easy, going back to the old neighborhood. Not when I fought so hard to get out.
...IT'S ART.
SNIFF
YOU GOTTA HAVE A NOSE FOR IT...
Thankfully, I got a partner to watch my back.

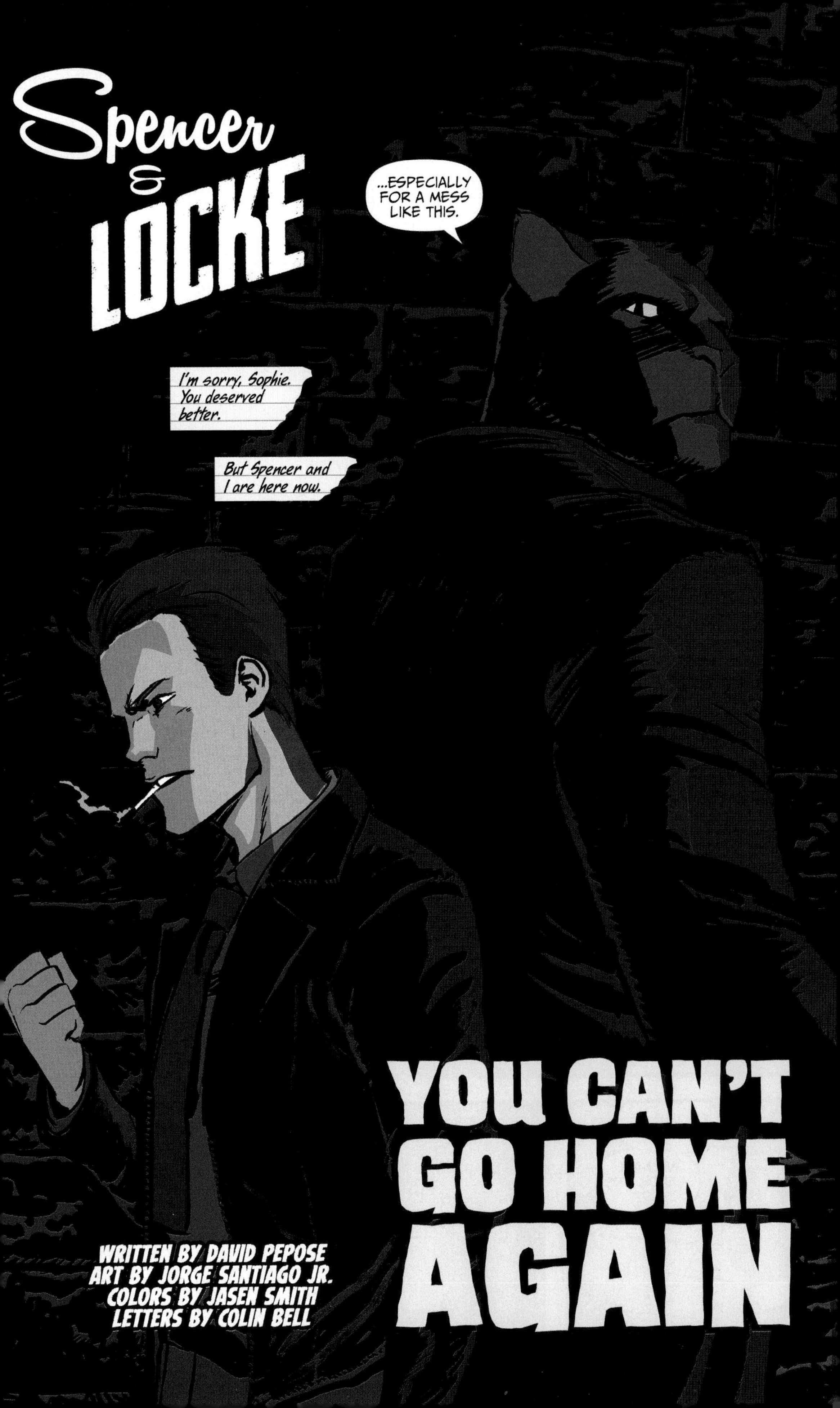

Spencer & LOCKE
...ESPECIALLY FOR A MESS LIKE THIS.
I'm sorry, Sophie. You deserved better.
But Spencer and I are here now.
YOU CAN'T GO HOME AGAIN
WRITTEN BY DAVID PEPOSE
ART BY JORGE SANTIAGO JR.
COLORS BY JASEN SMITH
LETTERS BY COLIN BELL

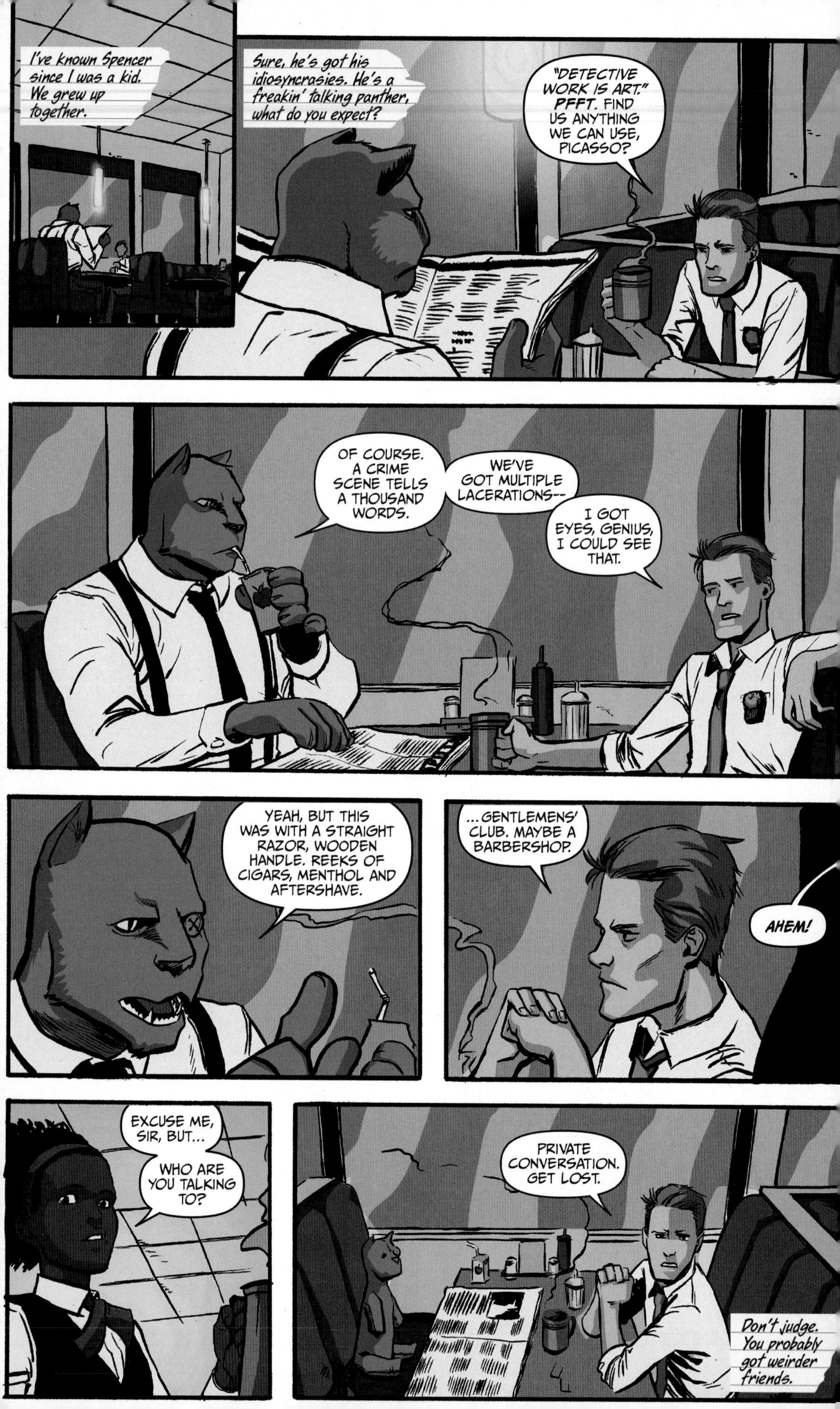
I've known Spencer since I was a kid. We grew up together.
Sure, he's got his idiosyncrasies. He's a freakin' talking panther, what do you expect?
"DETECTIVE WORK IS ART." PFFT. FIND US ANYTHING WE CAN USE, PICASSO?
OF COURSE. A CRIME SCENE TELLS A THOUSAND WORDS.
WE'VE GOT MULTIPLE LACERATIONS--
I GOT EYES, GENIUS, I COULD SEE THAT.
YEAH, BUT THIS WAS WITH A STRAIGHT RAZOR, WOODEN HANDLE. REEKS OF CIGARS, MENTHOL AND AFTERSHAVE.
...GENTLEMENS' CLUB. MAYBE A BARBERSHOP.
AHEM!
EXCUSE ME, SIR, BUT...
WHO ARE YOU TALKING TO?
PRIVATE CONVERSATION. GET LOST.
Don't judge. You probably got weirder friends.

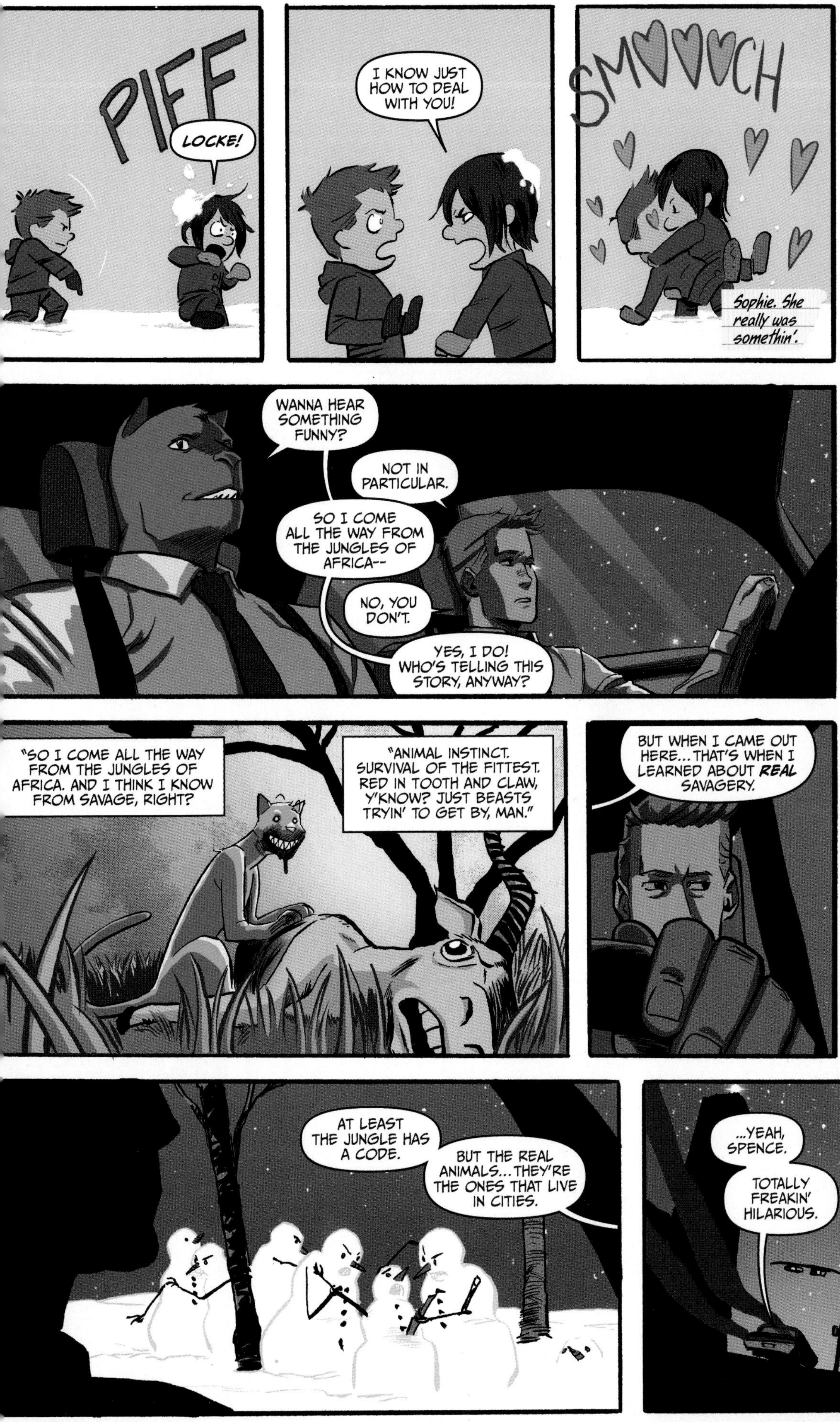
PIFF
LOCKE!
I KNOW JUST HOW TO DEAL WITH YOU!
SMOOCH
Sophie. She really was somethin'.
WANNA HEAR SOMETHING FUNNY?
NOT IN PARTICULAR.
SO I COME ALL THE WAY FROM THE JUNGLES OF AFRICA--
NO, YOU DON'T.
YES, I DO! WHO'S TELLING THIS STORY, ANYWAY?
"SO I COME ALL THE WAY FROM THE JUNGLES OF AFRICA. AND I THINK I KNOW FROM SAVAGE, RIGHT?
"ANIMAL INSTINCT. SURVIVAL OF THE FITTEST. RED IN TOOTH AND CLAW, Y'KNOW? JUST BEASTS TRYIN' TO GET BY, MAN."
BUT WHEN I CAME OUT HERE... THAT'S WHEN I LEARNED ABOUT REAL SAVAGERY.
AT LEAST THE JUNGLE HAS A CODE.
BUT THE REAL ANIMALS... THEY'RE THE ONES THAT LIVE IN CITIES.
...YEAH, SPENCE.
TOTALLY FREAKIN' HILARIOUS.

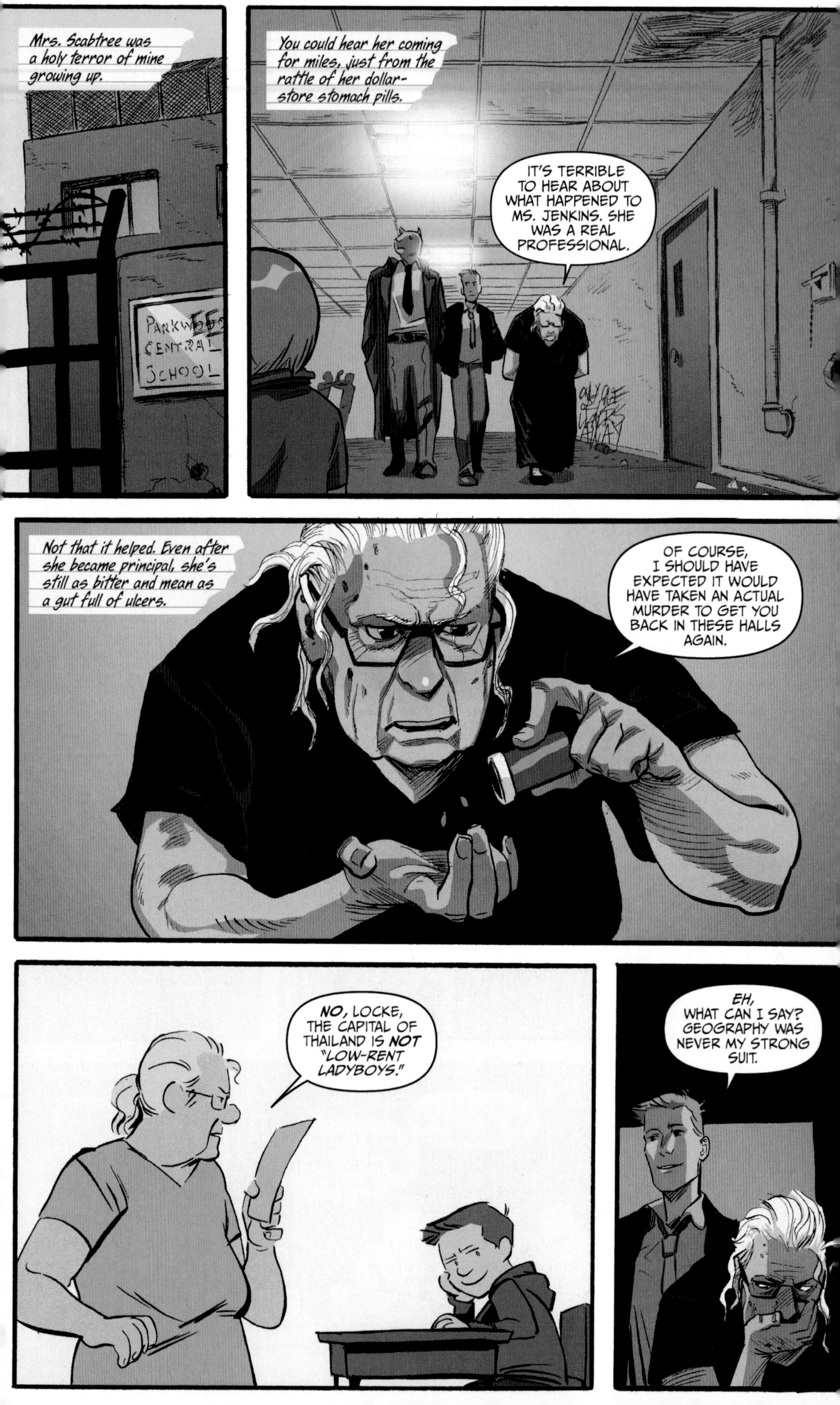

Mrs. Scabtree was a holy terror of mine growing up.
PARKWOOD CENTRAL SCHOOL
You could hear her coming for miles, just from the rattle of her dollar-store stomach pills.
IT'S TERRIBLE TO HEAR ABOUT WHAT HAPPENED TO MS. JENKINS. SHE WAS A REAL PROFESSIONAL.
Not that it helped. Even after she became principal, she's still as bitter and mean as a gut full of ulcers.
OF COURSE, I SHOULD HAVE EXPECTED IT WOULD HAVE TAKEN AN ACTUAL MURDER TO GET YOU BACK IN THESE HALLS AGAIN.
NO, LOCKE, THE CAPITAL OF THAILAND IS *NOT* "LOW-RENT LADYBOYS."
EH, WHAT CAN I SAY? GEOGRAPHY WAS NEVER MY STRONG SUIT.

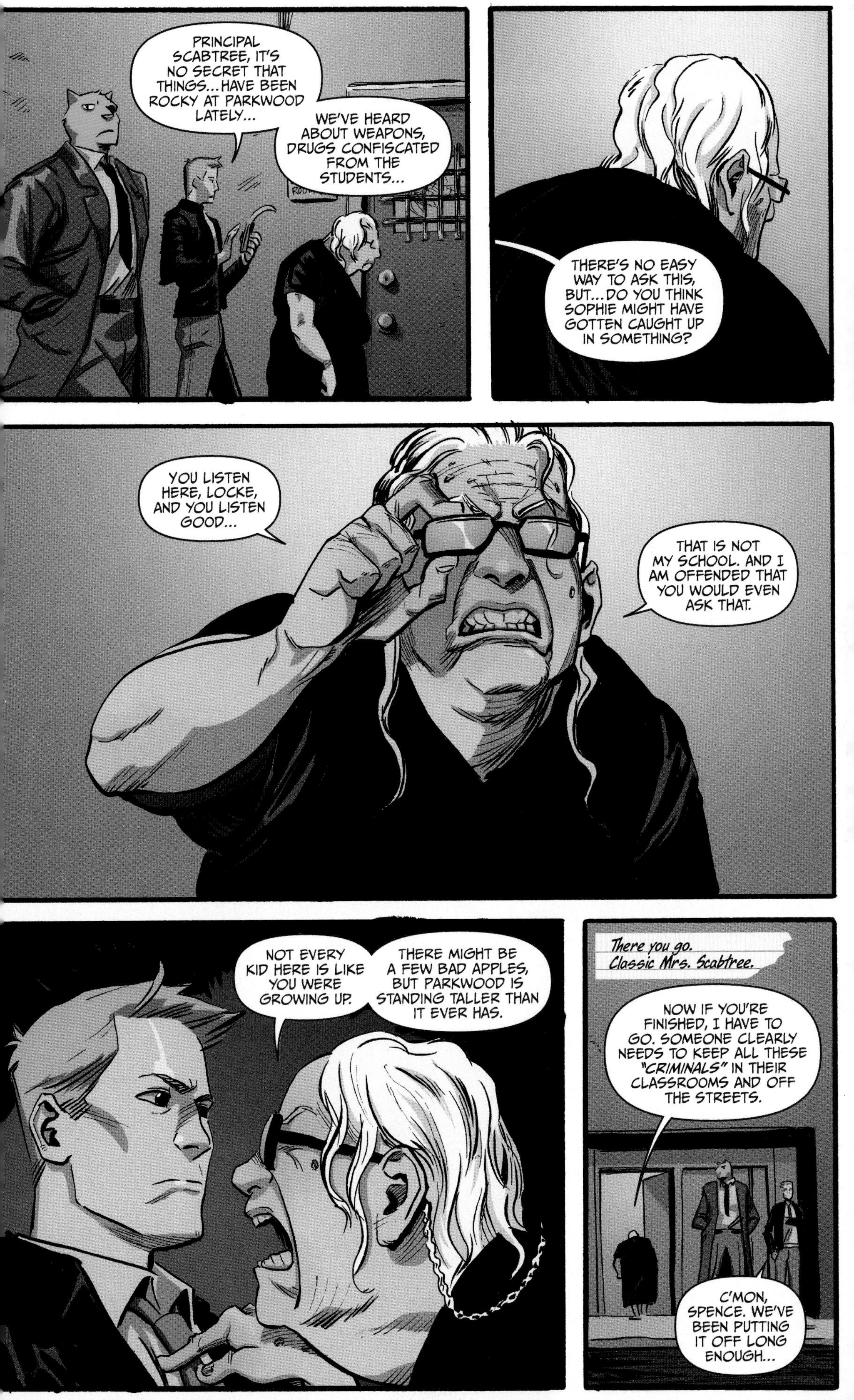
PRINCIPAL SCABTREE, IT'S NO SECRET THAT THINGS...HAVE BEEN ROCKY AT PARKWOOD LATELY...
WE'VE HEARD ABOUT WEAPONS, DRUGS CONFISCATED FROM THE STUDENTS...
THERE'S NO EASY WAY TO ASK THIS, BUT...DO YOU THINK SOPHIE MIGHT HAVE GOTTEN CAUGHT UP IN SOMETHING?
YOU LISTEN HERE, LOCKE, AND YOU LISTEN GOOD...
THAT IS NOT MY SCHOOL. AND I AM OFFENDED THAT YOU WOULD EVEN ASK THAT.
NOT EVERY KID HERE IS LIKE YOU WERE GROWING UP.
THERE MIGHT BE A FEW BAD APPLES, BUT PARKWOOD IS STANDING TALLER THAN IT EVER HAS.
There you go. Classic Mrs. Scabtree.
NOW IF YOU'RE FINISHED, I HAVE TO GO. SOMEONE CLEARLY NEEDS TO KEEP ALL THESE "CRIMINALS" IN THEIR CLASSROOMS AND OFF THE STREETS.
C'MON, SPENCE. WE'VE BEEN PUTTING IT OFF LONG ENOUGH...

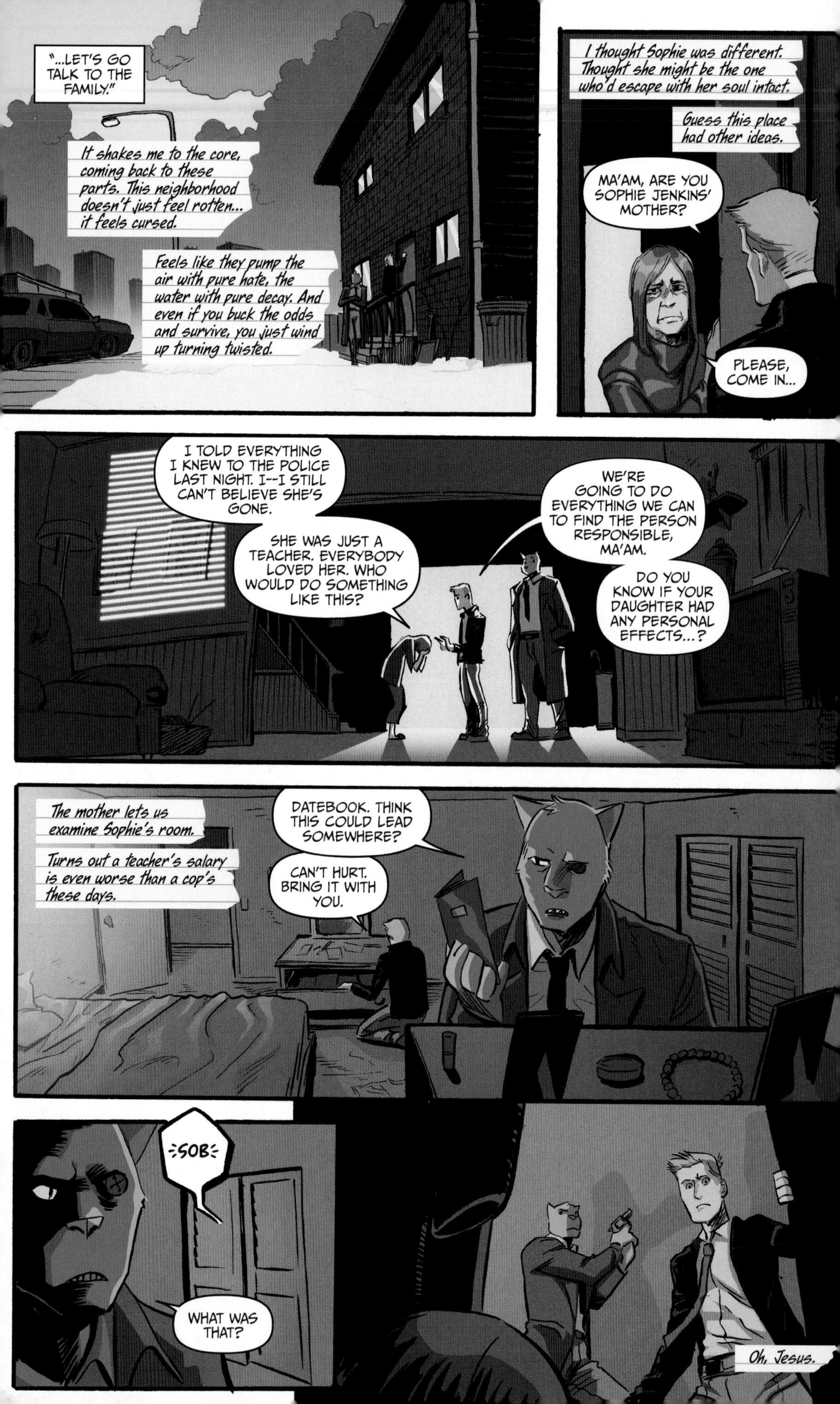
"...LET'S GO TALK TO THE FAMILY."
It shakes me to the core, coming back to these parts. This neighborhood doesn't just feel rotten... it feels cursed.
Feels like they pump the air with pure hate, the water with pure decay. And even if you buck the odds and survive, you just wind up turning twisted.
I thought Sophie was different. Thought she might be the one who'd escape with her soul intact.
Guess this place had other ideas.
MA'AM, ARE YOU SOPHIE JENKINS' MOTHER?
PLEASE, COME IN...
I TOLD EVERYTHING I KNEW TO THE POLICE LAST NIGHT. I--I STILL CAN'T BELIEVE SHE'S GONE.
SHE WAS JUST A TEACHER. EVERYBODY LOVED HER. WHO WOULD DO SOMETHING LIKE THIS?
WE'RE GOING TO DO EVERYTHING WE CAN TO FIND THE PERSON RESPONSIBLE, MA'AM.
DO YOU KNOW IF YOUR DAUGHTER HAD ANY PERSONAL EFFECTS...?
The mother lets us examine Sophie's room.
Turns out a teacher's salary is even worse than a cop's these days.
DATEBOOK. THINK THIS COULD LEAD SOMEWHERE?
CAN'T HURT. BRING IT WITH YOU.
SOB
WHAT WAS THAT?
Oh, Jesus.

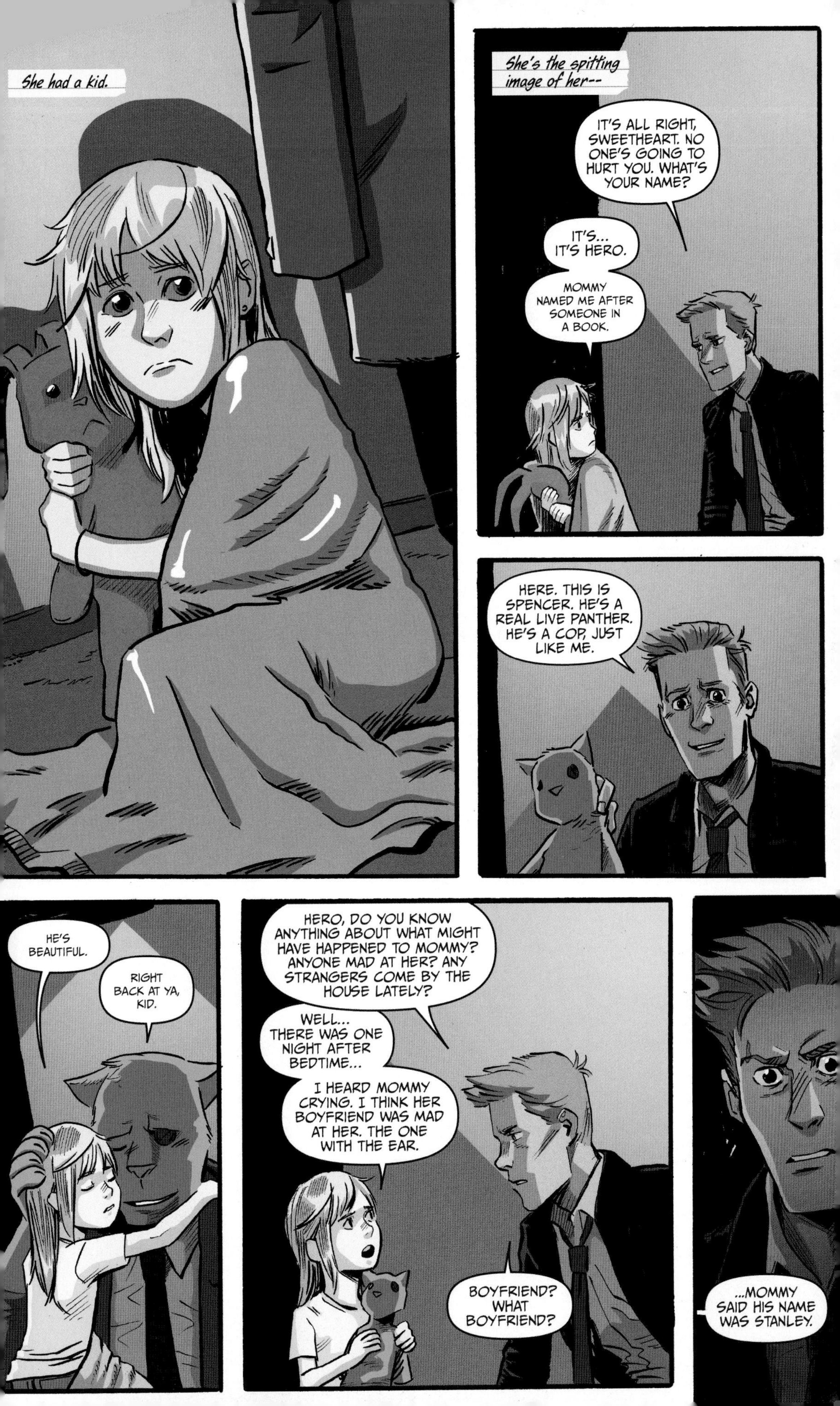

She had a kid.
She's the spitting image of her--
IT'S ALL RIGHT, SWEETHEART. NO ONE'S GOING TO HURT YOU. WHAT'S YOUR NAME?
IT'S... IT'S HERO.
MOMMY NAMED ME AFTER SOMEONE IN A BOOK.
HERE. THIS IS SPENCER. HE'S A REAL LIVE PANTHER. HE'S A COP, JUST LIKE ME.
HE'S BEAUTIFUL.
RIGHT BACK AT YA, KID.
HERO, DO YOU KNOW ANYTHING ABOUT WHAT MIGHT HAVE HAPPENED TO MOMMY? ANYONE MAD AT HER? ANY STRANGERS COME BY THE HOUSE LATELY?
WELL... THERE WAS ONE NIGHT AFTER BEDTIME...
I HEARD MOMMY CRYING. I THINK HER BOYFRIEND WAS MAD AT HER. THE ONE WITH THE EAR.
BOYFRIEND? WHAT BOYFRIEND?
...MOMMY SAID HIS NAME WAS STANLEY.

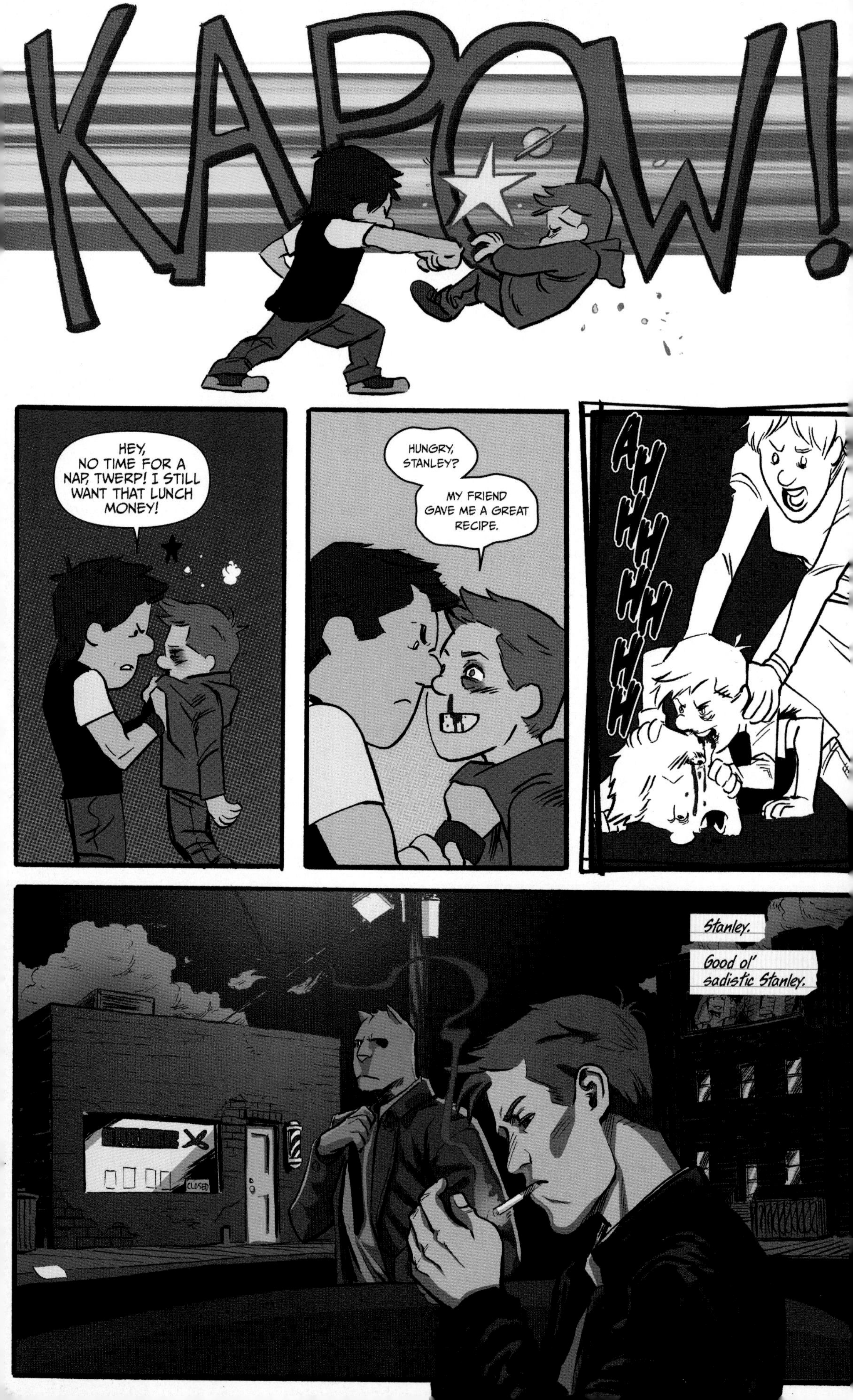
KAPOW!
HEY, NO TIME FOR A NAP, TWERP! I STILL WANT THAT LUNCH MONEY!
HUNGRY, STANLEY?
MY FRIEND GAVE ME A GREAT RECIPE.
AHHHHHHH
Stanley.
Good ol' sadistic Stanley.
CLOSED

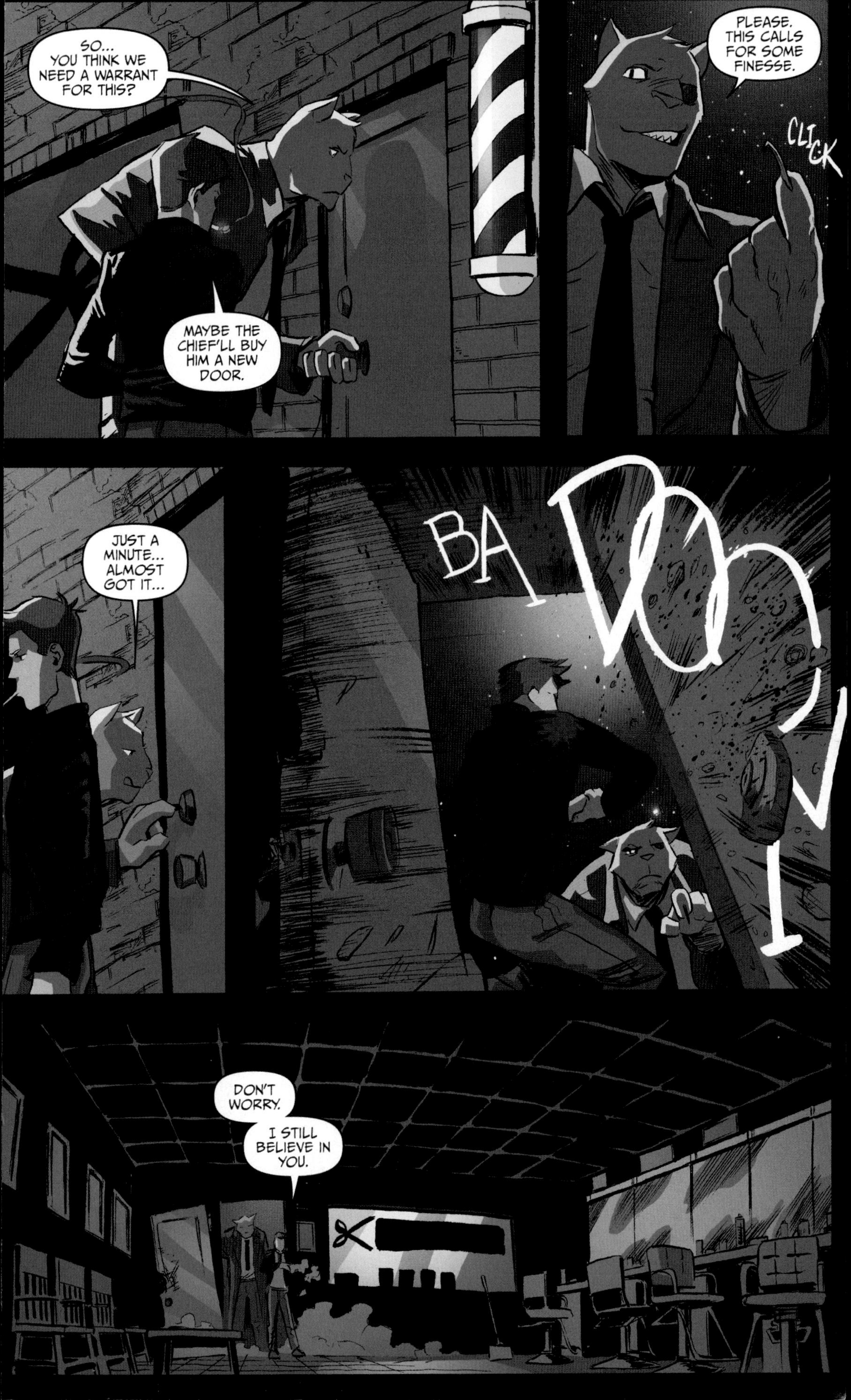
SO... YOU THINK WE NEED A WARRANT FOR THIS?
MAYBE THE CHIEF'LL BUY HIM A NEW DOOR.
PLEASE. THIS CALLS FOR SOME FINESSE.
CLICK
JUST A MINUTE... ALMOST GOT IT...
BA
DON'T WORRY.
I STILL BELIEVE IN YOU.

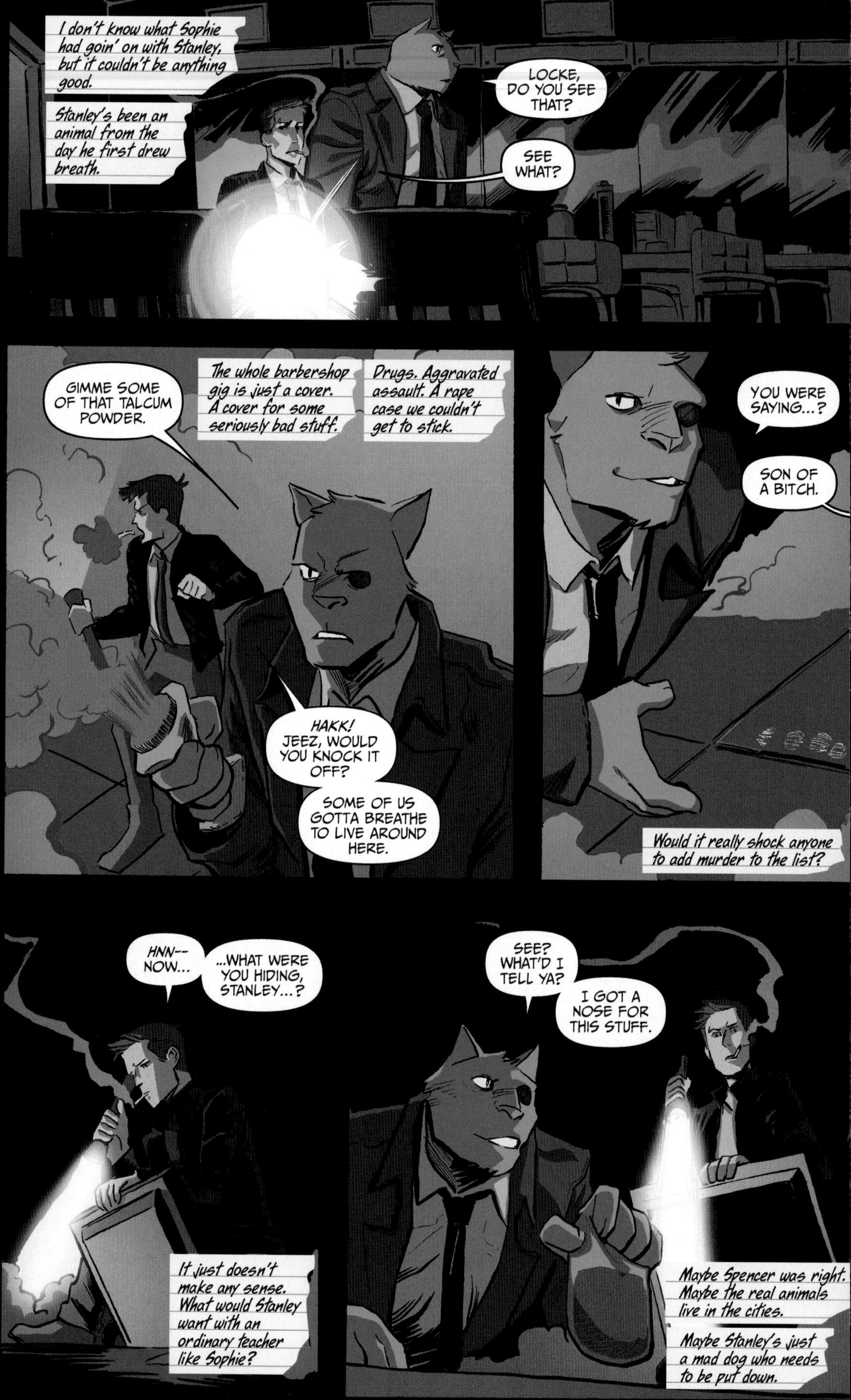

I don't know what Sophie had goin' on with Stanley, but it couldn't be anything good.
Stanley's been an animal from the day he first drew breath.
LOCKE, DO YOU SEE THAT?
SEE WHAT?
GIMME SOME OF THAT TALCUM POWDER.
The whole barbershop gig is just a cover. A cover for some seriously bad stuff.
Drugs. Aggravated assault. A rape case we couldn't get to stick.
HAKK! JEEZ, WOULD YOU KNOCK IT OFF?
SOME OF US GOTTA BREATHE TO LIVE AROUND HERE.
YOU WERE SAYING...?
SON OF A BITCH.
Would it really shock anyone to add murder to the list?
HNN-- NOW...
...WHAT WERE YOU HIDING, STANLEY...?
It just doesn't make any sense. What would Stanley want with an ordinary teacher like Sophie?
SEE? WHAT'D I TELL YA?
I GOT A NOSE FOR THIS STUFF.
Maybe Spencer was right. Maybe the real animals live in the cities.
Maybe Stanley's just a mad dog who needs to be put down.

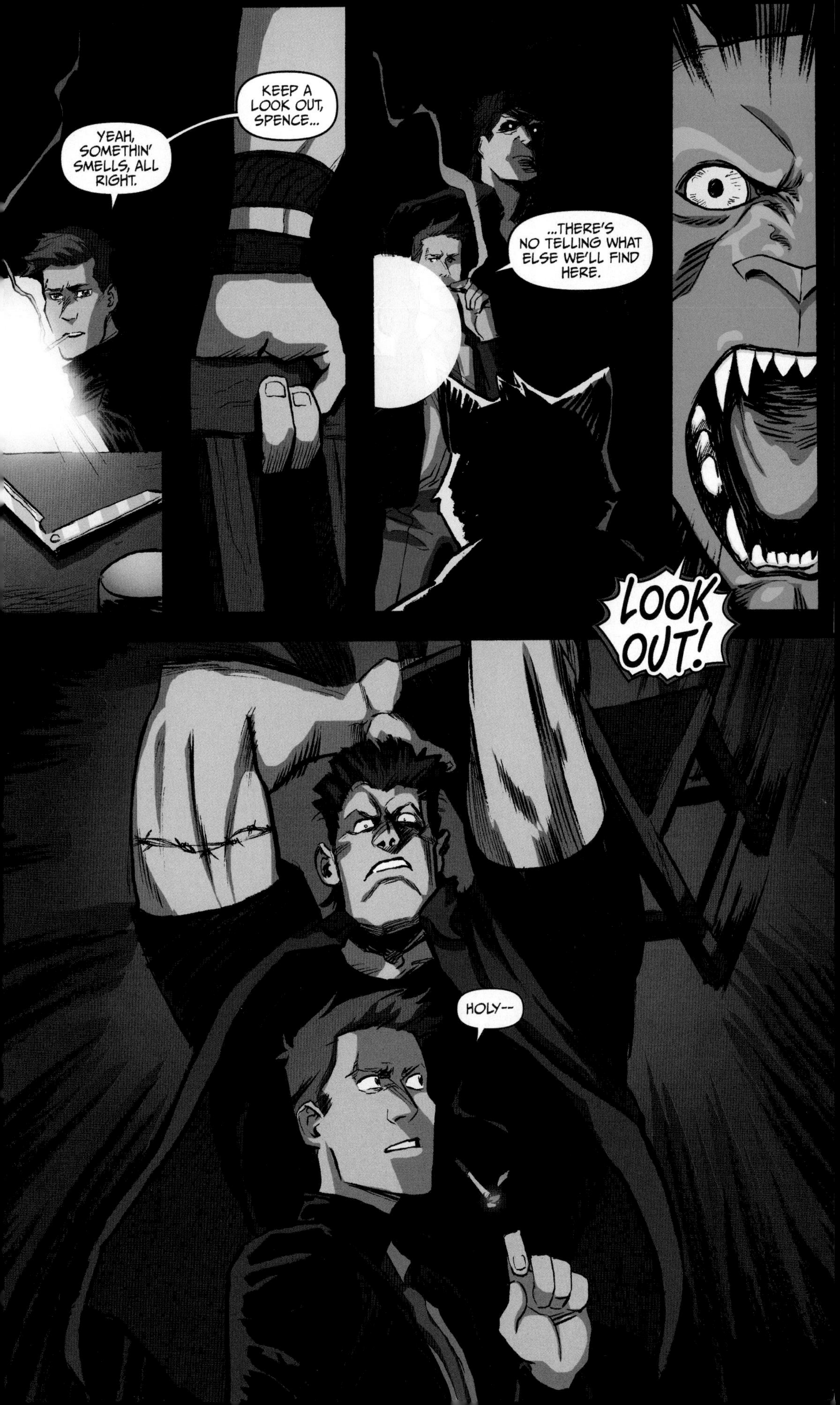
YEAH, SOMETHIN' SMELLS, ALL RIGHT.
KEEP A LOOK OUT, SPENCE...
...THERE'S NO TELLING WHAT ELSE WE'LL FIND HERE.
LOOK OUT!
HOLY--

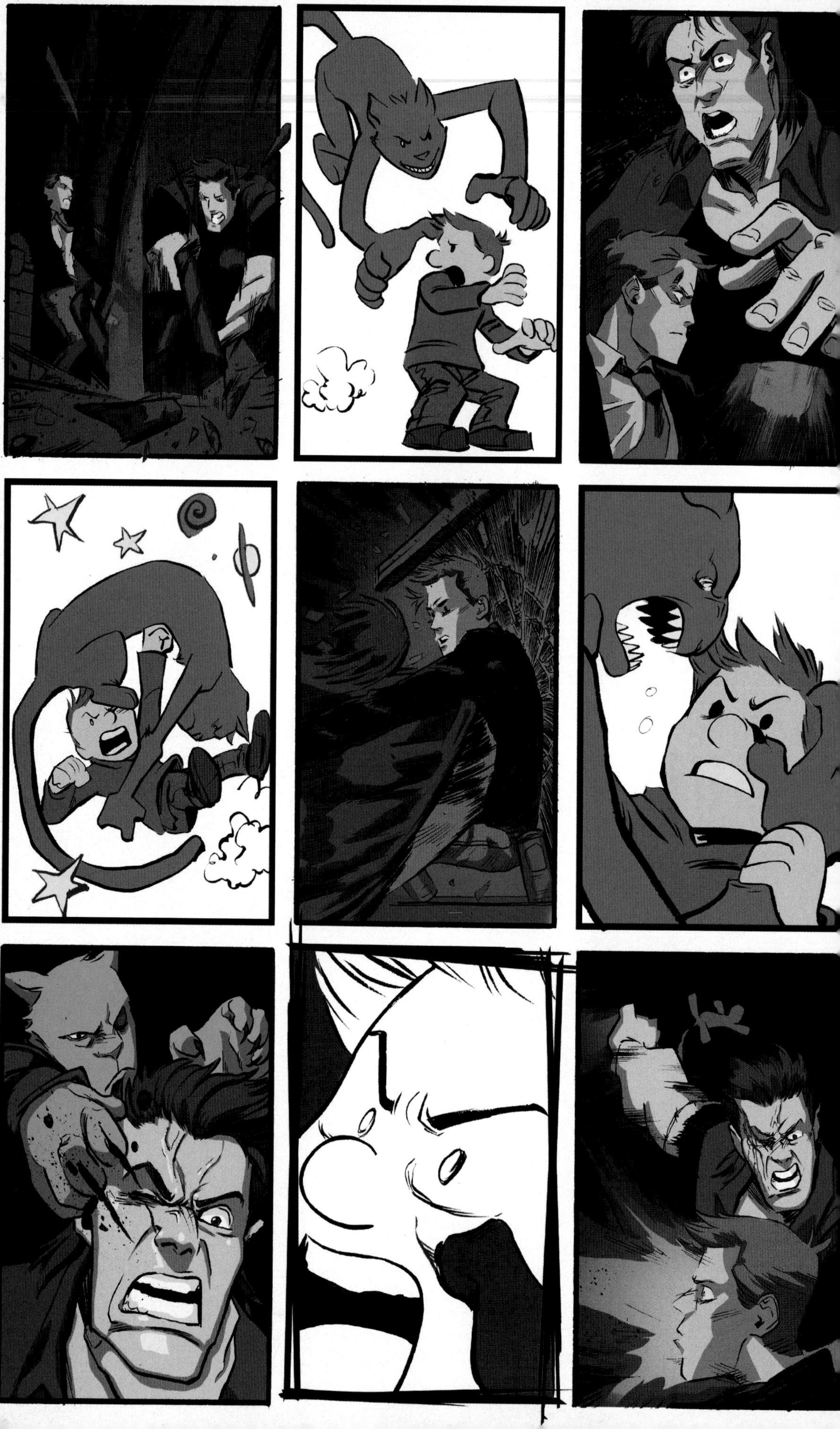

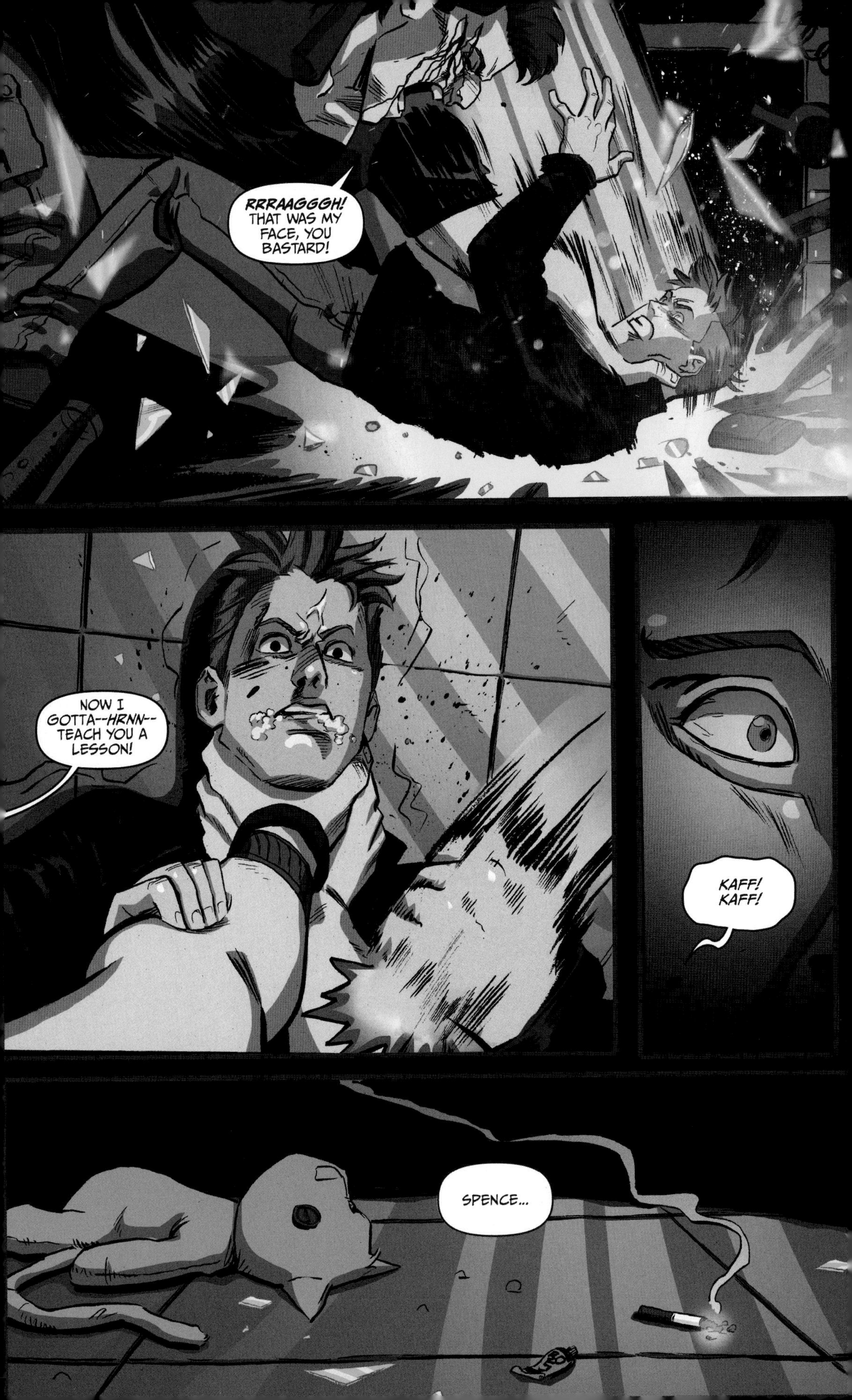
RRRAAGGGH! THAT WAS MY FACE, YOU BASTARD!
NOW I GOTTA--HRNN-- TEACH YOU A LESSON!
KAFF! KAFF!
SPENCE...

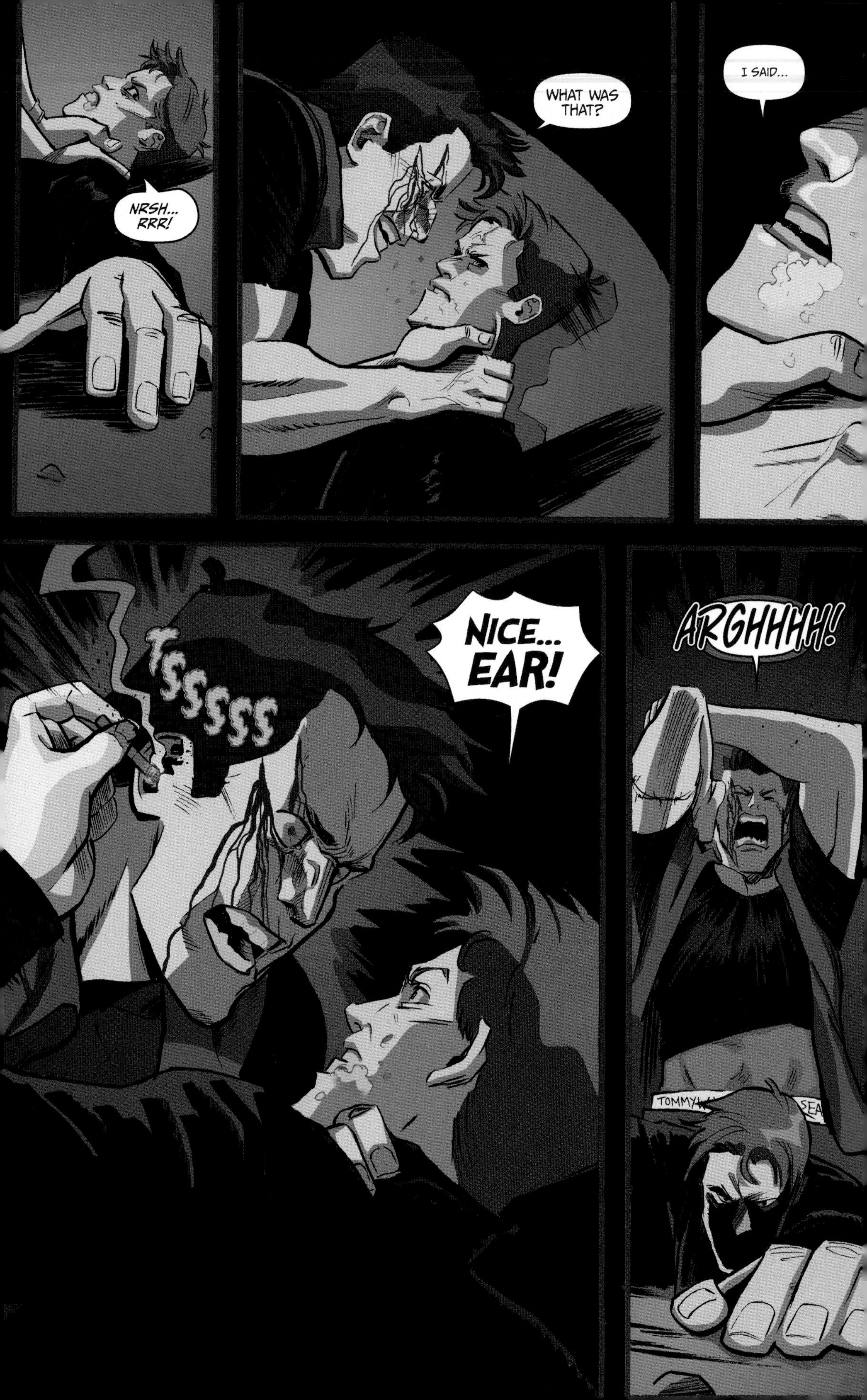
NRSH... RRR!
WHAT WAS THAT?
I SAID...
TSSSSS
NICE... EAR!
ARGHHHH!
TOMMY
SEA

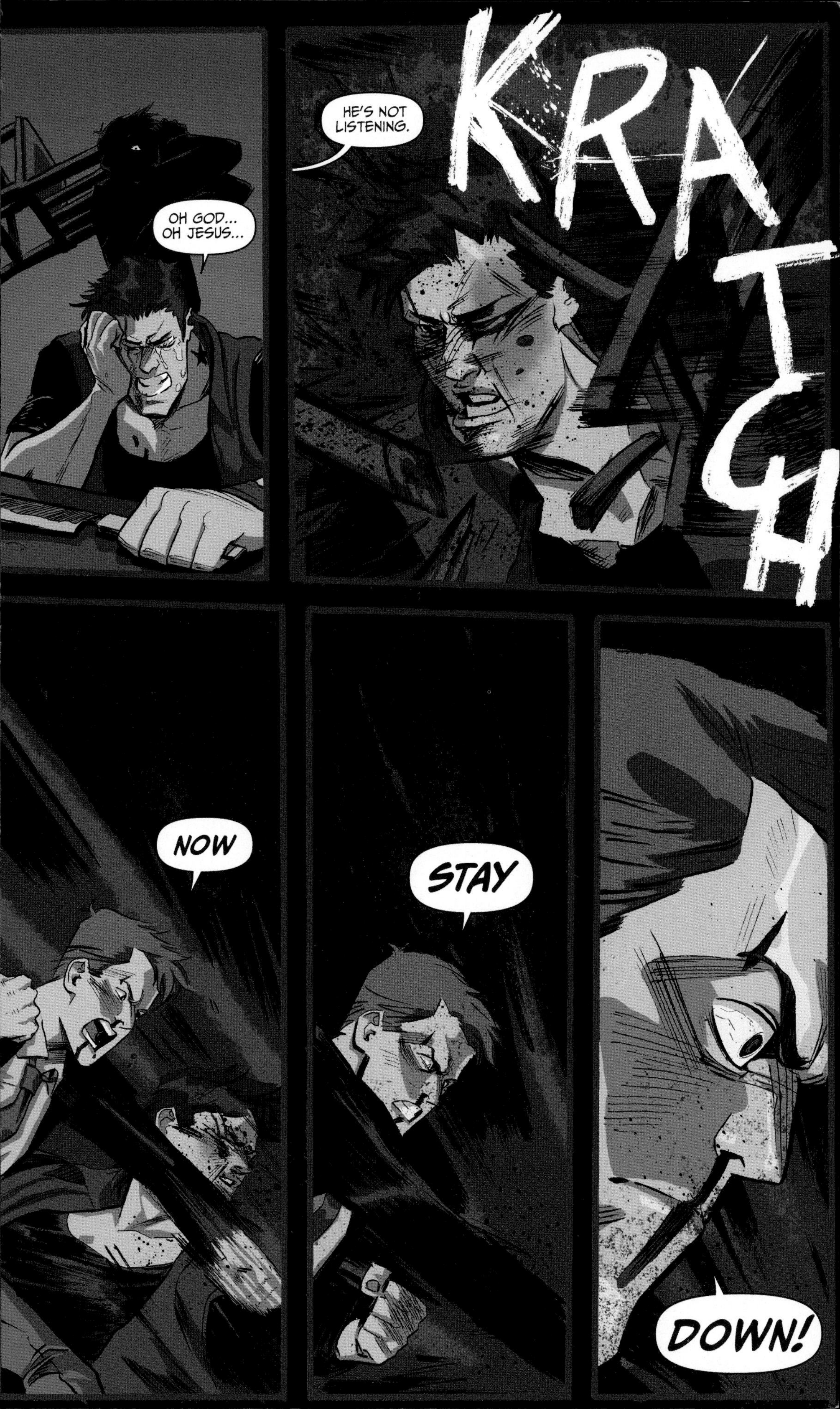
OH GOD...
OH JESUS...
HE'S NOT LISTENING.
KRATCH
NOW
STAY
DOWN!

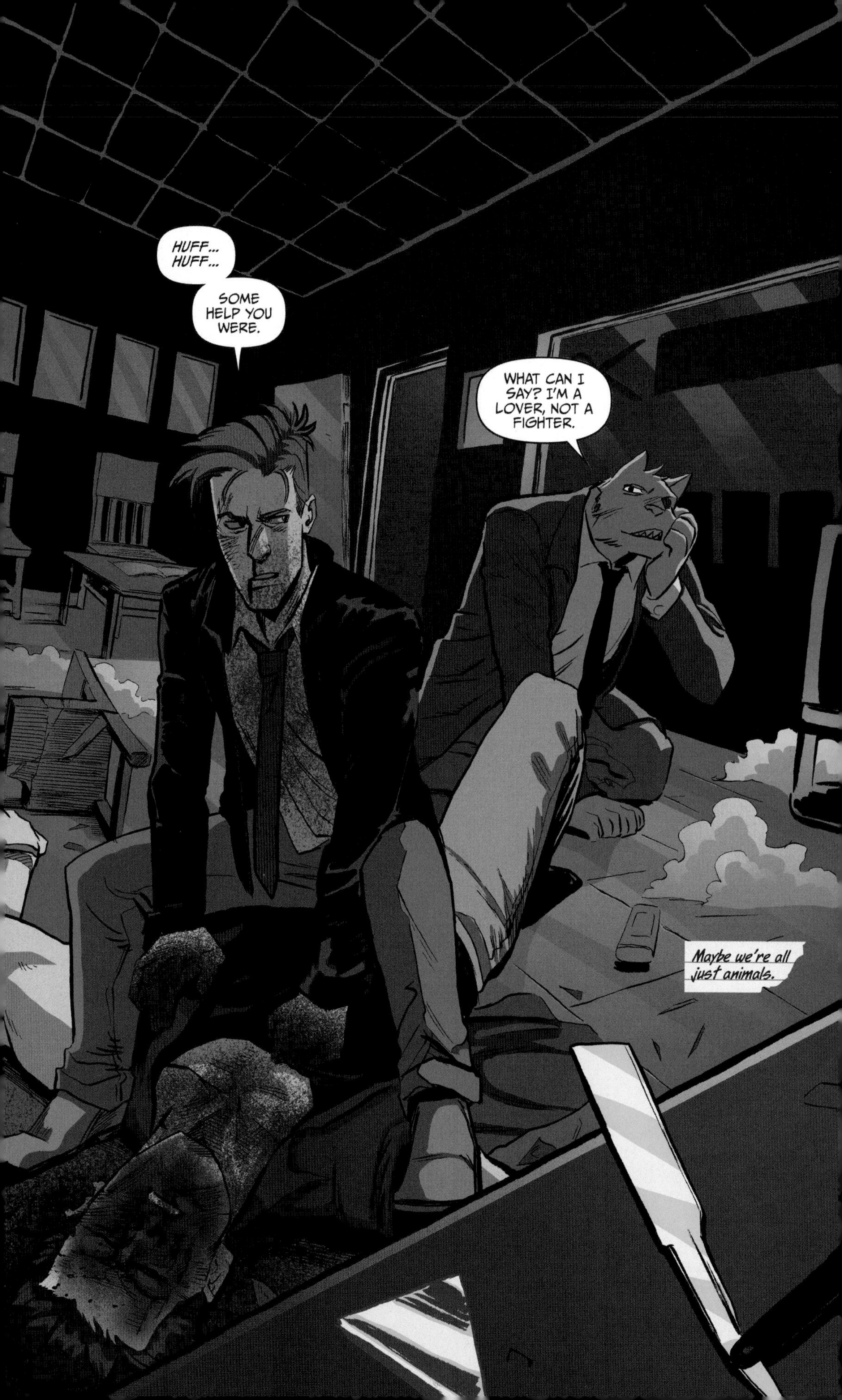
HUFF... HUFF...
SOME HELP YOU WERE.
WHAT CAN I SAY? I'M A LOVER, NOT A FIGHTER.
Maybe we're all just animals.

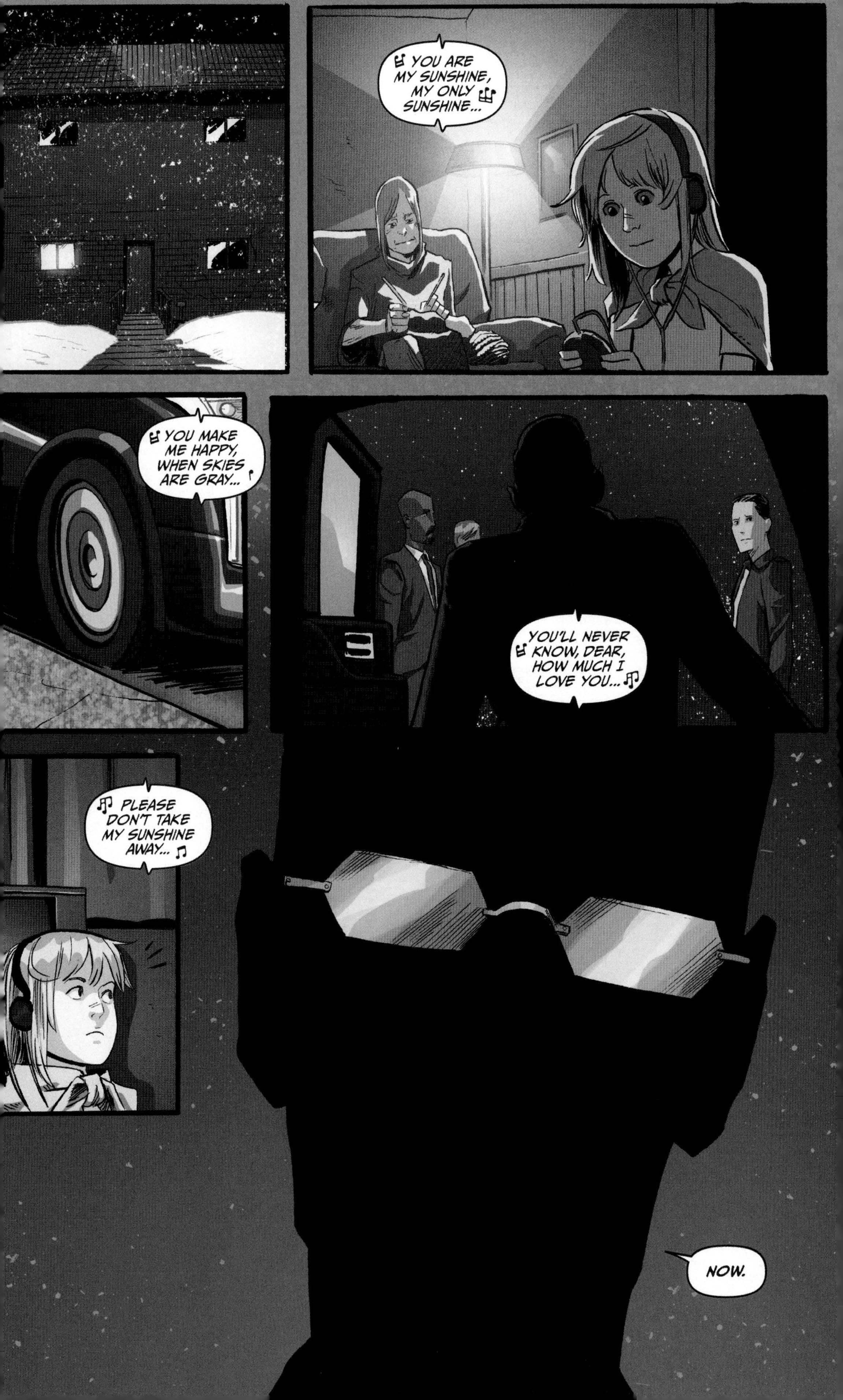
YOU ARE MY SUNSHINE, MY ONLY SUNSHINE...
YOU MAKE ME HAPPY, WHEN SKIES ARE GRAY...
YOU'LL NEVER KNOW, DEAR, HOW MUCH I LOVE YOU...
PLEASE DON'T TAKE MY SUNSHINE AWAY...
NOW.

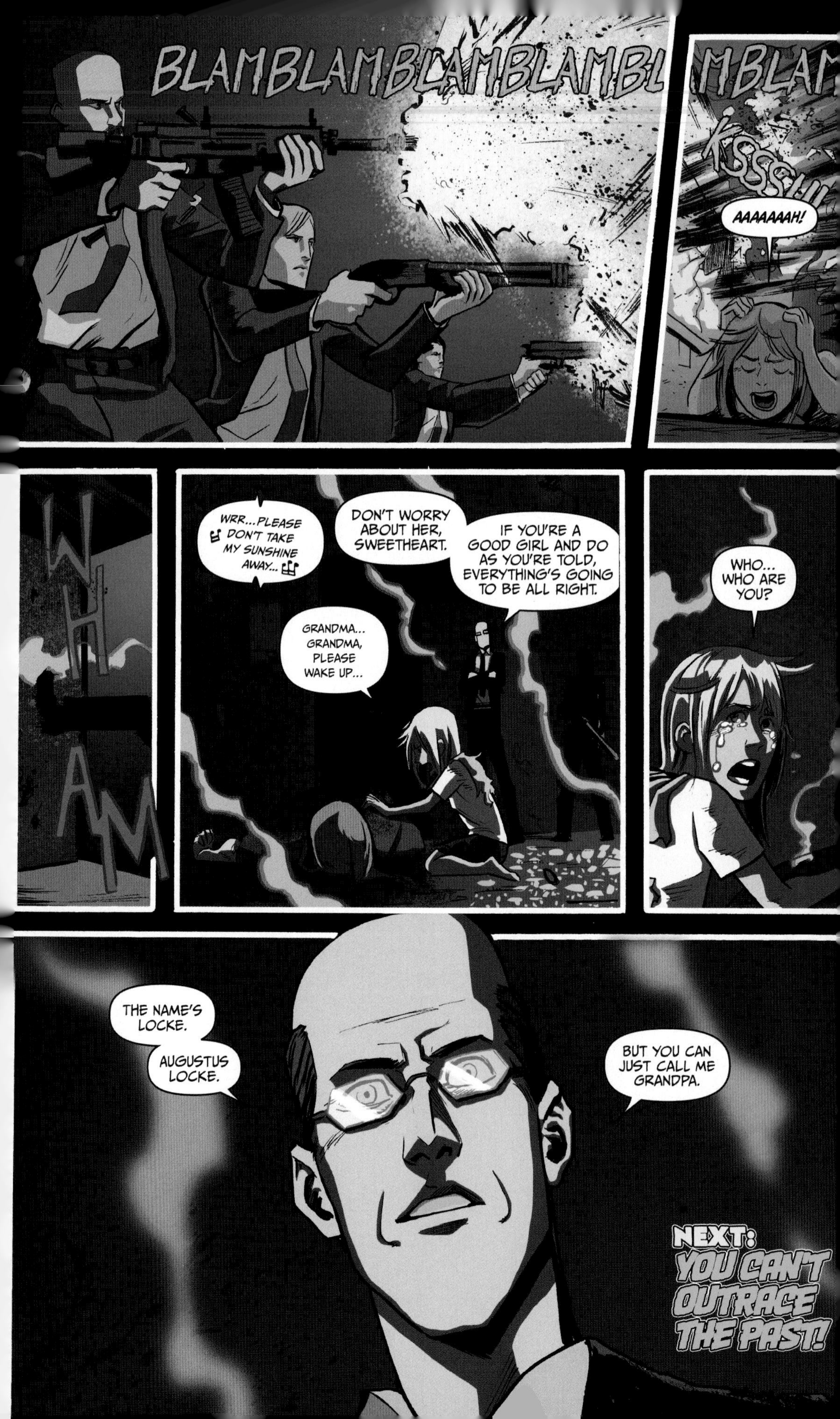
BLAMBLAMBLAMBLAMBL
MBLAM
KSSSH!!
AAAAAAAH!
WHAM
WRR...PLEASE DON'T TAKE MY SUNSHINE AWAY...
DON'T WORRY ABOUT HER, SWEETHEART.
IF YOU'RE A GOOD GIRL AND DO AS YOU'RE TOLD, EVERYTHING'S GOING TO BE ALL RIGHT.
GRANDMA... GRANDMA, PLEASE WAKE UP...
WHO... WHO ARE YOU?
THE NAME'S LOCKE.
AUGUSTUS LOCKE.
BUT YOU CAN JUST CALL ME GRANDPA.
NEXT: YOU CAN'T OUTRACE THE PAST!

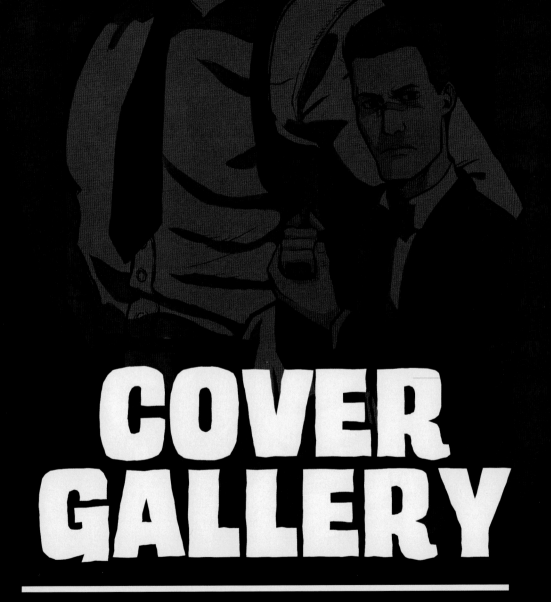

COVER GALLERY

COVER A - JORGE SANTIAGO, JR.
COVER B - MAAN HOUSE
COVER C - JOE MULVEY

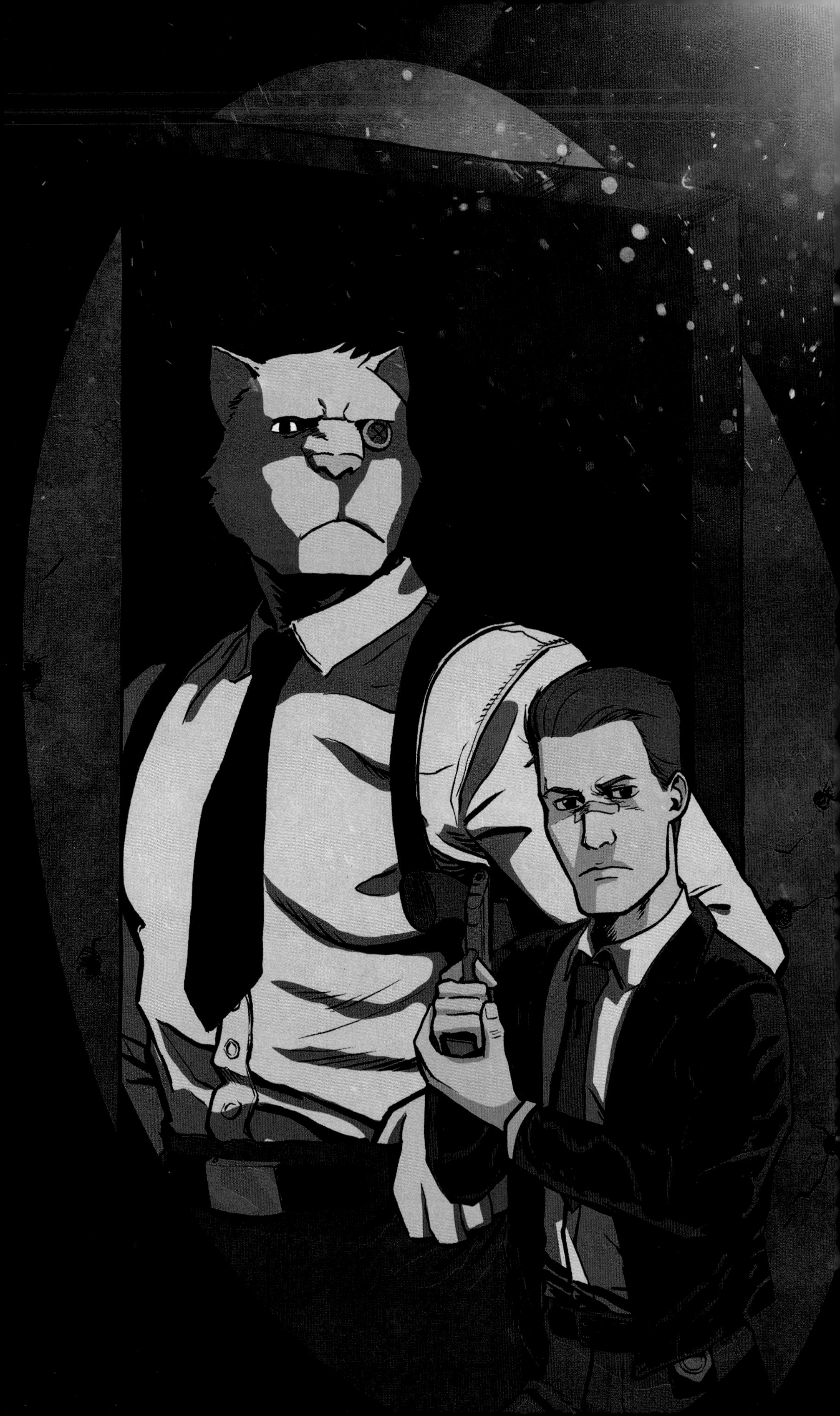

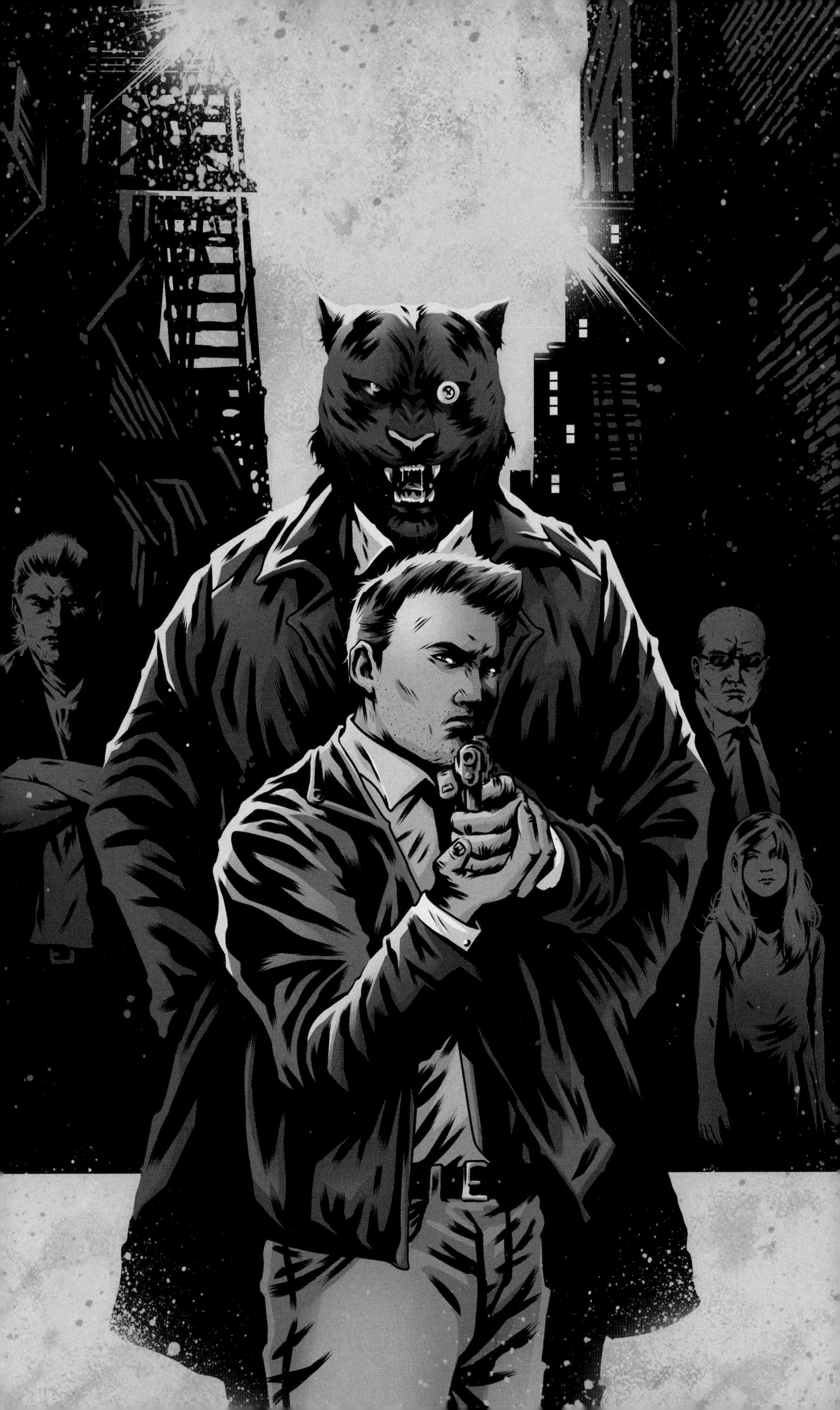

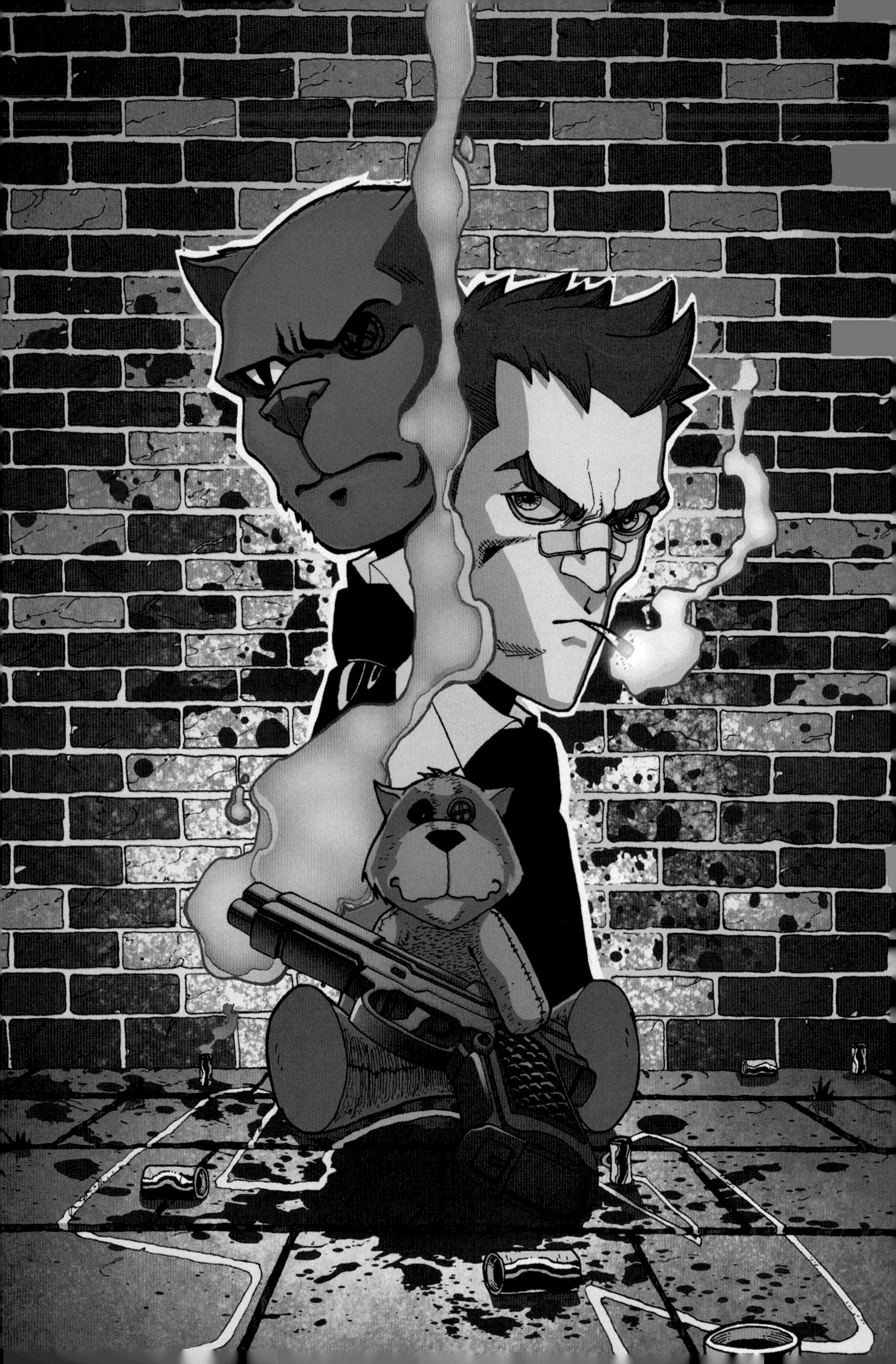

CHARACTER DESIGNS

BY JORGE SANTIAGO, JR.

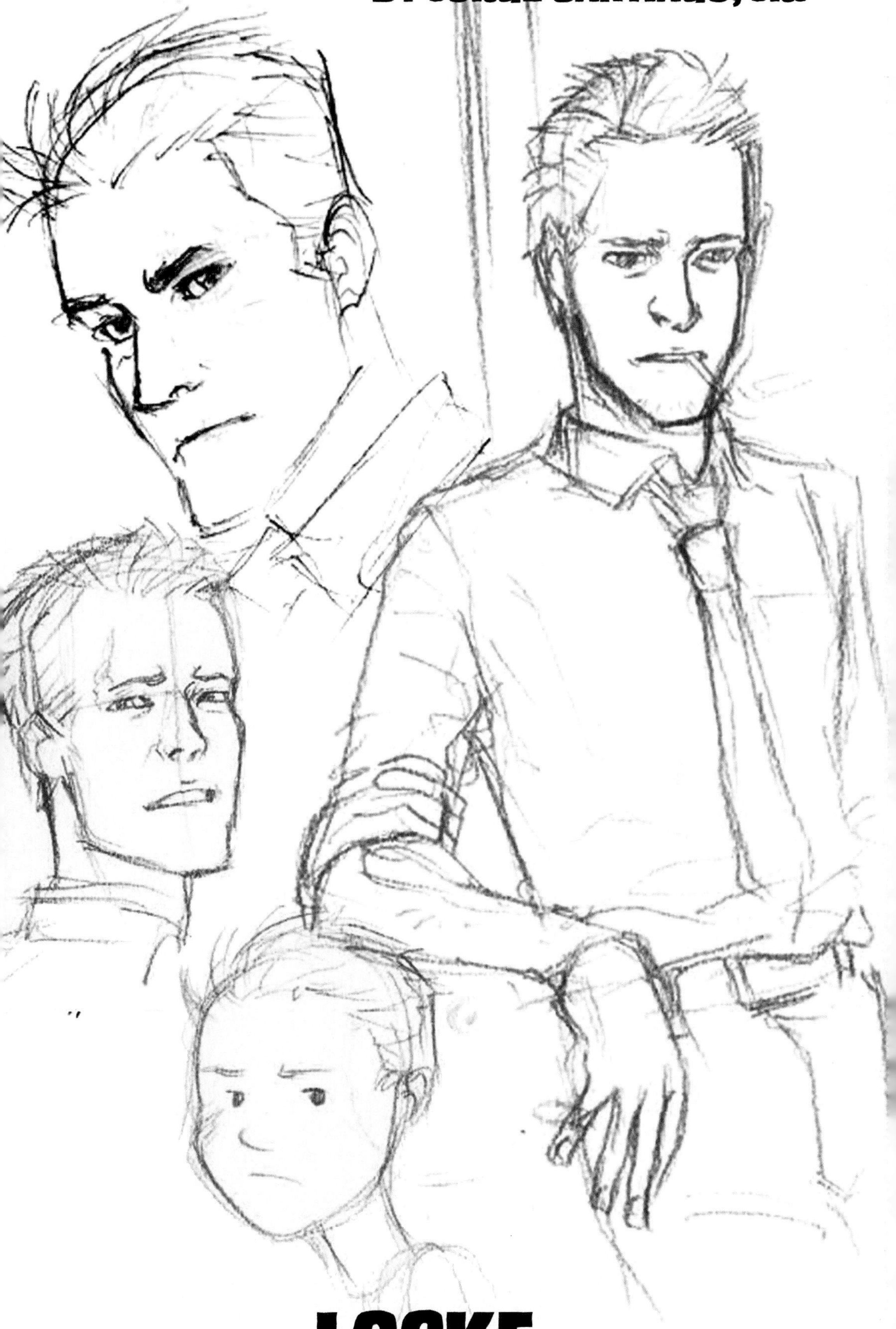

LOCKE

SPENCER

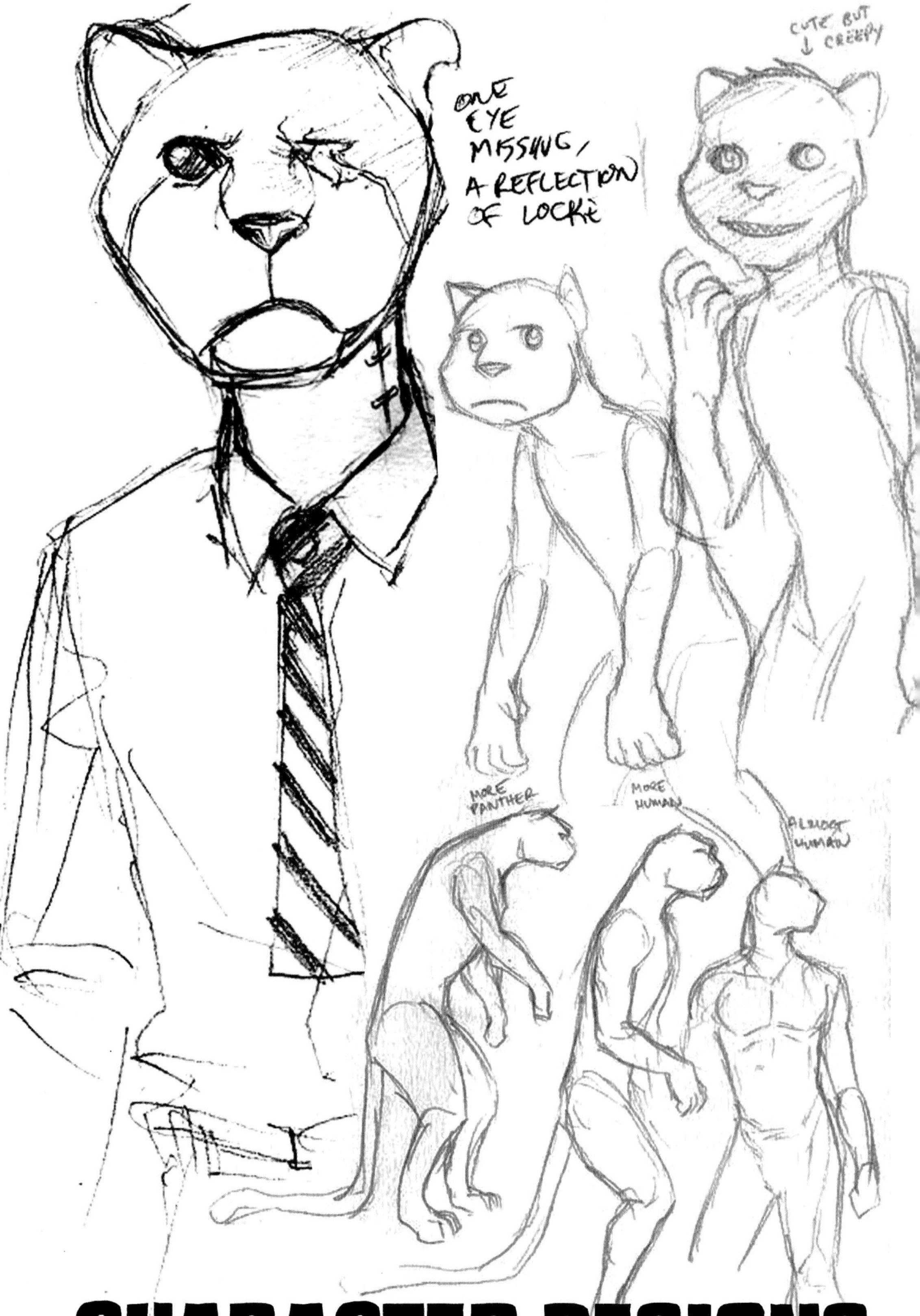
ONE EYE MISSING, A REFLECTION OF LOCKE
CUTE BUT CREEPY
MORE PANTHER
MORE HUMAN
ALMOST HUMAN

CHARACTER DESIGNS

BY JORGE SANTIAGO, JR.

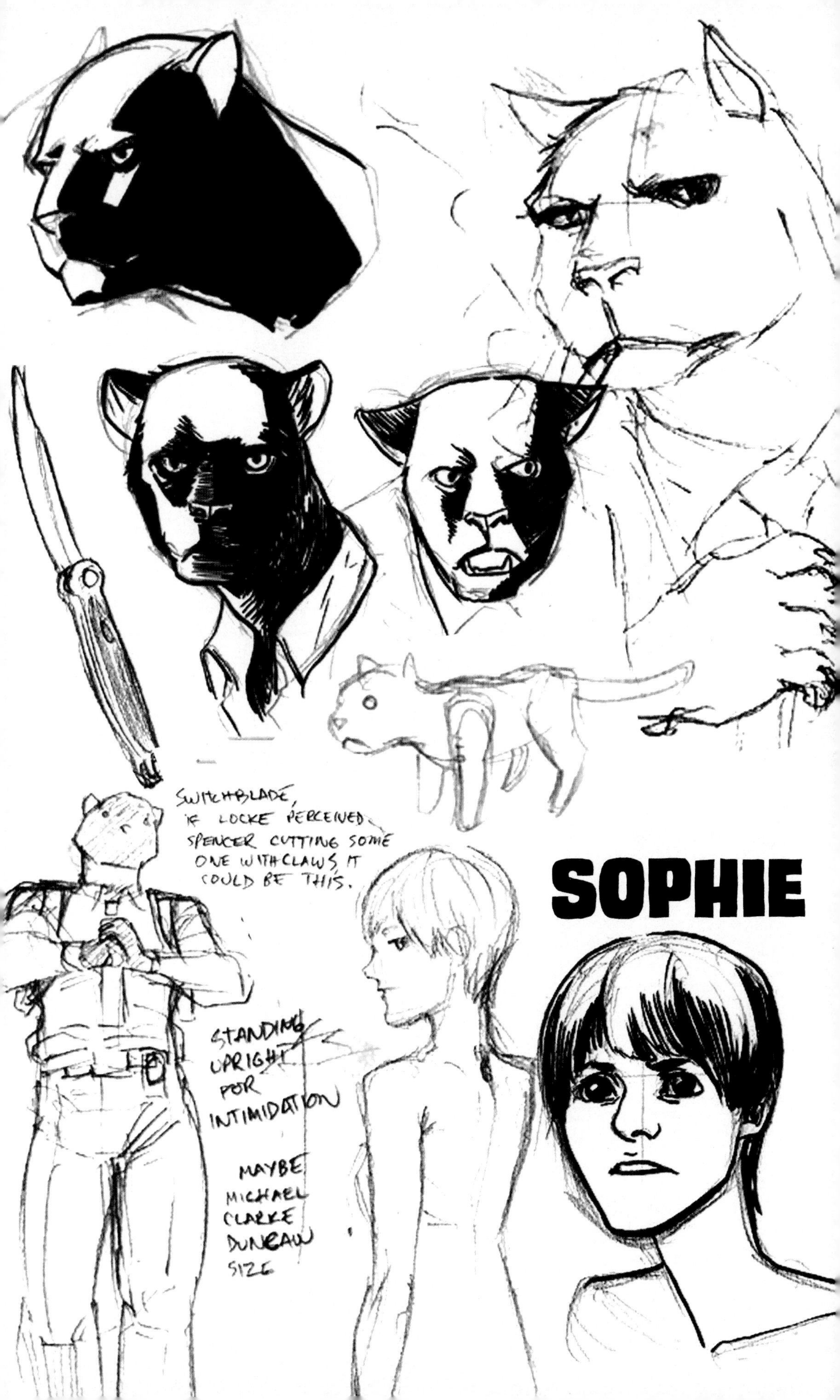
SWITCHBLADE,
IF LOCKE PERCEIVED
SPENCER CUTTING SOME
ONE WITH CLAWS, IT
COULD BE THIS.
SOPHIE
STANDING
UPRIGHT
FOR
INTIMIDATION
MAYBE
MICHAEL
CLARKE
DUNCAN
SIZE

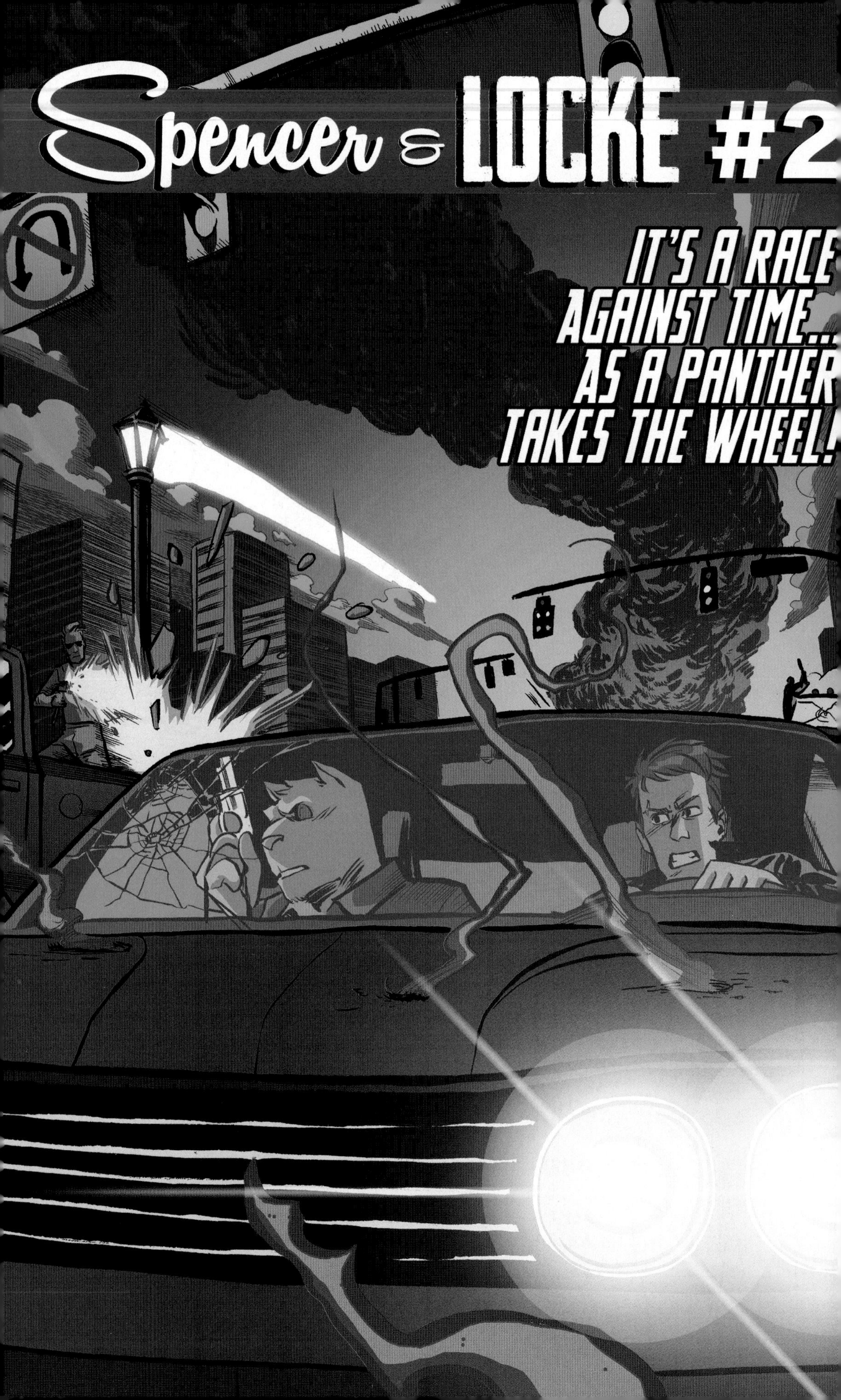
Spencer & LOCKE #2
IT'S A RACE AGAINST TIME... AS A PANTHER TAKES THE WHEEL!

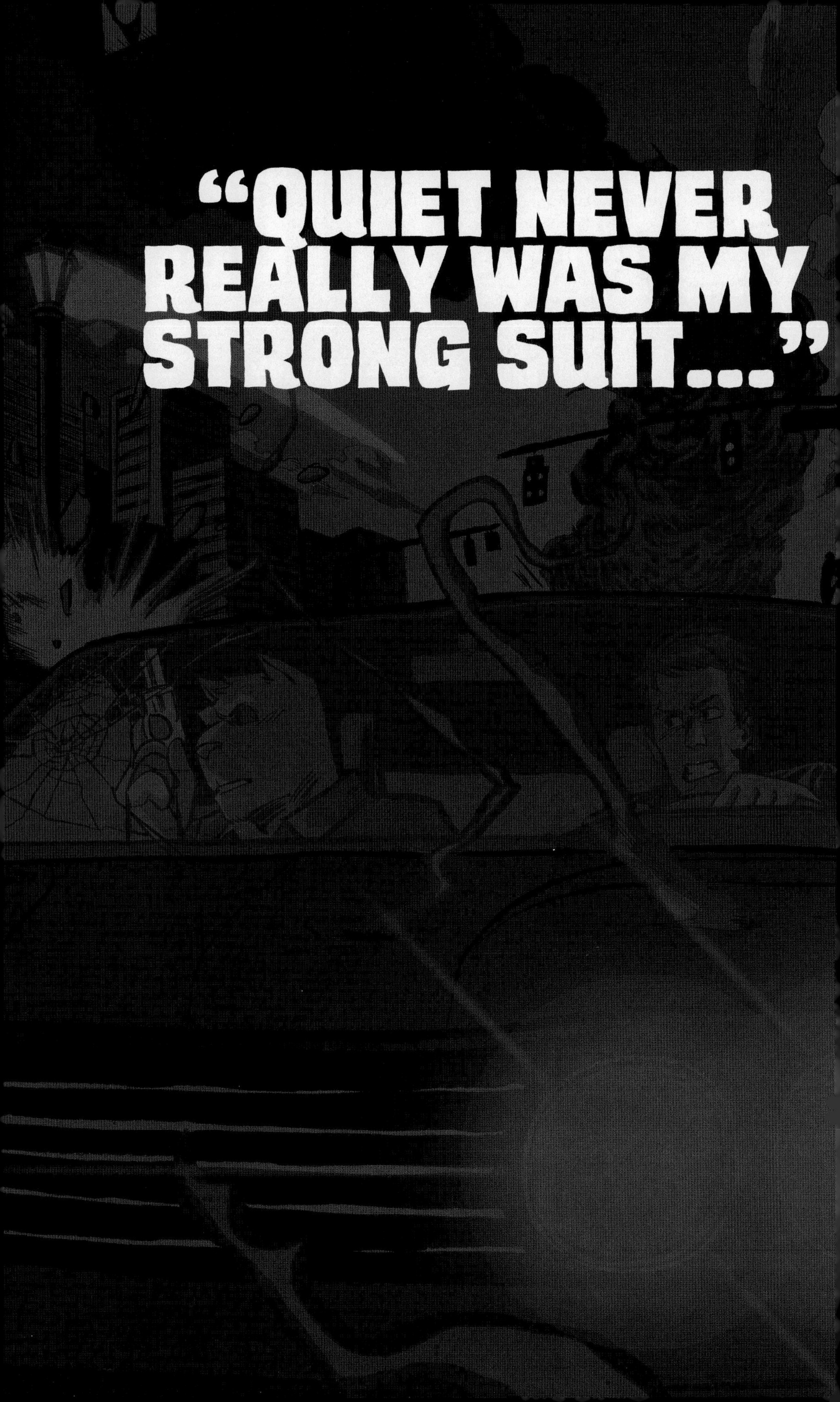
"QUIET NEVER REALLY WAS MY STRONG SUIT...."

Spencer & Locke 2

WRITTEN BY
DAVID PEPOSE

ART BY
JORGE SANTIAGO, JR.

COLORS BY
JASEN SMITH

LETTERS BY
COLIN BELL

SPENCER & LOCKE #2, May 2017. Copyright David Pepose, 2017. Published by Action Lab Entertainment.
All rights reserved. All characters are fictional. Any likeness to anyone living or undead is purely coincidental.
No part of this publication may be reproduced or transmitted without permission, except for small excerpts
for review purposes. Printed in Canada. First Printing.

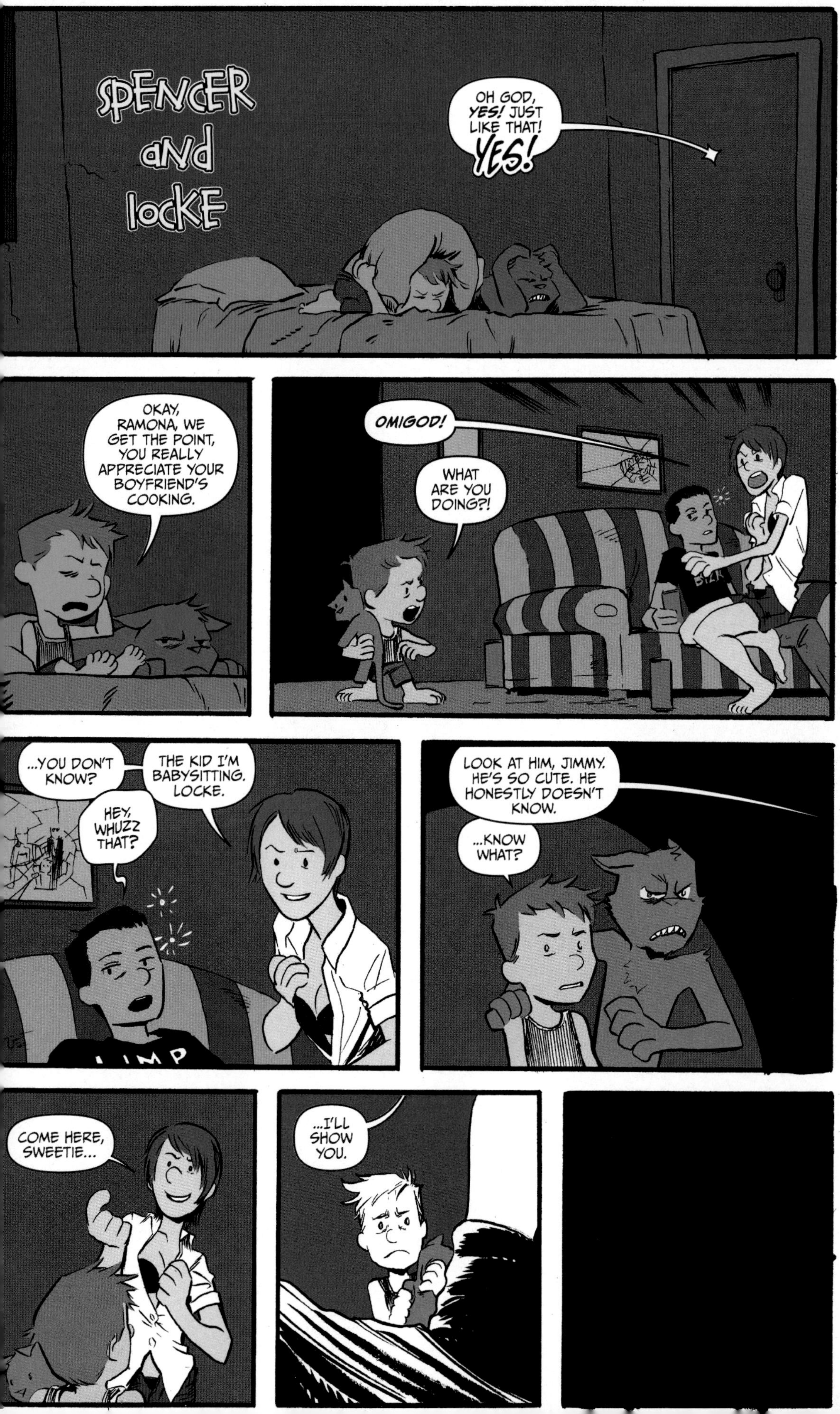
SPENCER and LOCKE
OH GOD, YES! JUST LIKE THAT! YES!
OKAY, RAMONA, WE GET THE POINT, YOU REALLY APPRECIATE YOUR BOYFRIEND'S COOKING.
OMIGOD!
WHAT ARE YOU DOING?!
...YOU DON'T KNOW?
THE KID I'M BABYSITTING. LOCKE.
HEY, WHUZZ THAT?
LOOK AT HIM, JIMMY. HE'S SO CUTE. HE HONESTLY DOESN'T KNOW.
...KNOW WHAT?
COME HERE, SWEETIE...
...I'LL SHOW YOU.

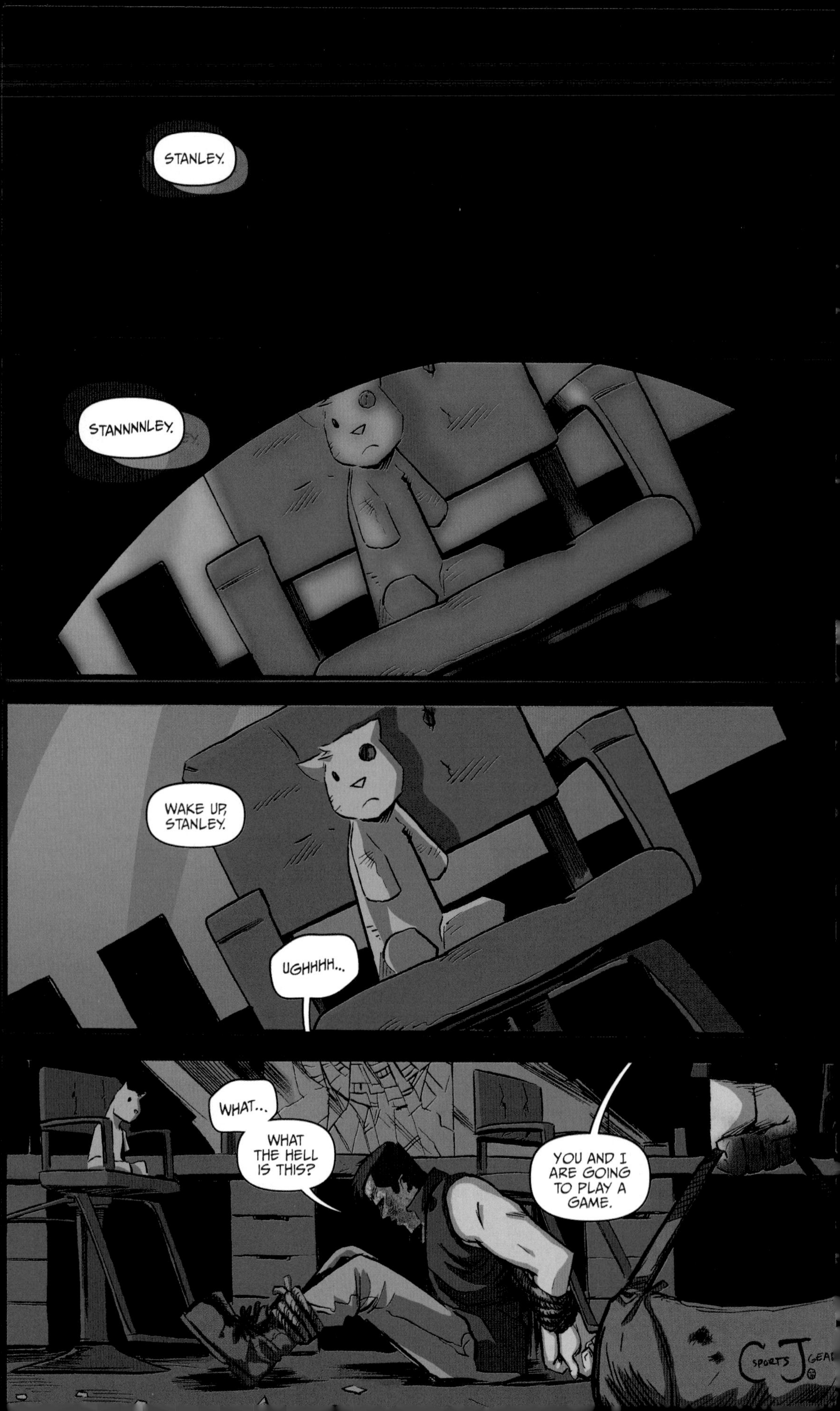
STANLEY.
STANNNNLEY.
WAKE UP, STANLEY.
UGHHHH...
WHAT...
WHAT THE HELL IS THIS?
YOU AND I ARE GOING TO PLAY A GAME.
CJ SPORTS GEAR

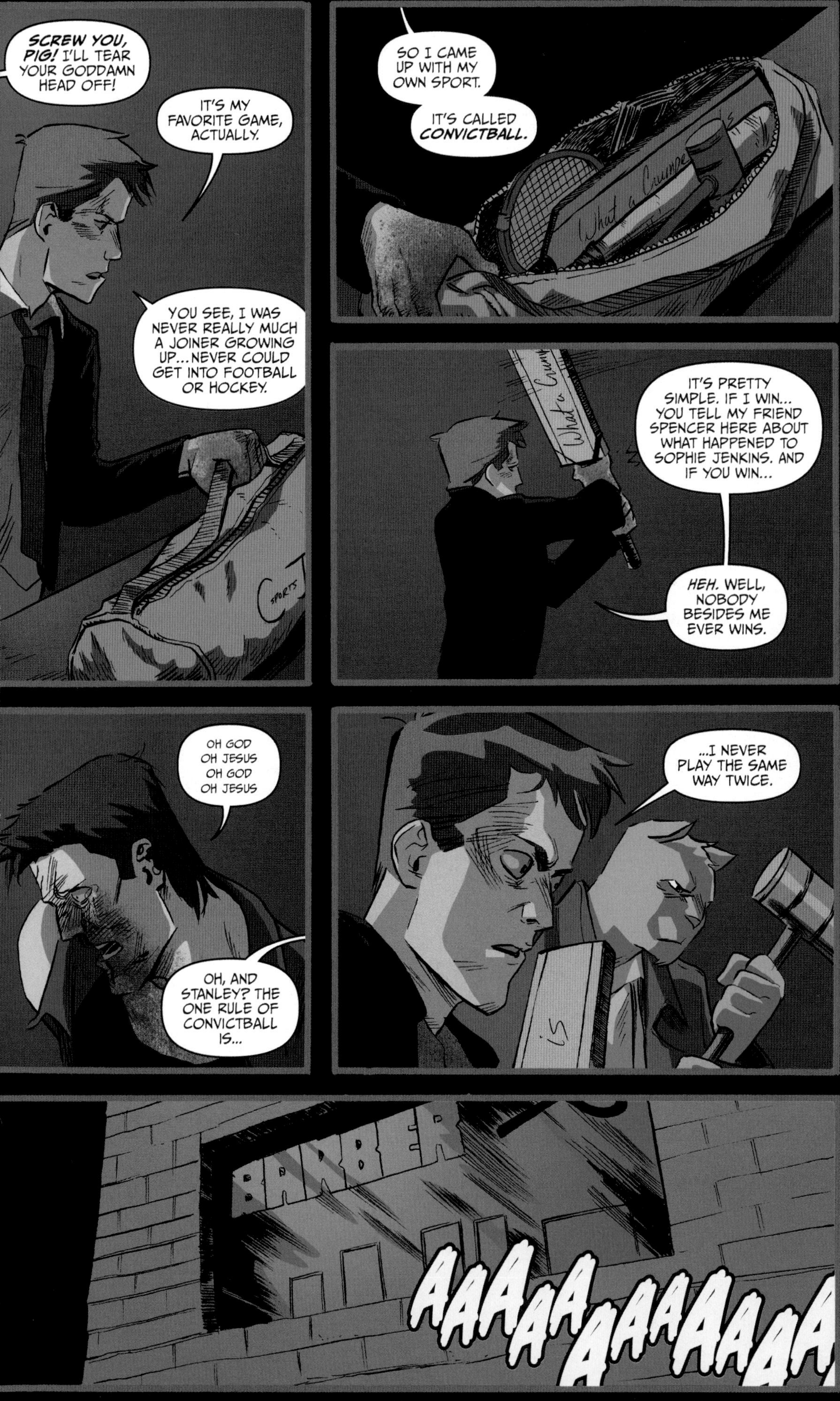
SCREW YOU, PIG! I'LL TEAR YOUR GODDAMN HEAD OFF!
IT'S MY FAVORITE GAME, ACTUALLY.
YOU SEE, I WAS NEVER REALLY MUCH A JOINER GROWING UP...NEVER COULD GET INTO FOOTBALL OR HOCKEY.
SPORTS
SO I CAME UP WITH MY OWN SPORT.
IT'S CALLED CONVICTBALL.
IT'S PRETTY SIMPLE. IF I WIN... YOU TELL MY FRIEND SPENCER HERE ABOUT WHAT HAPPENED TO SOPHIE JENKINS. AND IF YOU WIN...
HEH. WELL, NOBODY BESIDES ME EVER WINS.
OH GOD OH JESUS OH GOD OH JESUS
OH, AND STANLEY? THE ONE RULE OF CONVICTBALL IS...
...I NEVER PLAY THE SAME WAY TWICE.
BARBER
AAAAAAAAAAAA

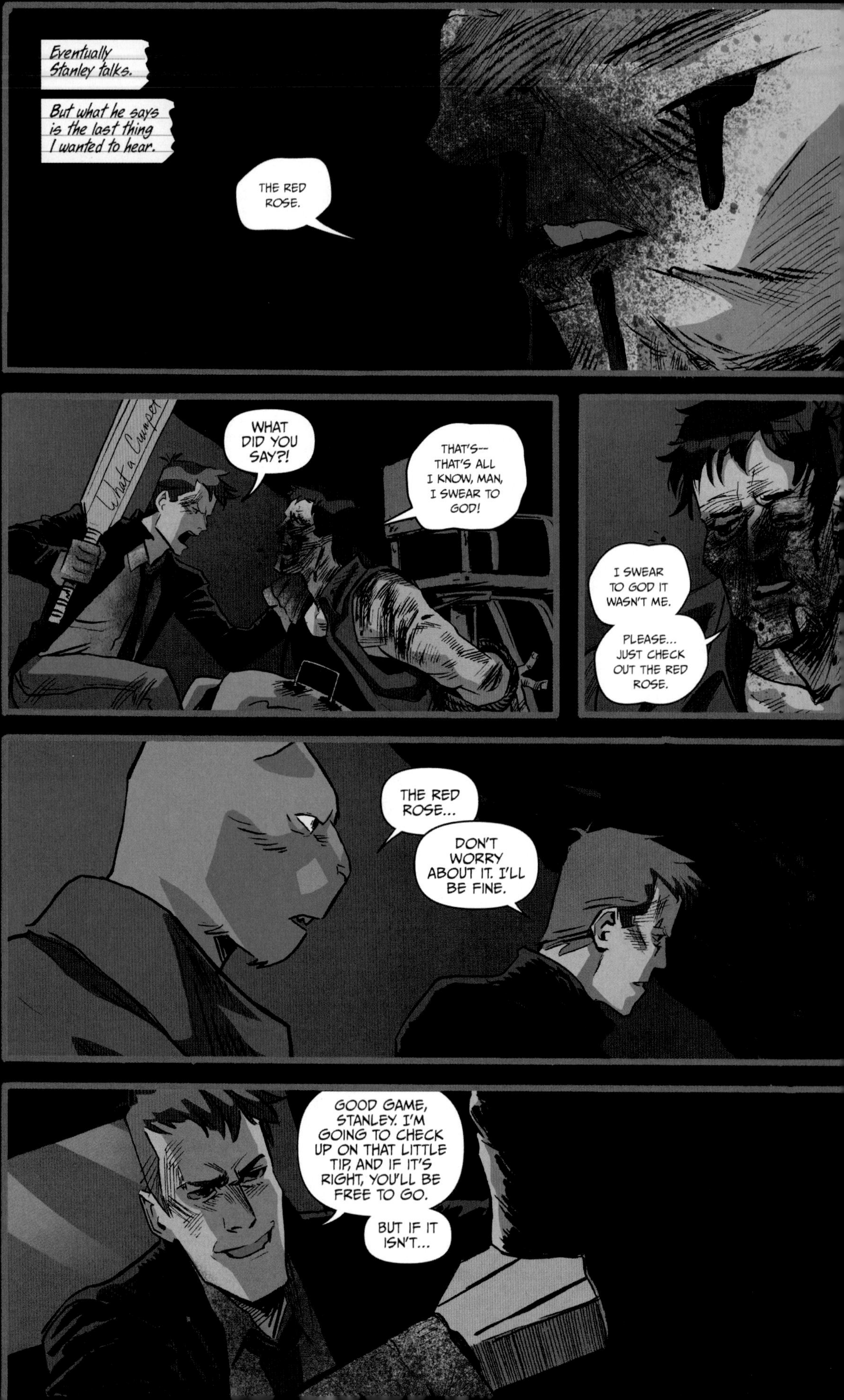
Eventually Stanley talks.
But what he says is the last thing I wanted to hear.
THE RED ROSE.
WHAT DID YOU SAY?!
THAT'S-- THAT'S ALL I KNOW, MAN, I SWEAR TO GOD!
I SWEAR TO GOD IT WASN'T ME.
PLEASE... JUST CHECK OUT THE RED ROSE.
THE RED ROSE...
DON'T WORRY ABOUT IT. I'LL BE FINE.
GOOD GAME, STANLEY. I'M GOING TO CHECK UP ON THAT LITTLE TIP, AND IF IT'S RIGHT, YOU'LL BE FREE TO GO.
BUT IF IT ISN'T...

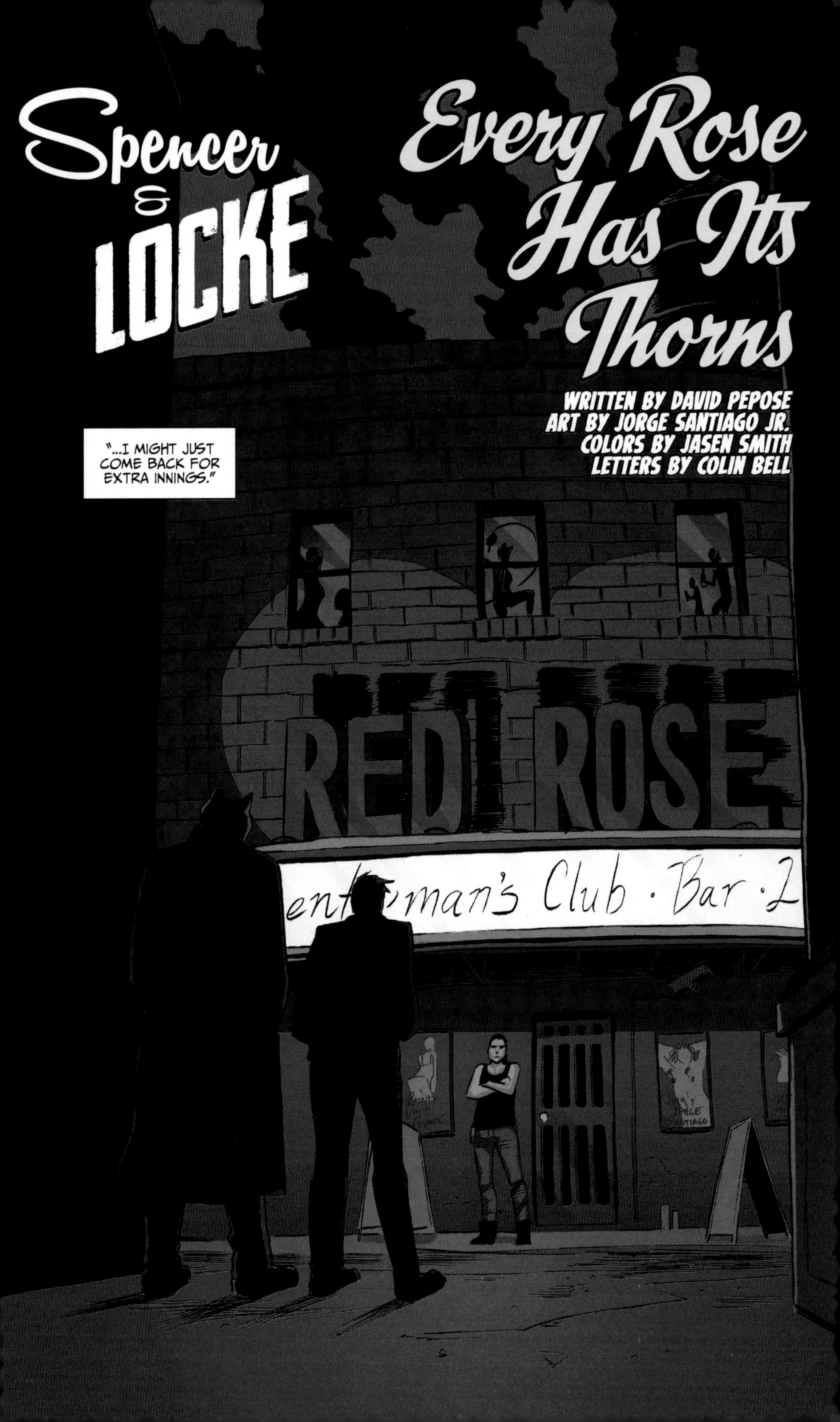
Spencer & LOCKE
Every Rose Has Its Thorns
WRITTEN BY DAVID PEPOSE
ART BY JORGE SANTIAGO JR.
COLORS BY JASEN SMITH
LETTERS BY COLIN BELL
"...I MIGHT JUST COME BACK FOR EXTRA INNINGS."
RED ROSE
man's Club · Bar ·

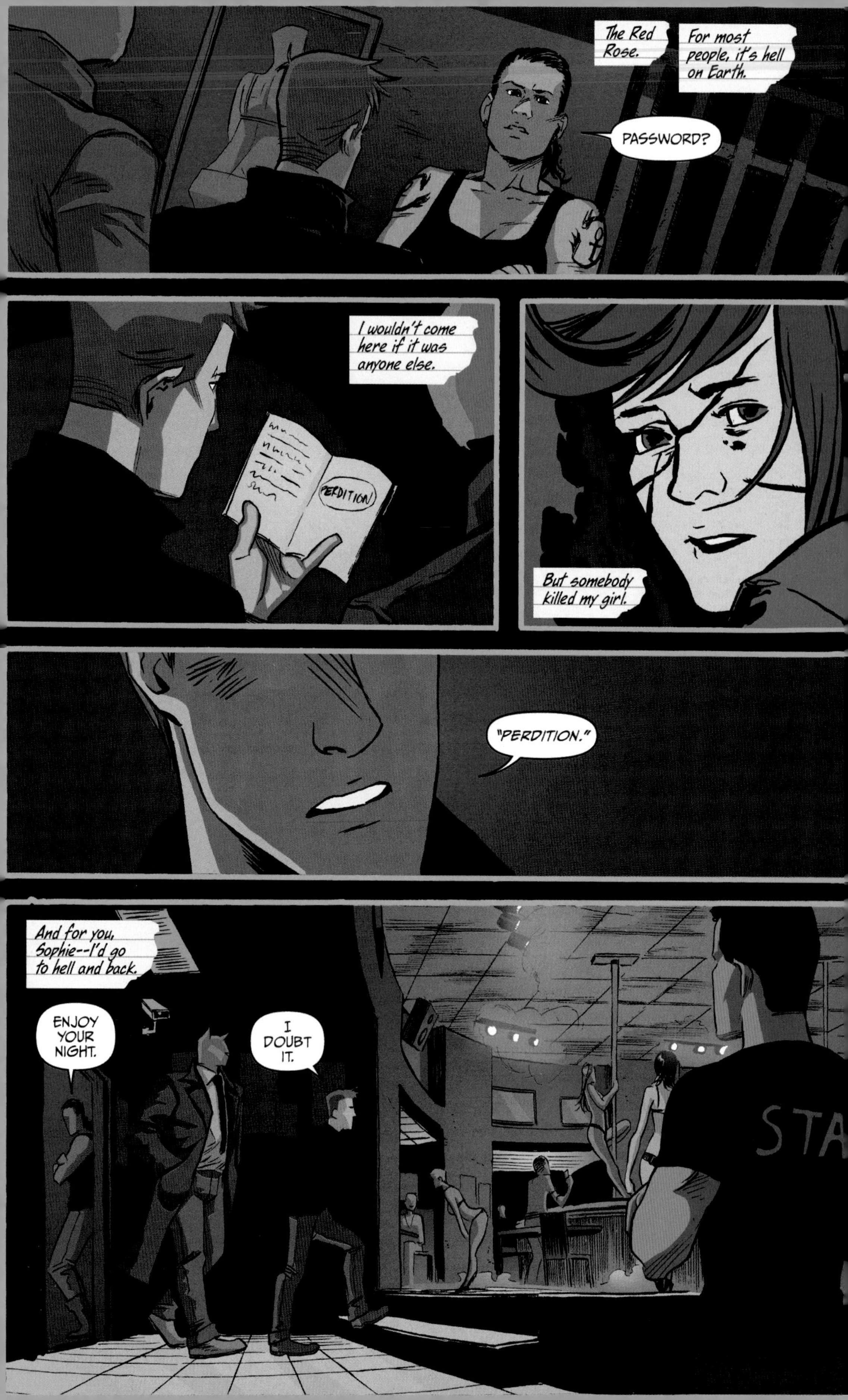
The Red Rose.
For most people, it's hell on Earth.
PASSWORD?
I wouldn't come here if it was anyone else.
PERDITION
But somebody killed my girl.
"PERDITION."
And for you, Sophie--I'd go to hell and back.
ENJOY YOUR NIGHT.
I DOUBT IT.

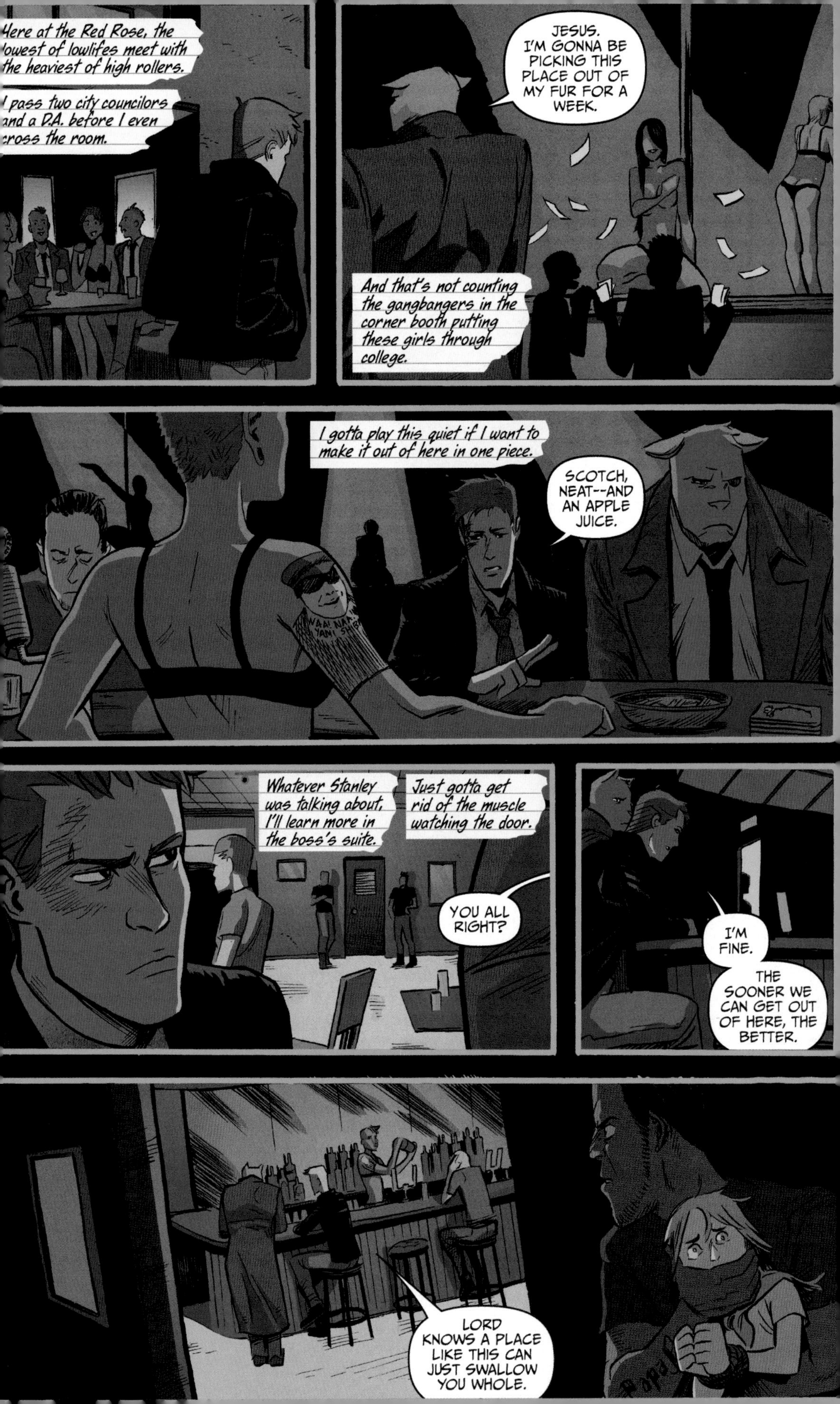
Here at the Red Rose, the lowest of lowlifes meet with the heaviest of high rollers.
I pass two city councilors and a D.A. before I even cross the room.
JESUS. I'M GONNA BE PICKING THIS PLACE OUT OF MY FUR FOR A WEEK.
And that's not counting the gangbangers in the corner booth putting these girls through college.
I gotta play this quiet if I want to make it out of here in one piece.
SCOTCH, NEAT--AND AN APPLE JUICE.
Whatever Stanley was talking about, I'll learn more in the boss's suite.
Just gotta get rid of the muscle watching the door.
YOU ALL RIGHT?
I'M FINE.
THE SOONER WE CAN GET OUT OF HERE, THE BETTER.
LORD KNOWS A PLACE LIKE THIS CAN JUST SWALLOW YOU WHOLE.

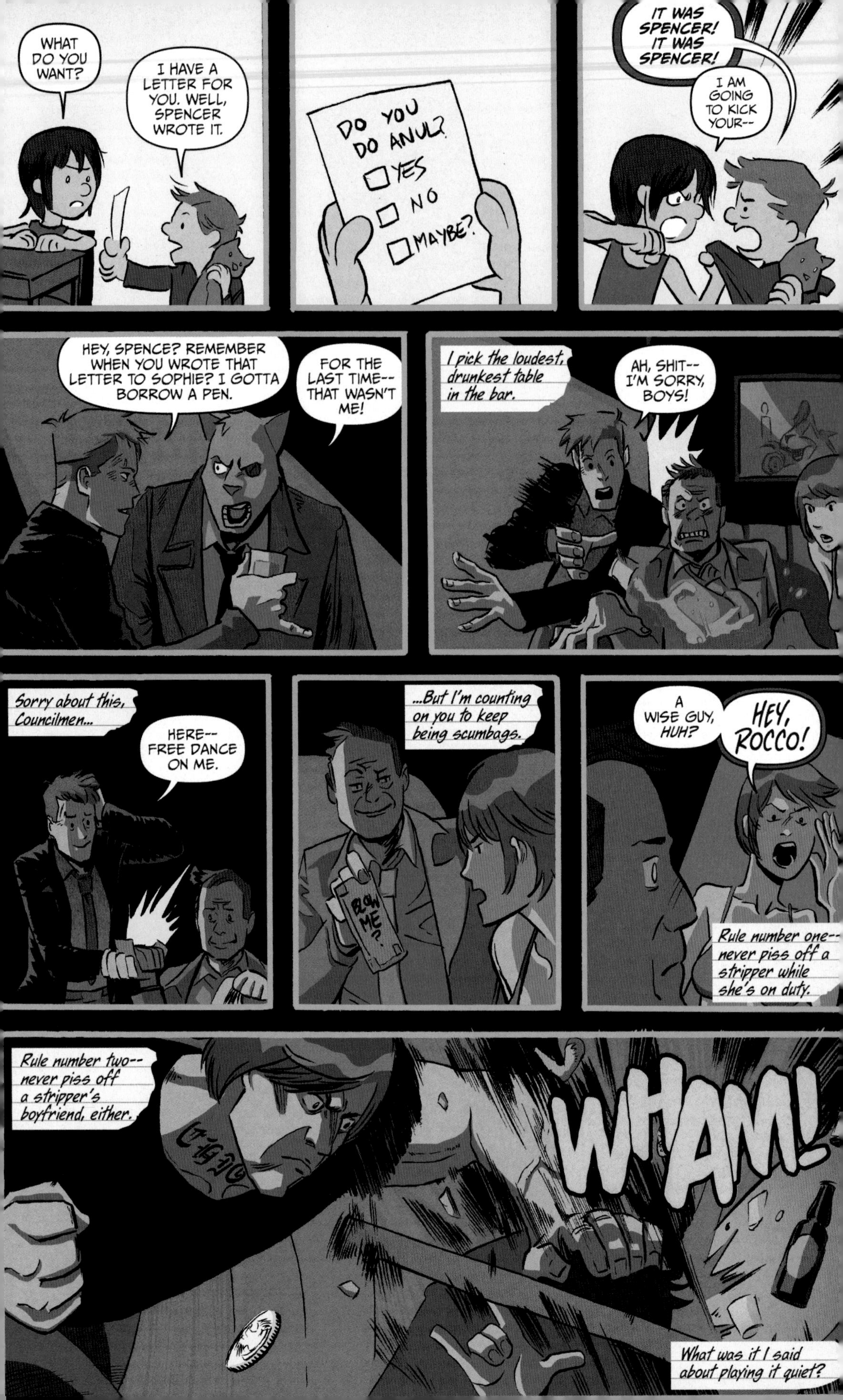
WHAT DO YOU WANT?
I HAVE A LETTER FOR YOU. WELL, SPENCER WROTE IT.
DO YOU DO ANUL?
YES
NO
MAYBE?
IT WAS SPENCER! IT WAS SPENCER!
I AM GOING TO KICK YOUR--
HEY, SPENCE? REMEMBER WHEN YOU WROTE THAT LETTER TO SOPHIE? I GOTTA BORROW A PEN.
FOR THE LAST TIME-- THAT WASN'T ME!
I pick the loudest, drunkest table in the bar.
AH, SHIT-- I'M SORRY, BOYS!
Sorry about this, Councilmen...
HERE-- FREE DANCE ON ME.
...But I'm counting on you to keep being scumbags.
BLOW ME?
A WISE GUY, HUH?
HEY, ROCCO!
Rule number one-- never piss off a stripper while she's on duty.
Rule number two-- never piss off a stripper's boyfriend, either.
WHAM!
What was it I said about playing it quiet?

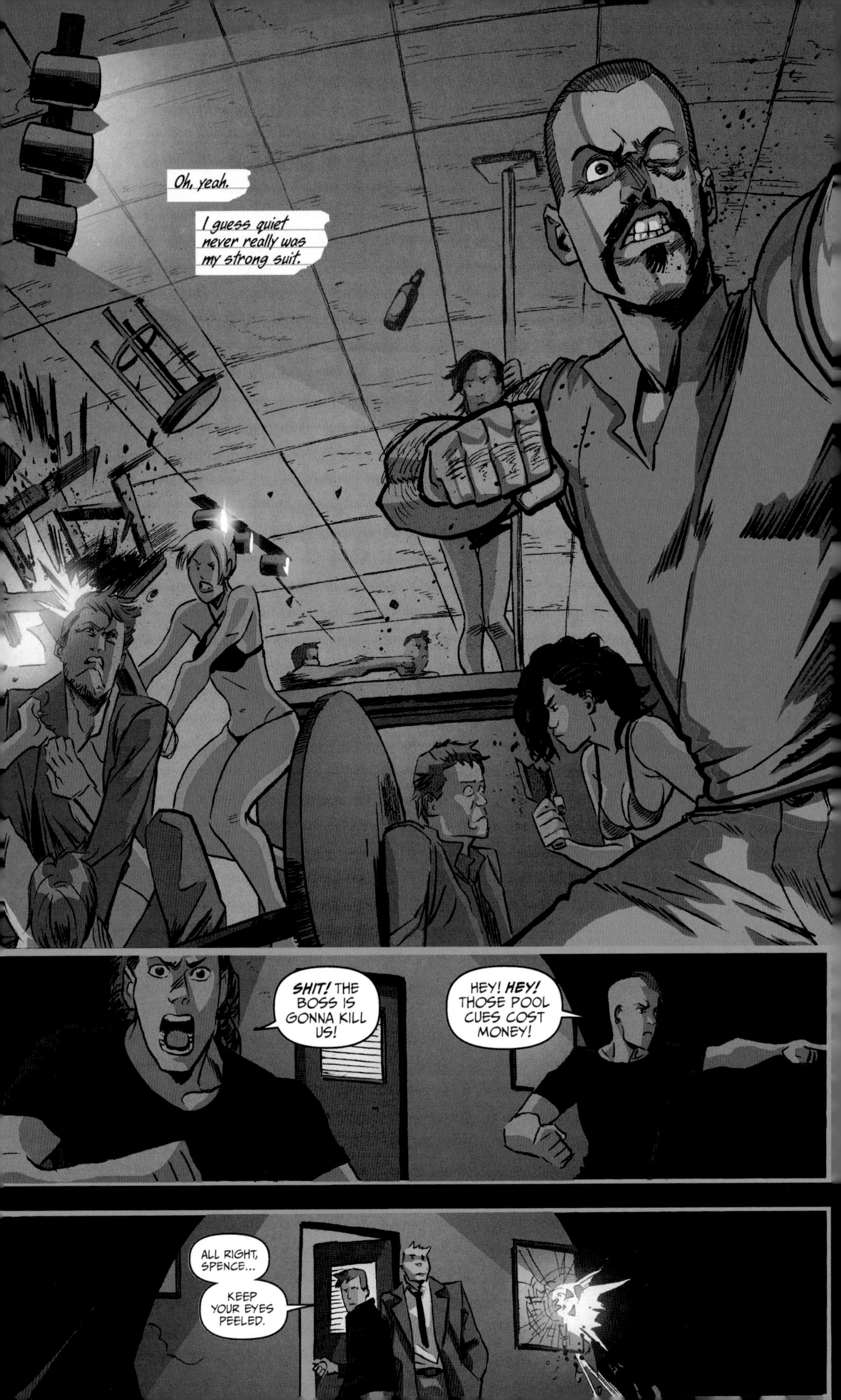
Oh, yeah.
I guess quiet never really was my strong suit.
SHIT! THE BOSS IS GONNA KILL US!
HEY! HEY! THOSE POOL CUES COST MONEY!
ALL RIGHT, SPENCE...
KEEP YOUR EYES PEELED.

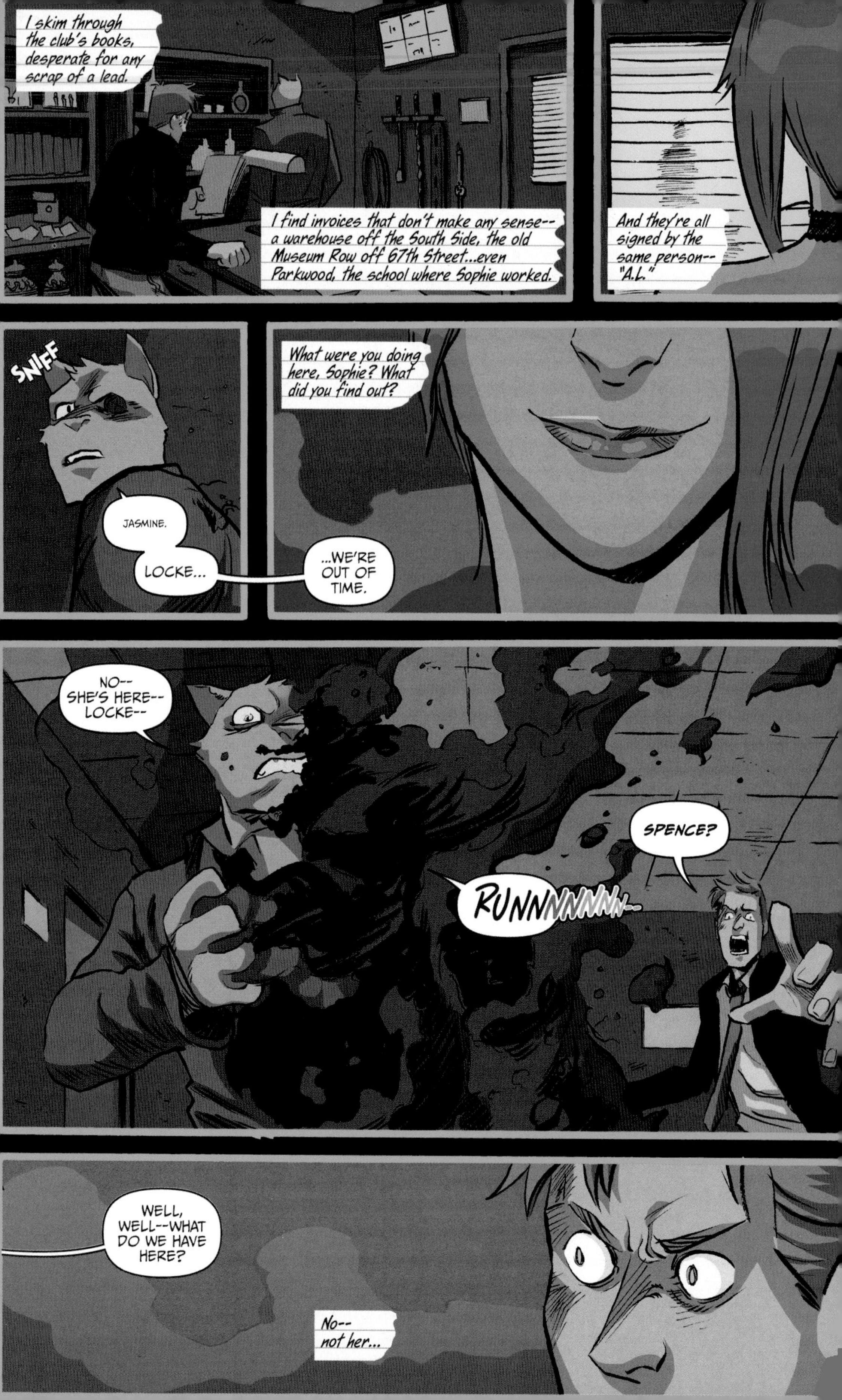
I skim through the club's books, desperate for any scrap of a lead.
I find invoices that don't make any sense--a warehouse off the South Side, the old Museum Row off 67th Street...even Parkwood, the school where Sophie worked.
And they're all signed by the same person--"A.L."
SNIFF
What were you doing here, Sophie? What did you find out?
JASMINE.
LOCKE...
...WE'RE OUT OF TIME.
NO--SHE'S HERE--LOCKE--
SPENCE?
RUNNNNNNNN--
WELL, WELL--WHAT DO WE HAVE HERE?
No--not her...

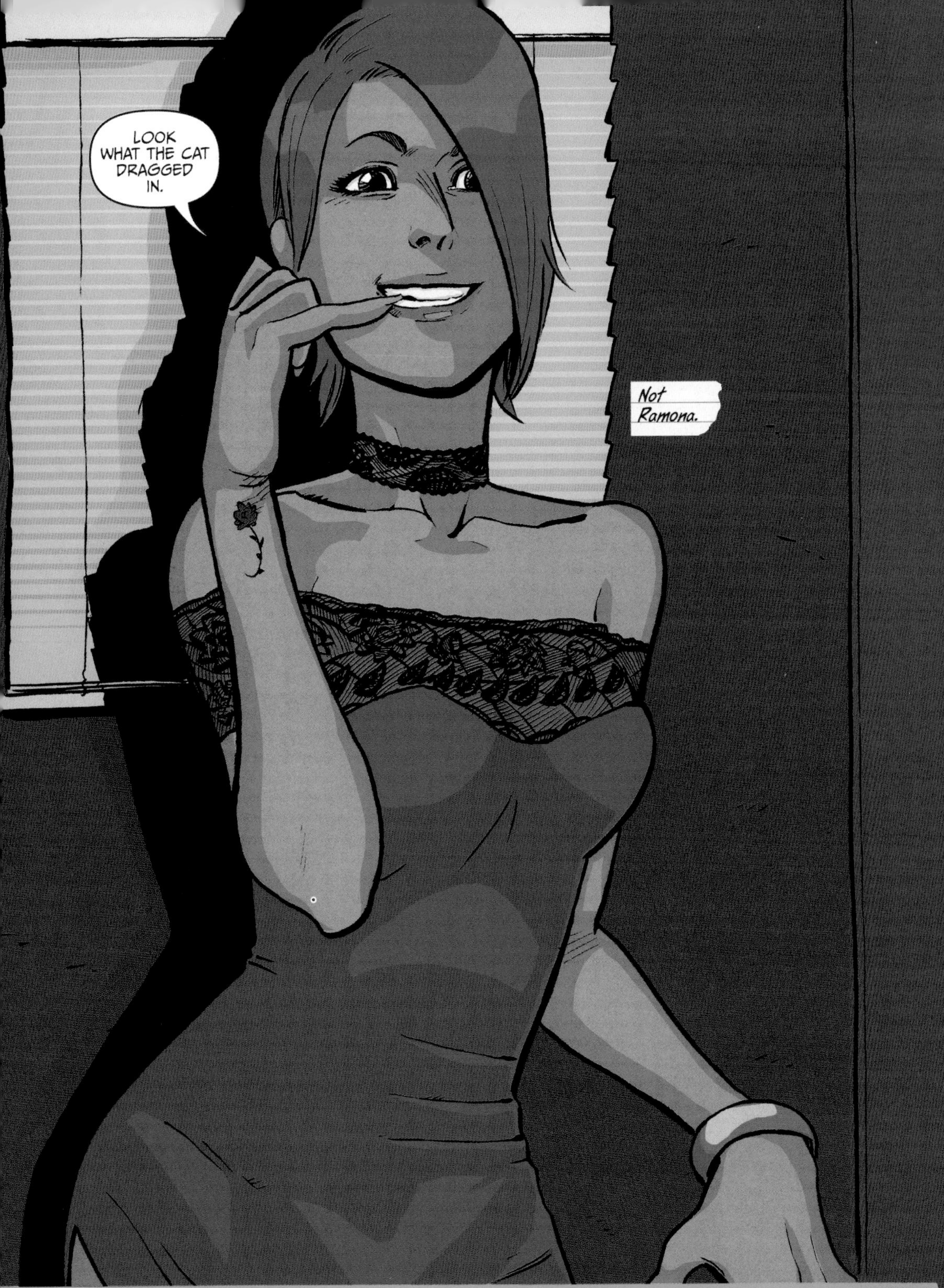
LOOK WHAT THE CAT DRAGGED IN.
Not Ramona.

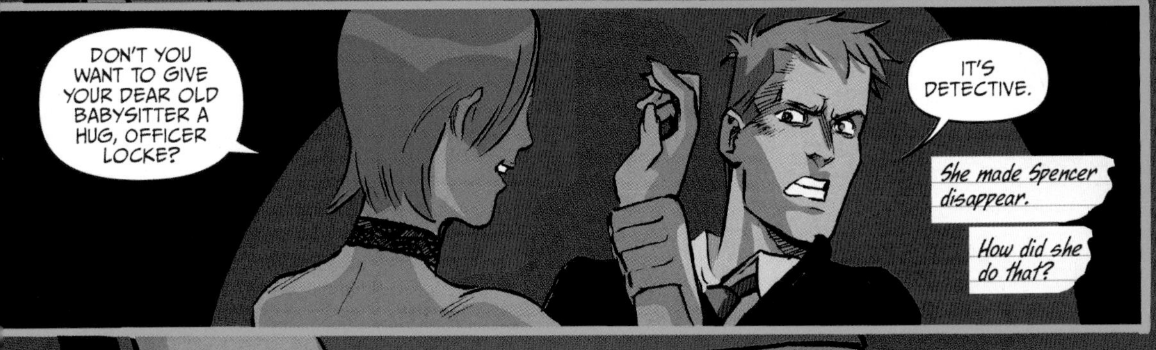
DON'T YOU WANT TO GIVE YOUR DEAR OLD BABYSITTER A HUG, OFFICER LOCKE?
IT'S DETECTIVE.
She made Spencer disappear.
How did she do that?

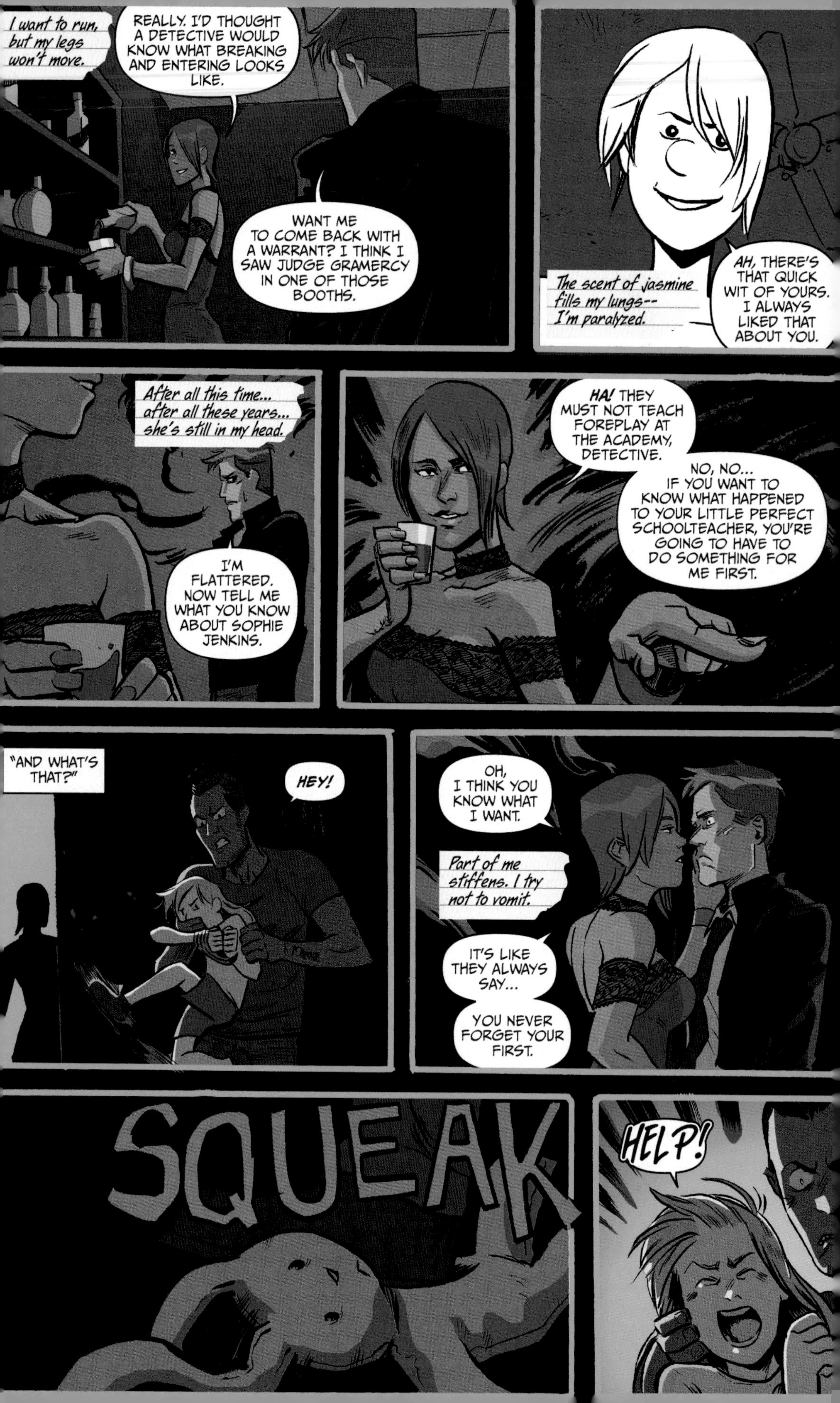

I want to run, but my legs won't move.
REALLY. I'D THOUGHT A DETECTIVE WOULD KNOW WHAT BREAKING AND ENTERING LOOKS LIKE.
WANT ME TO COME BACK WITH A WARRANT? I THINK I SAW JUDGE GRAMERCY IN ONE OF THOSE BOOTHS.
The scent of jasmine fills my lungs-- I'm paralyzed.
AH, THERE'S THAT QUICK WIT OF YOURS. I ALWAYS LIKED THAT ABOUT YOU.
After all this time... after all these years... she's still in my head.
I'M FLATTERED. NOW TELL ME WHAT YOU KNOW ABOUT SOPHIE JENKINS.
HA! THEY MUST NOT TEACH FOREPLAY AT THE ACADEMY, DETECTIVE.
NO, NO... IF YOU WANT TO KNOW WHAT HAPPENED TO YOUR LITTLE PERFECT SCHOOLTEACHER, YOU'RE GOING TO HAVE TO DO SOMETHING FOR ME FIRST.
"AND WHAT'S THAT?"
HEY!
OH, I THINK YOU KNOW WHAT I WANT.
Part of me stiffens. I try not to vomit.
IT'S LIKE THEY ALWAYS SAY...
YOU NEVER FORGET YOUR FIRST.
SQUEAK
HELP!

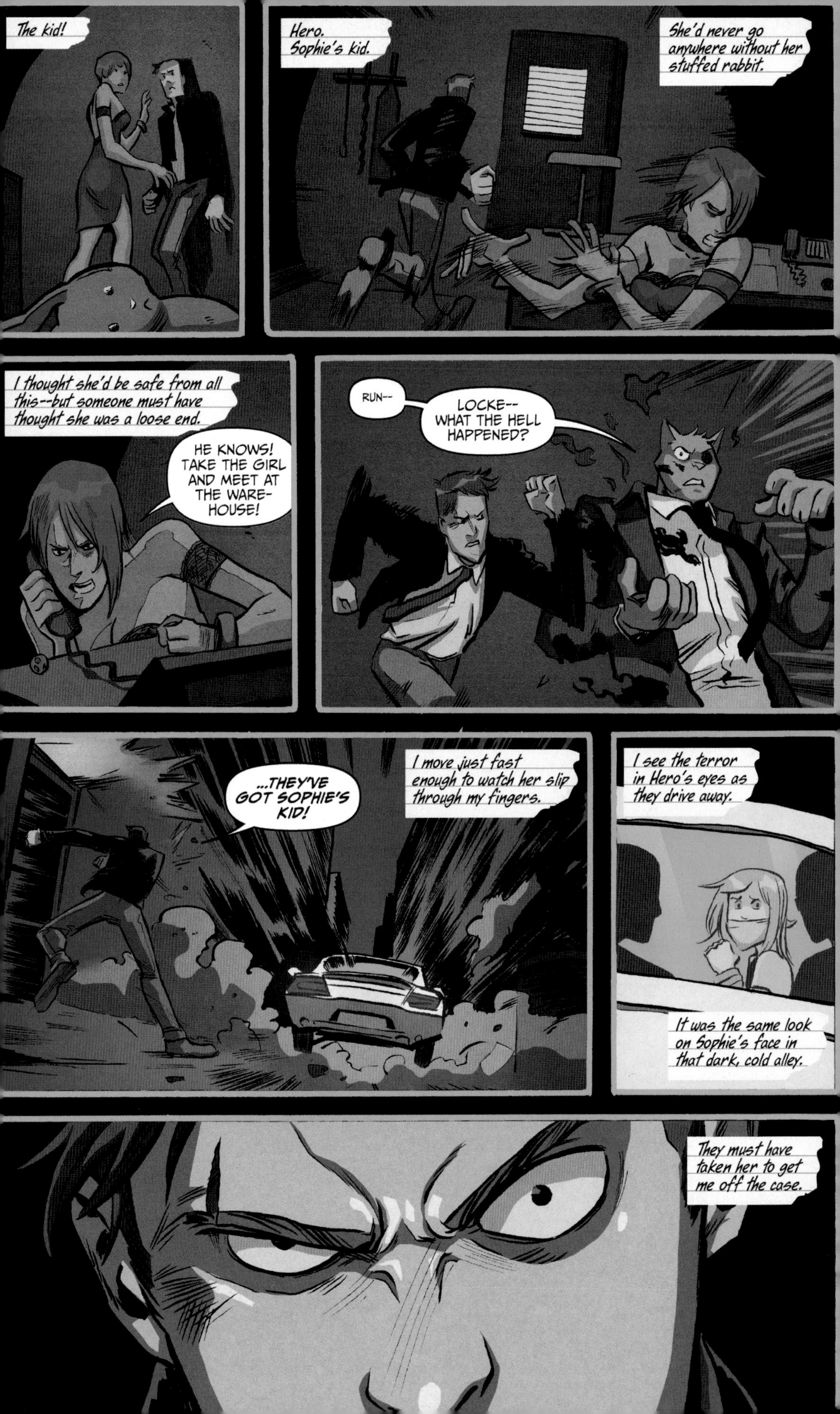
The kid!
Hero.
Sophie's kid.
She'd never go anywhere without her stuffed rabbit.
I thought she'd be safe from all this--but someone must have thought she was a loose end.
HE KNOWS! TAKE THE GIRL AND MEET AT THE WARE-HOUSE!
RUN--
LOCKE--
WHAT THE HELL HAPPENED?
...THEY'VE GOT SOPHIE'S KID!
I move just fast enough to watch her slip through my fingers.
I see the terror in Hero's eyes as they drive away.
It was the same look on Sophie's face in that dark, cold alley.
They must have taken her to get me off the case.

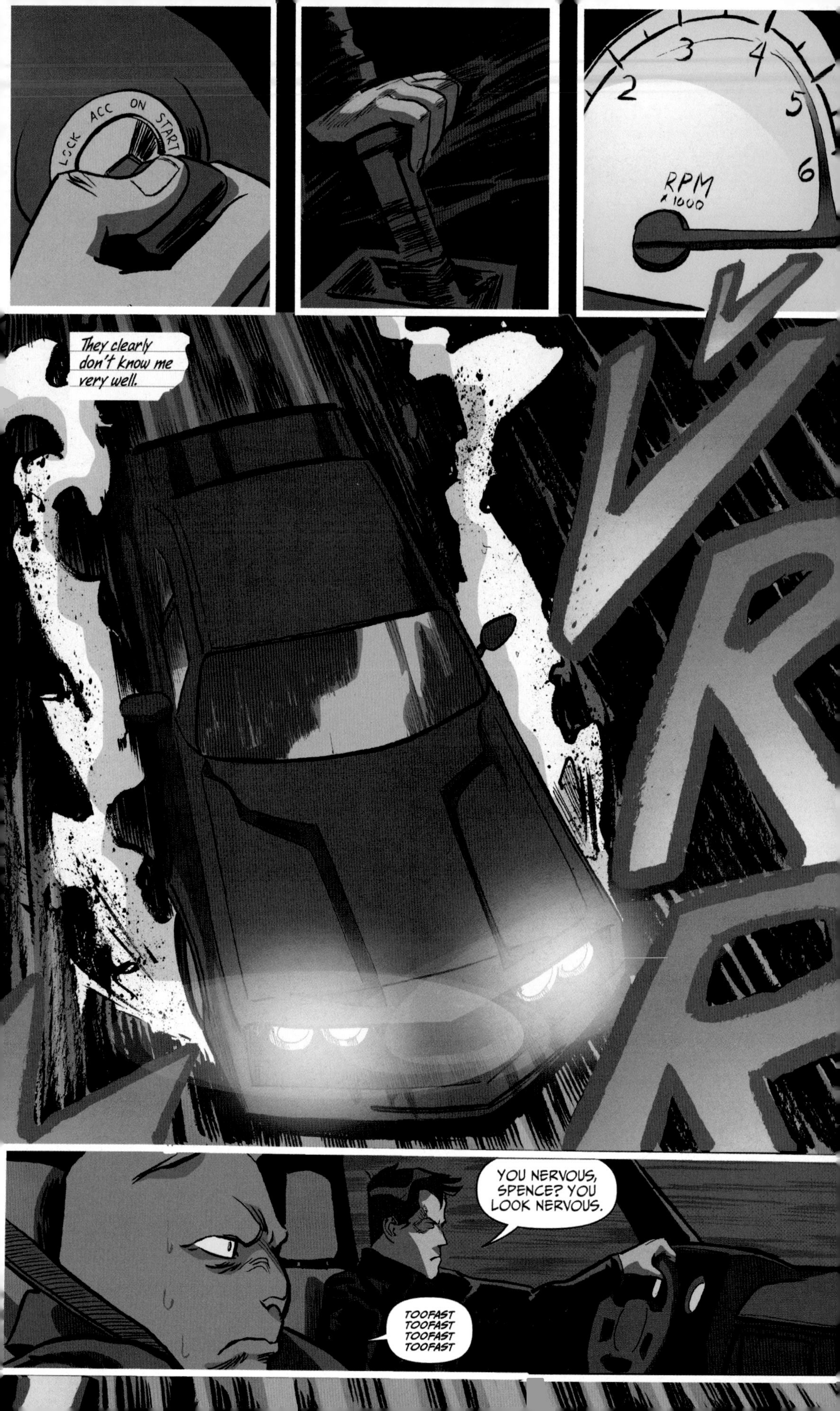
LOCK ACC ON START
2 3 4 5 6
RPM x1000
They clearly don't know me very well.
YOU NERVOUS, SPENCE? YOU LOOK NERVOUS.
TOOFAST TOOFAST TOOFAST TOOFAST

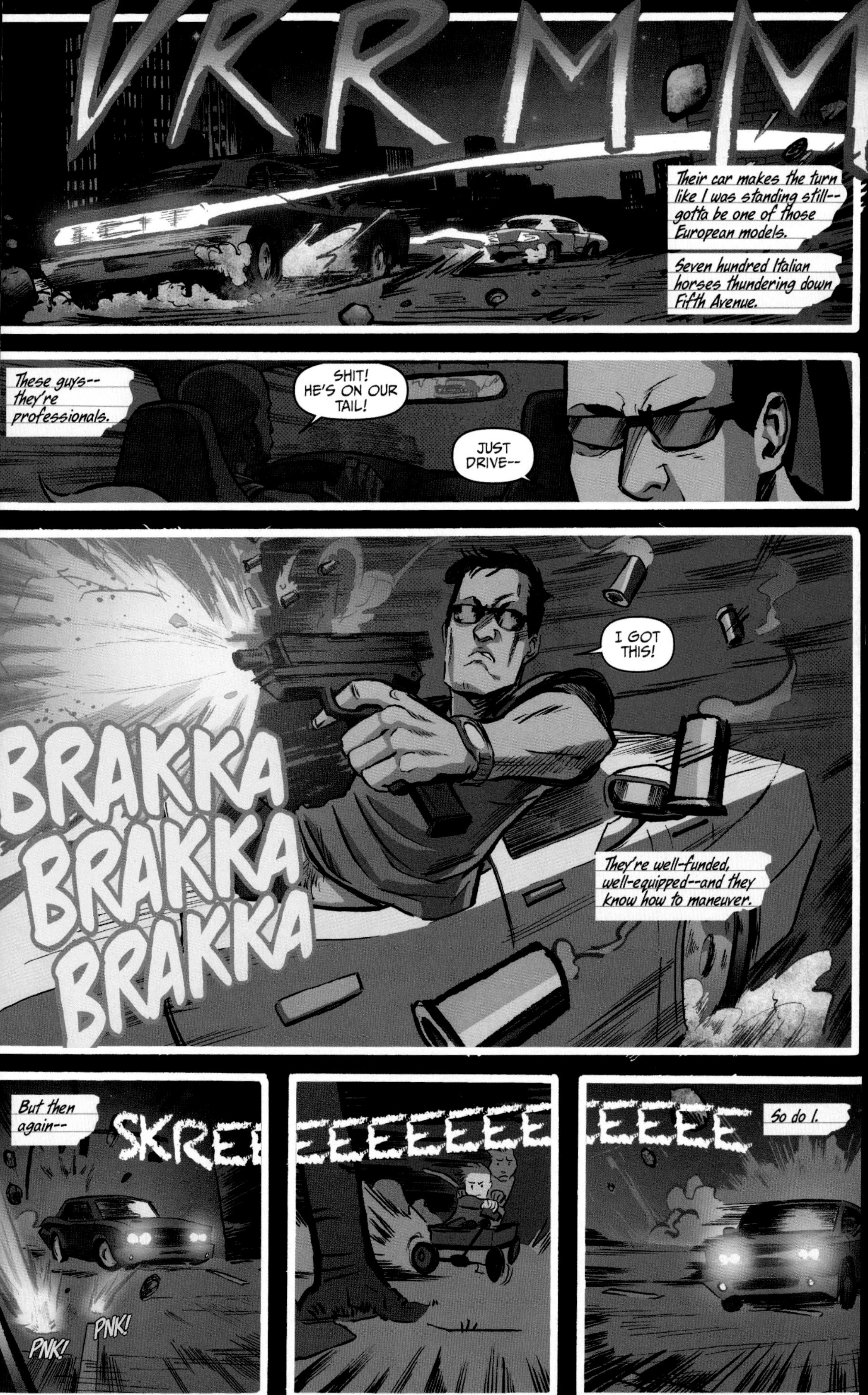
VRRMM
Their car makes the turn like I was standing still--gotta be one of those European models.
Seven hundred Italian horses thundering down Fifth Avenue.
These guys--they're professionals.
SHIT! HE'S ON OUR TAIL!
JUST DRIVE--
I GOT THIS!
BRAKKA BRAKKA BRAKKA
They're well-funded, well-equipped--and they know how to maneuver.
But then again--
SKREEEEEEEEEEEEEE
So do I.
PNK!
PNK!

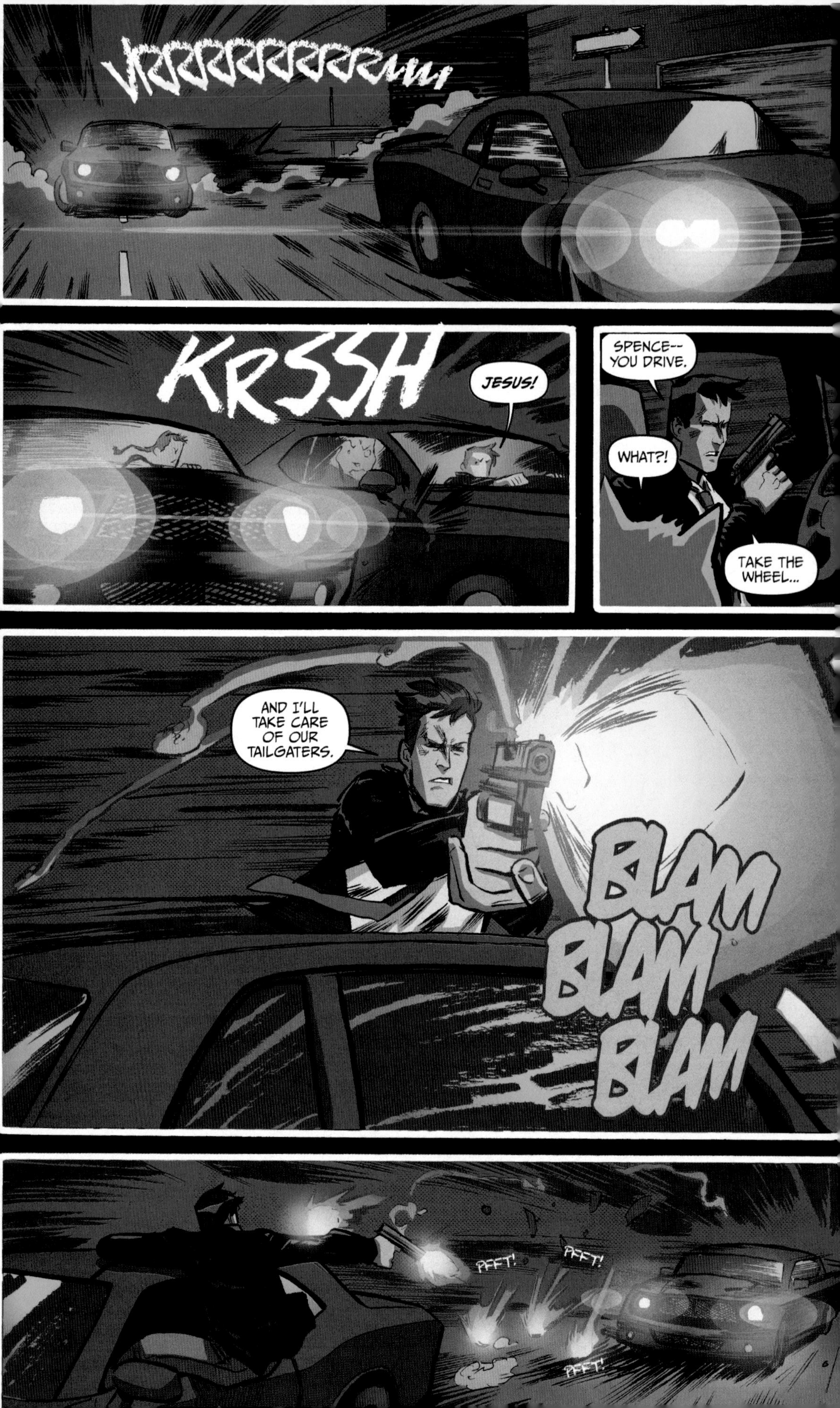

VRRRRRRRRRMM
KRSSH
JESUS!
SPENCE-- YOU DRIVE.
WHAT?!
TAKE THE WHEEL...
AND I'LL TAKE CARE OF OUR TAILGATERS.
BLAM BLAM BLAM
PFFT!
PFFT!
PFFT!

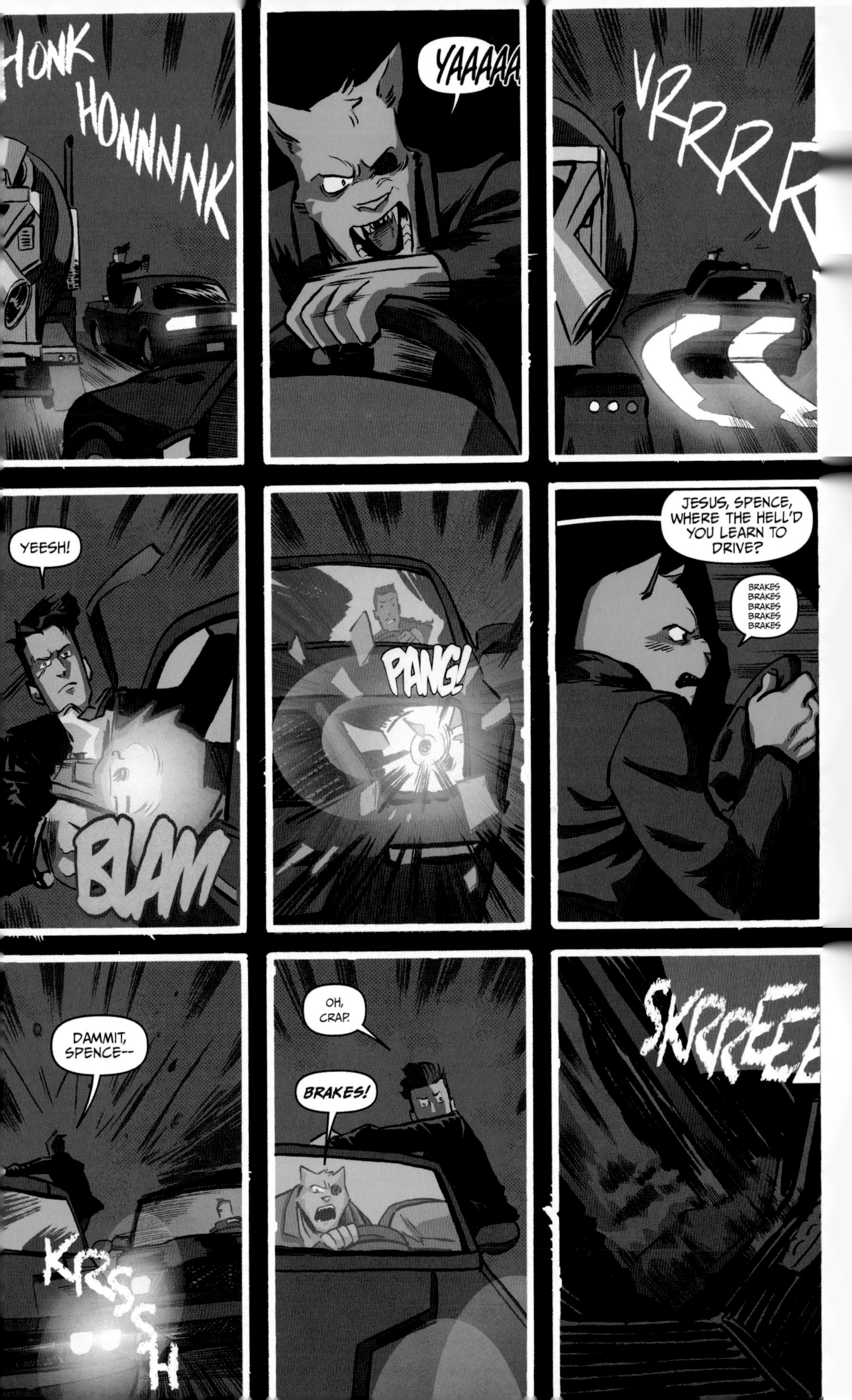

HONK
HONNNNNK
YAAAAA
VRRRRR
YEESH!
BLAM
PANG!
JESUS, SPENCE, WHERE THE HELL'D YOU LEARN TO DRIVE?
BRAKES BRAKES BRAKES BRAKES BRAKES
DAMMIT, SPENCE--
KRSSSH
OH, CRAP.
BRAKES!
SKREE

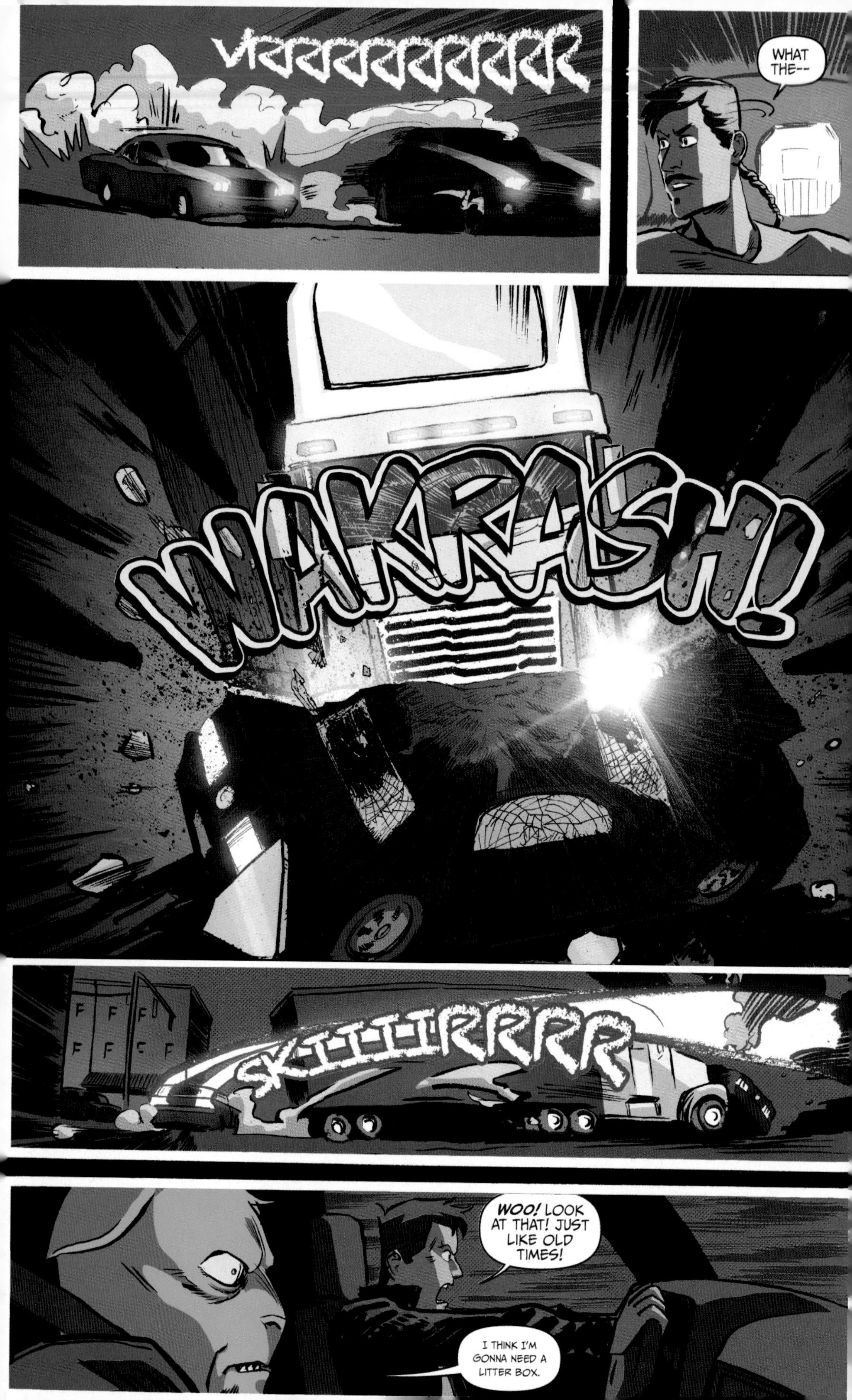
VRRRRRRRRRRRRR
WHAT THE--
WAKRASH!
SKIIIIIRRRR
WOO! LOOK AT THAT! JUST LIKE OLD TIMES!
I THINK I'M GONNA NEED A LITTER BOX.

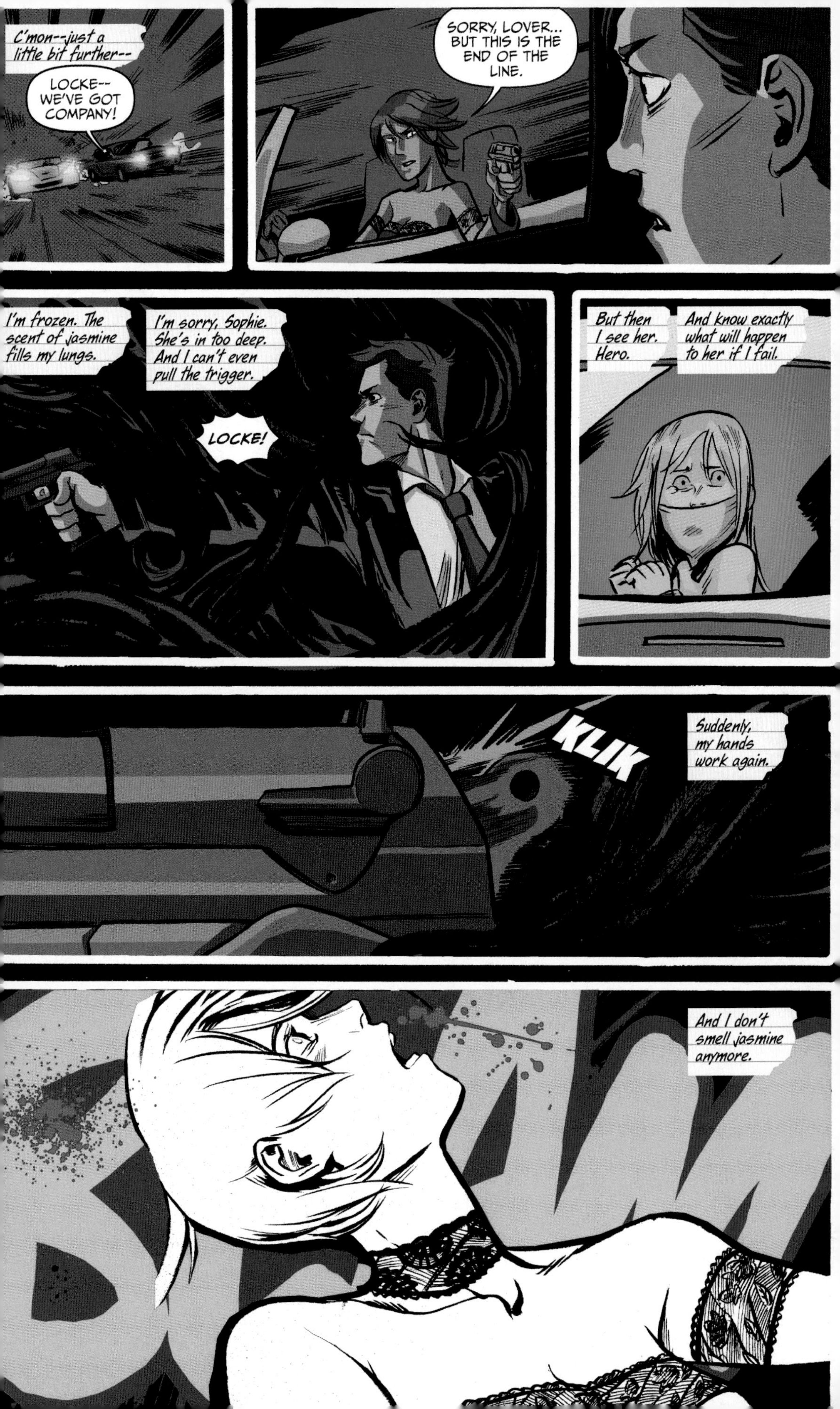
C'mon--just a little bit further--
LOCKE-- WE'VE GOT COMPANY!
SORRY, LOVER... BUT THIS IS THE END OF THE LINE.
I'm frozen. The scent of jasmine fills my lungs.
I'm sorry, Sophie. She's in too deep. And I can't even pull the trigger.
LOCKE!
But then I see her. Hero.
And know exactly what will happen to her if I fail.
KLIK
Suddenly, my hands work again.
And I don't smell jasmine anymore.

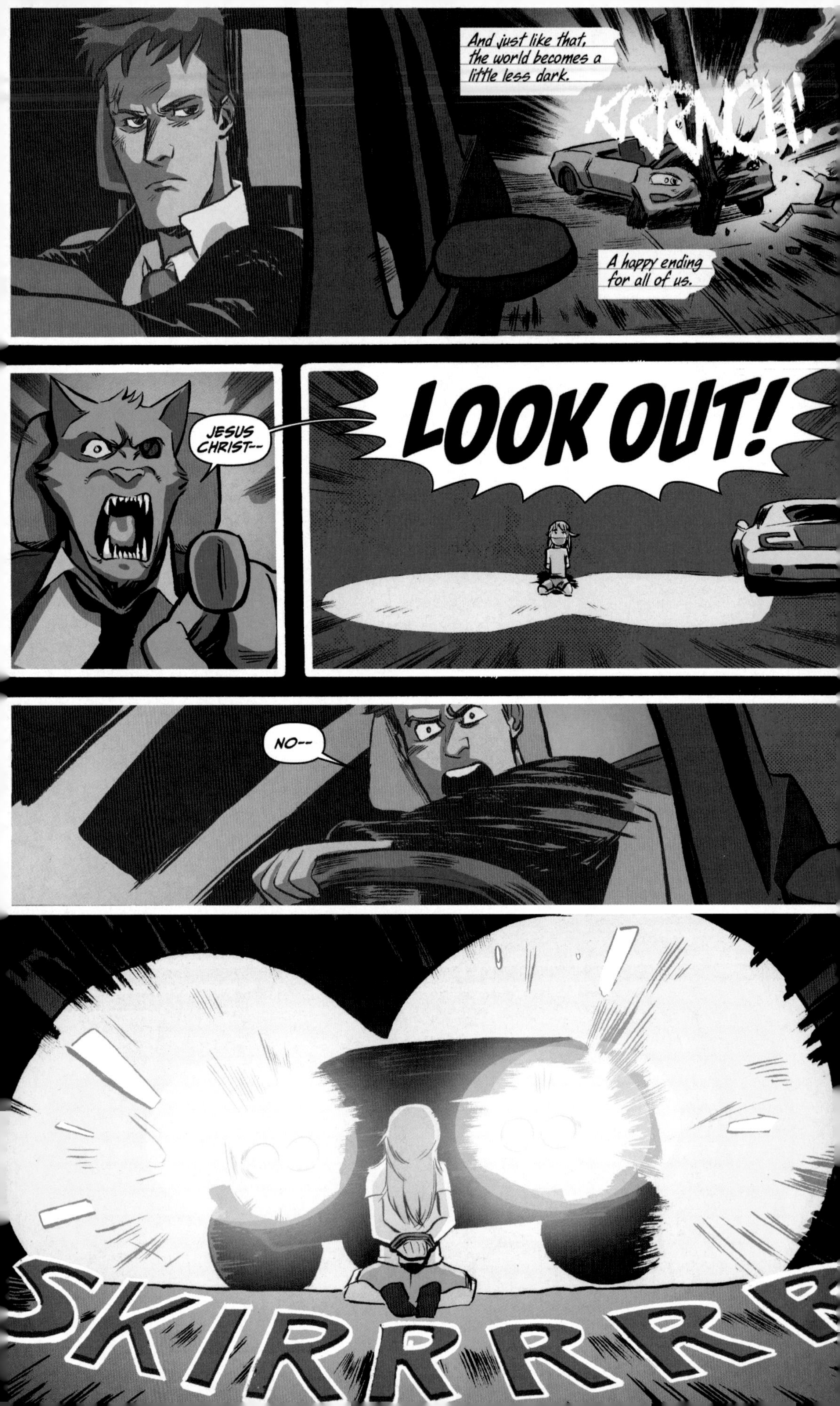
And just like that, the world becomes a little less dark.
KRRNCH!
A happy ending for all of us.
JESUS CHRIST--
LOOK OUT!
NO--
SKIRRRR

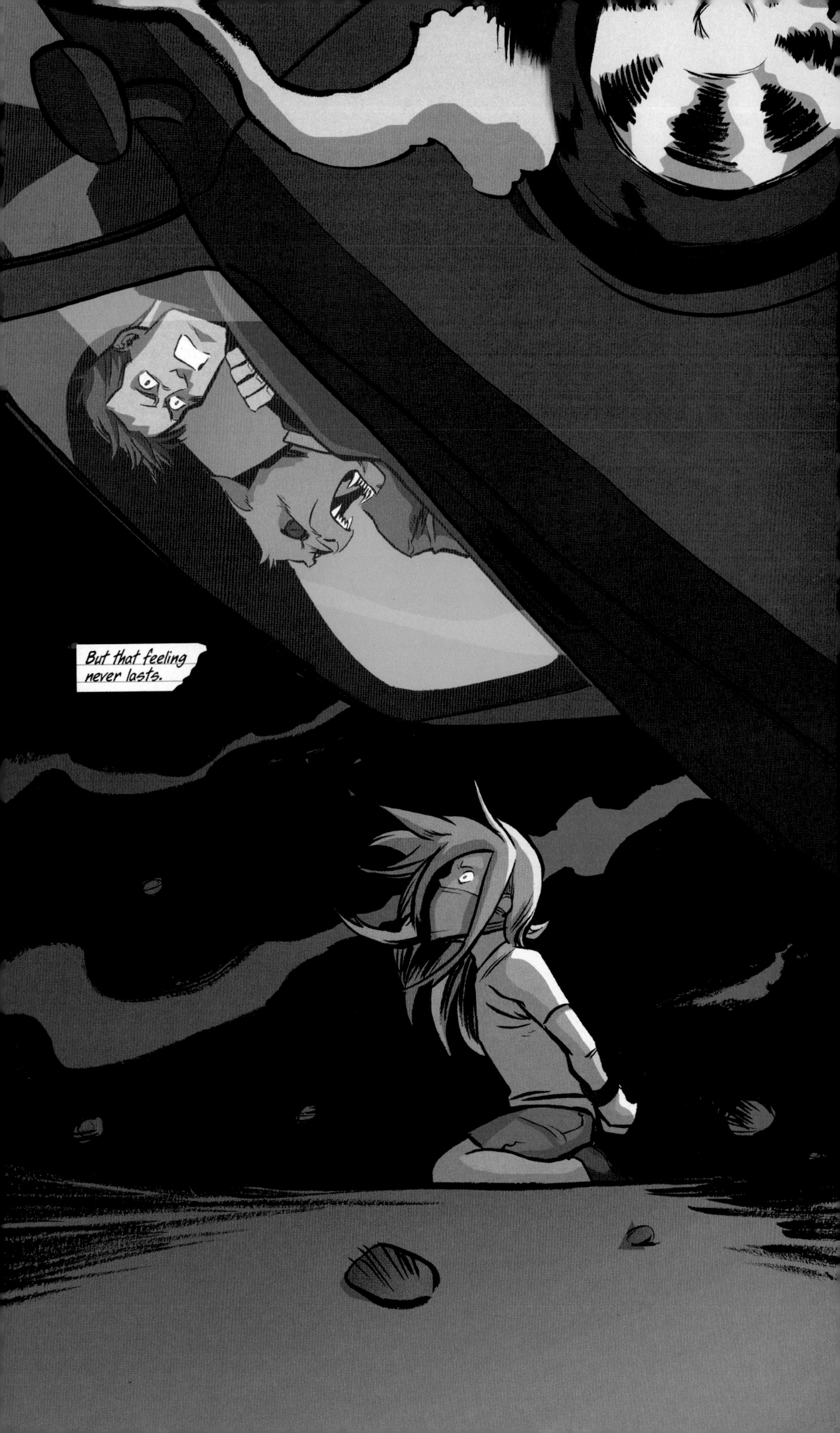
But that feeling never lasts.

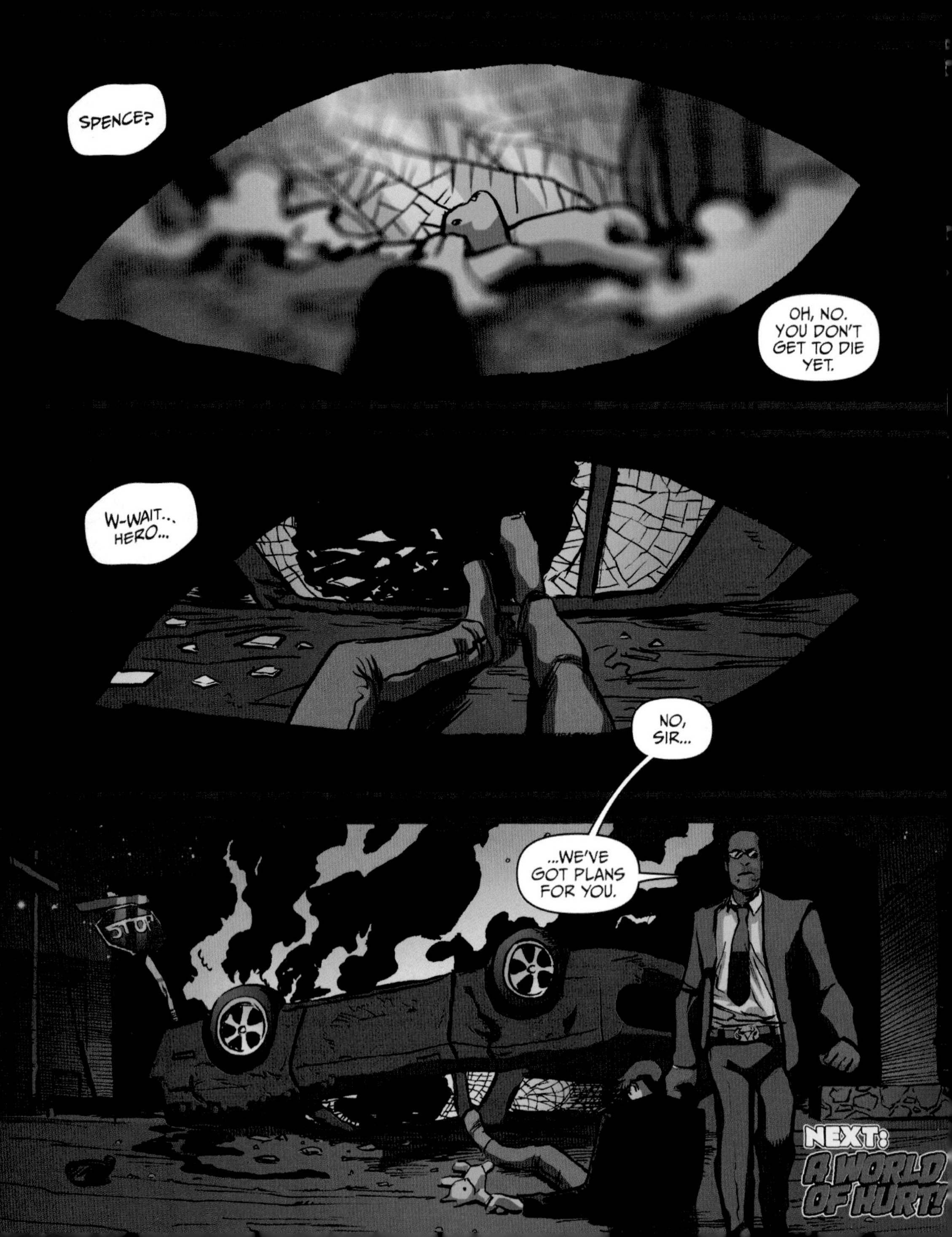
SPENCE?
OH, NO. YOU DON'T GET TO DIE YET.
W-WAIT... HERO...
NO, SIR...
...WE'VE GOT PLANS FOR YOU.
STOP
NEXT: A WORLD OF HURT!

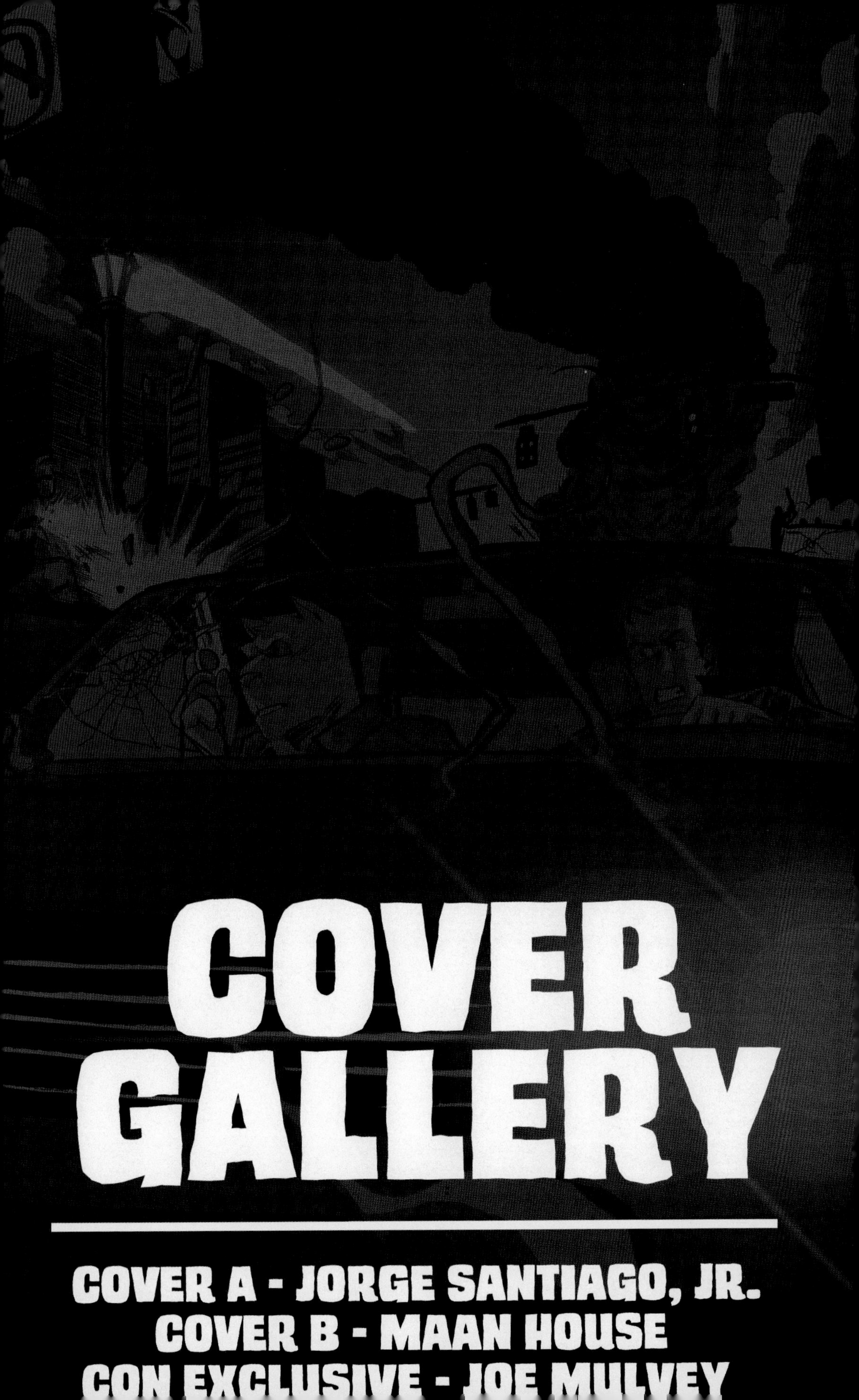

COVER GALLERY

COVER A - JORGE SANTIAGO, JR.
COVER B - MAAN HOUSE
CON EXCLUSIVE - JOE MULVEY

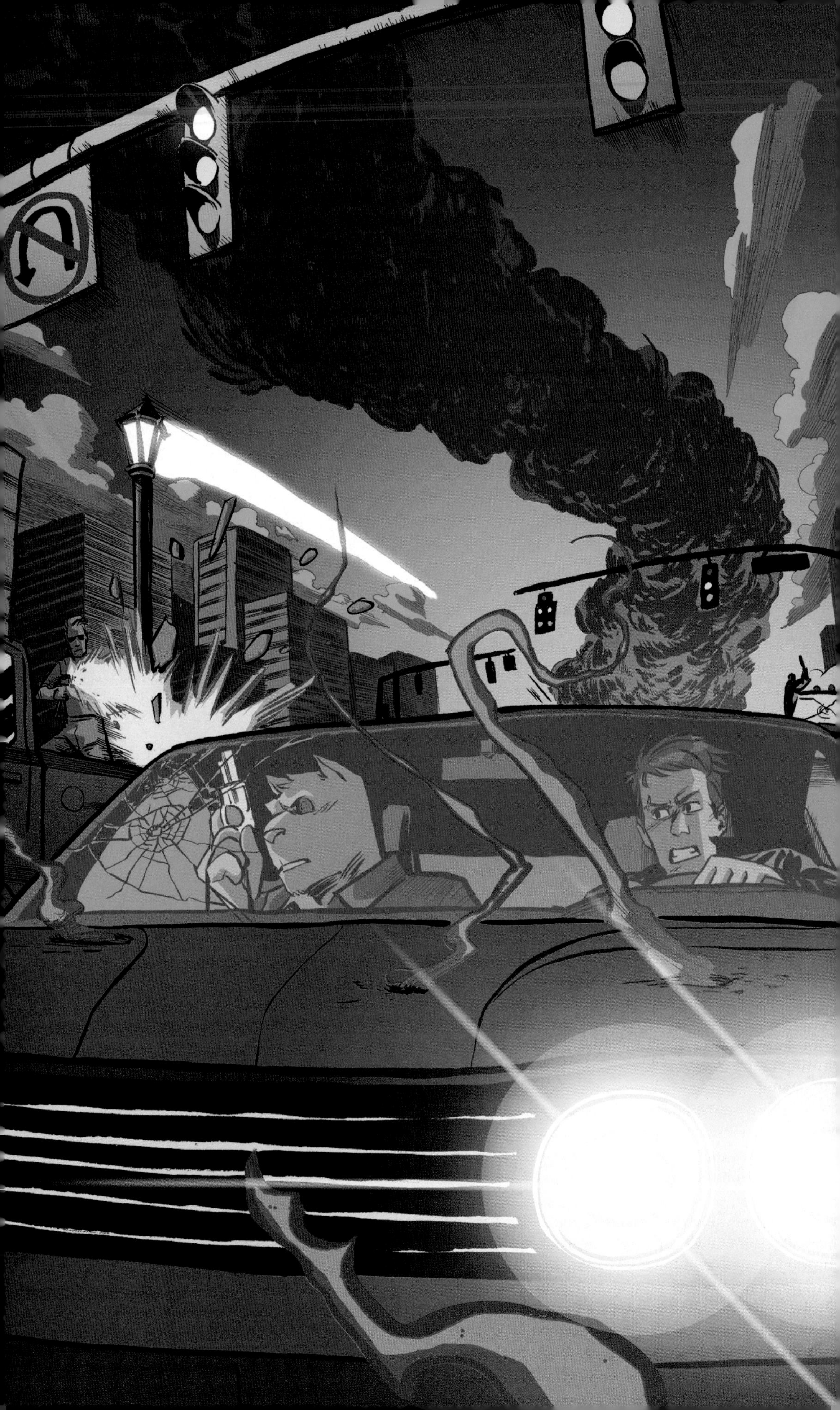

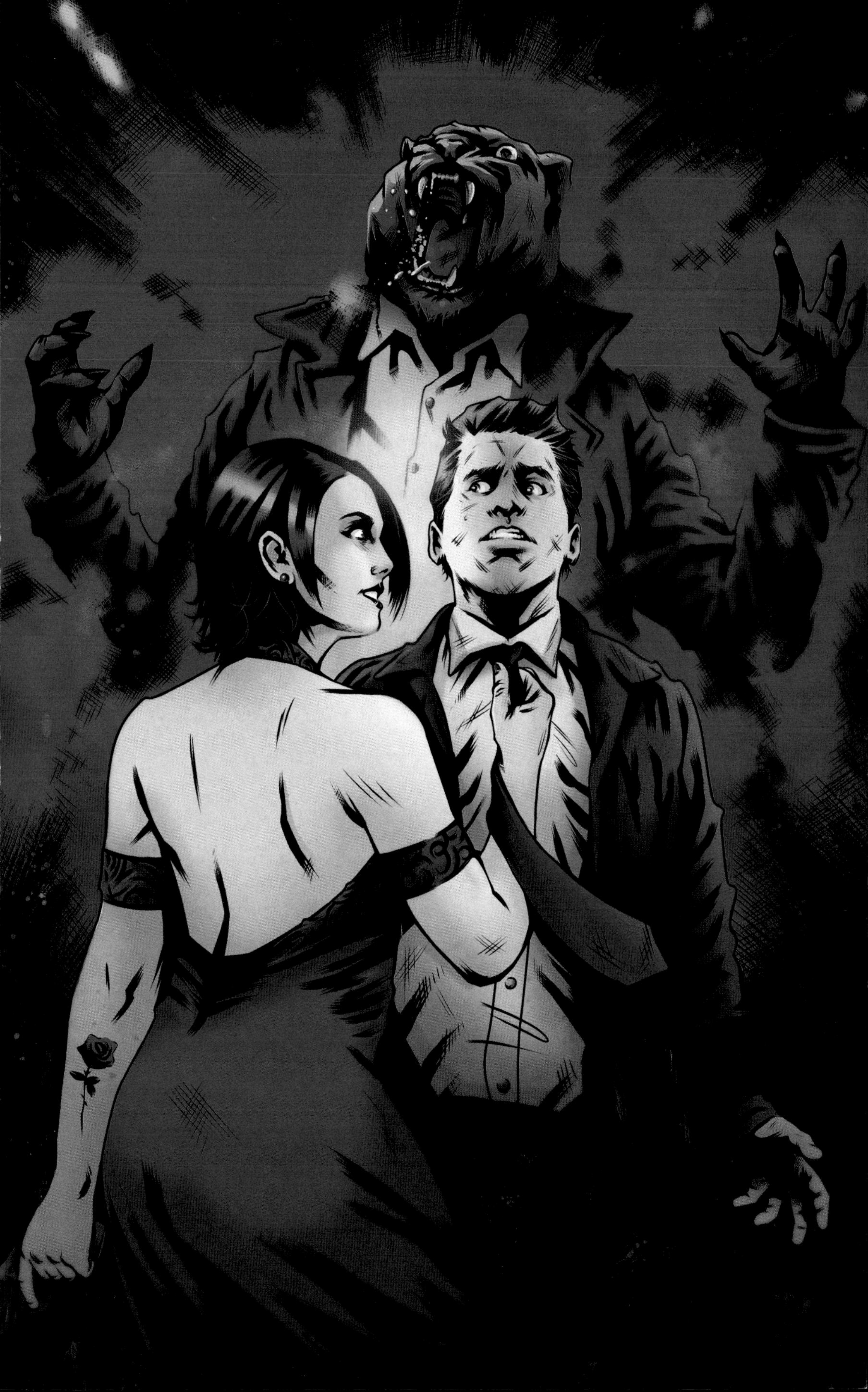

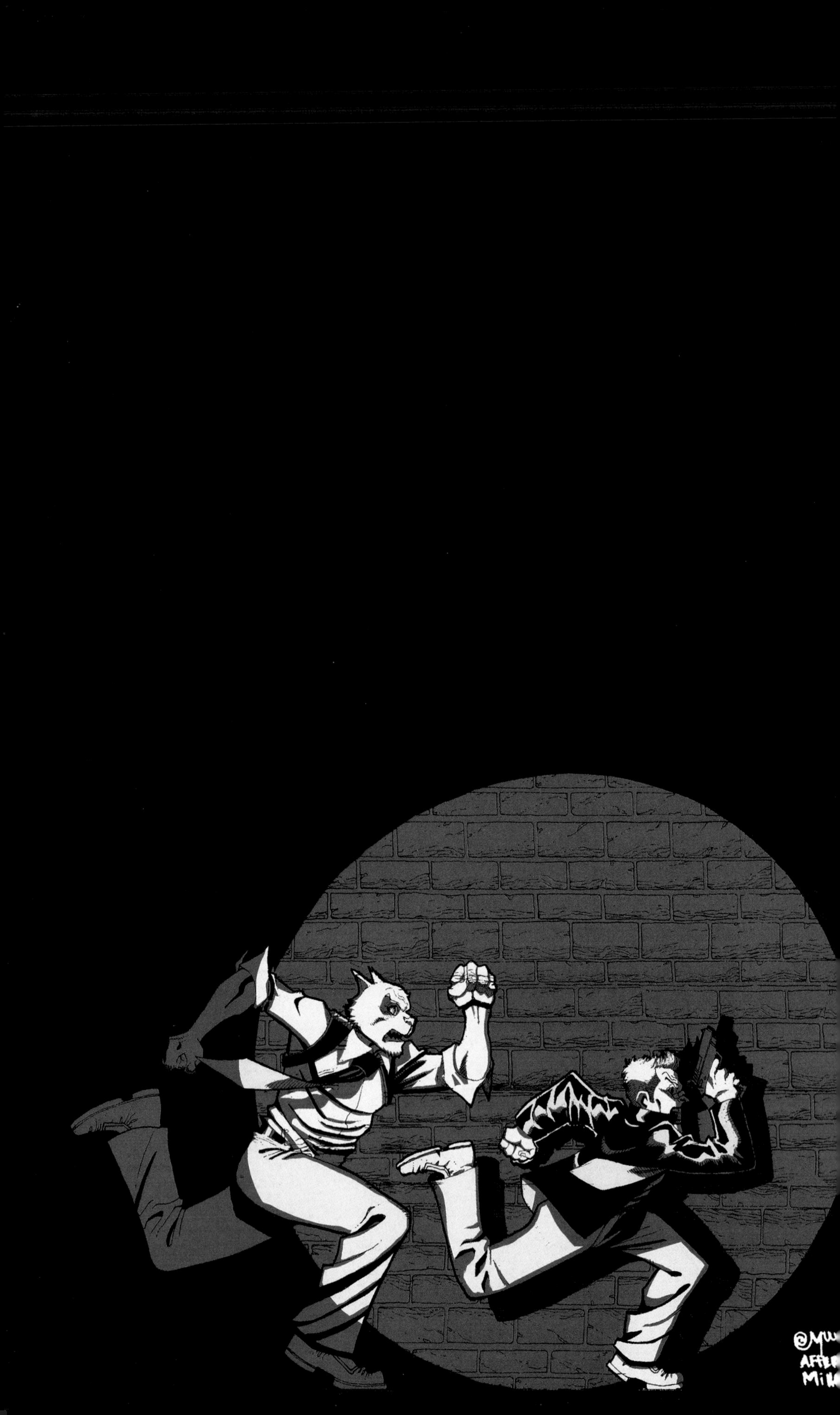

SCRIPT PAGES
BY DAVID PEPOSE

PAGE THIRTEEN:
Panel One: Tier one. Locke snaps out of his fear. He looks down at the pink rabbit doll, immediately recognizing it.

1 LOCKE CAP: The kid!

Panel Two: Shoving Ramona to the side, Locke runs from the office, chasing after the sound of the scream.

2 LOCKE CAP: Hero. Sophie's kid.

3 LOCKE CAP: She'd never go anywhere without her stuffed rabbit.

Panel Three: Tier two. Fuming, Ramona shouts into the phone on her desk.

4 LOCKE CAP: I thought she'd be safe from all this — but someone must have thought she was a loose end.

5 RAMONA: He knows! Take the girl and meet at the warehouse!

Panel Four: Locke races down the hallway, where Spencer begins to reform like mist. Spencer is shocked, like he just blacked out for a minute.

6 SPENCER (Smaller): Run—

7 SPENCER: Locke — what the hell happened?

Panel Five: Tier three. Locke bursts out of the back of the bar, where we see a white car zooming off into the distance. (Some sort of four-door, something that's classic and fast - in fact, all the cars should have that vintage quality. No Civics in this book!)

8 LOCKE: ...They've got Sophie's kid!

9 LOCKE CAP: I move just fast enough to watch her slip through my fingers.

Panel Six: Tears in her eyes, Hero stares at us from the back of the car.

10 LOCKE CAP: I see the terror in Hero's eyes as they drive away.

11 LOCKE CAP: It was the same look on Sophie's face in that dark, cold alley.

Panel Seven: Tier four. Thin letterbox panel Close-up on Locke's eyes, angry.

12 LOCKE CAP: They must have taken her to get me off the case.

SCRIPT PAGES
BY DAVID PEPOSE

PAGE FOURTEEN:
Panel One: Tier one. First three panels will be small, on one line. Locke twists the key into the ignition.

NO DIALOGUE

Panel Two: Locke shoves the stick shift into first gear.

NO DIALOGUE

Panel Three: The RPM dial goes to the redline.

NO DIALOGUE

Panel Four: Tier two. Big awesome shot of Spencer and Locke's red police cruiser (I'm thinking a classic Mustang or a Dodge Charger, but anything of that vintage will work) racing toward us like a bat out of hell

1 LOCKE CAP: They clearly don't know me very well

2 SFX: VRRRRRRRRRRRRMMMMMMM

Panel Five: Tier three. Inside the car, Locke is behind the wheel, while Spencer panics at how fast they're going.

3 LOCKE: You nervous, Spence? You look nervous.

4 SPENCER (Smaller): Toofasttoofasttoofasttoofast

SCRIPT PAGES
BY DAVID PEPOSE

PAGE FIFTEEN:
Panel One: The white getaway car's tail lights arc as the car swerves into a hard corner; Locke's red cruiser does the same.

1 SFX: VRRRRMMMMMMMM!

2 LOCKE CAP: Their car makes the turn like I was standing still — gotta be one of those European models.

3 LOCKE CAP: Seven hundred Italian horses thundering down Fifth Avenue.

Panel Two: Inside the white getaway car, the DRIVER looks in his rear view mirror to see Locke's red cruiser roaring towards them.

4 LOCKE CAP: These guys — they're professionals.

5 DRIVER: Shit! He's on our tail!

6 HENCHMAN: Just drive—

Panel Three: One of the other HENCHMEN leans out of the back window, firing an automatic rifle behind them!

7 HENCHMAN: I got this!

8 SFX: BRAKKABRAKKABRAKKABRAKKA

9 LOCKE CAP: They're well-funded, well-equipped — and they know how to maneuver.

Panel Four: Locke's red cruiser swerves through traffic to avoid the gunfire—

10 LOCKE CAP: But then again—

11 SFX: SKREEEEEEEEEE

Panel Five: Cut to flashback to young Locke and Spencer in their red wagon, making an impossible swerve—

NO DIALOGUE

Panel Six: Cut back to present-day, the red cruiser continues to swerve through another lane, still unscathed. The bullets hit the pavement just ahead of them.

12 LOCKE CAP: So do I.

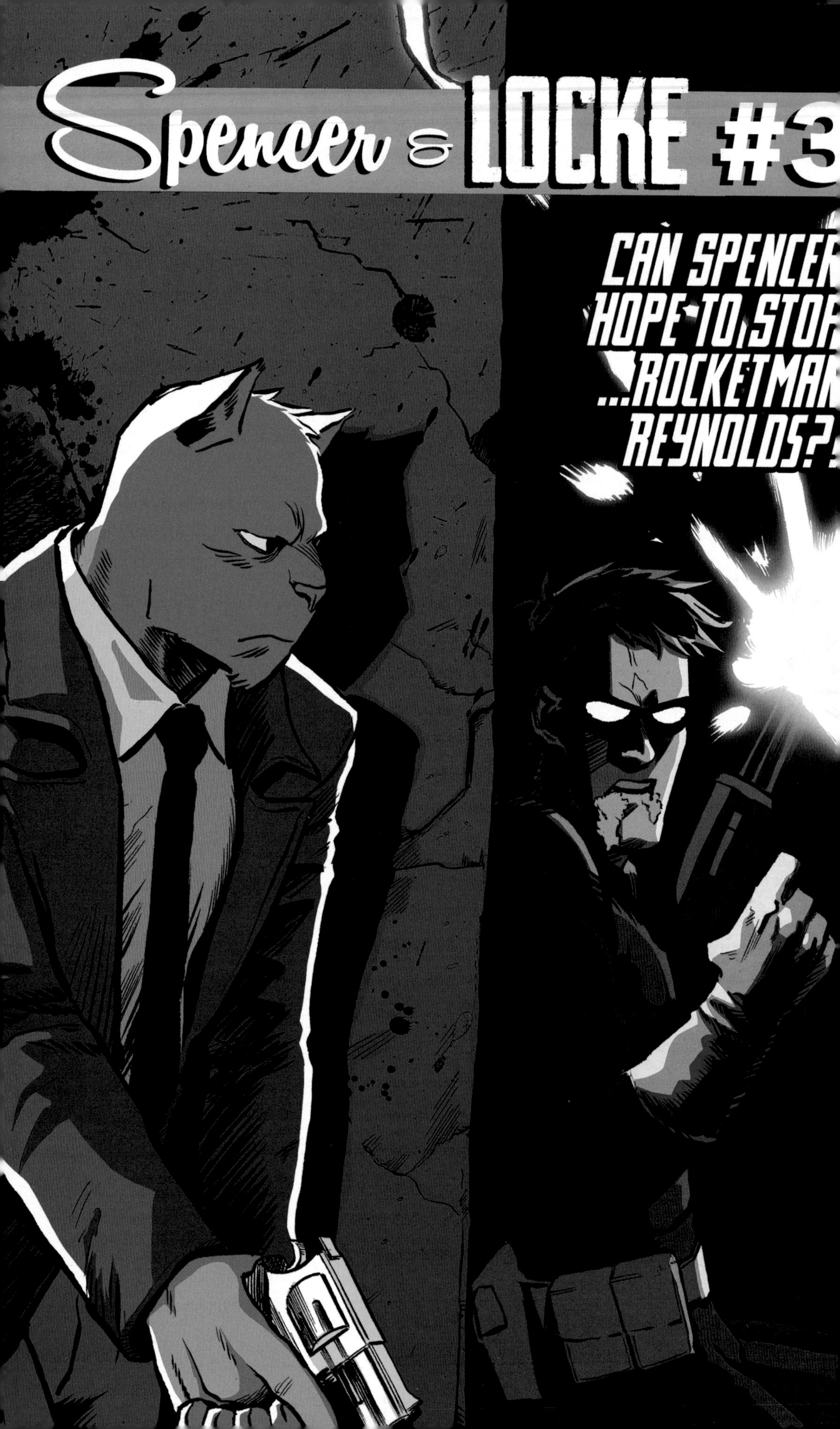
Spencer & LOCKE #3
CAN SPENCER HOPE TO STOP ...ROCKETMAN REYNOLDS?!

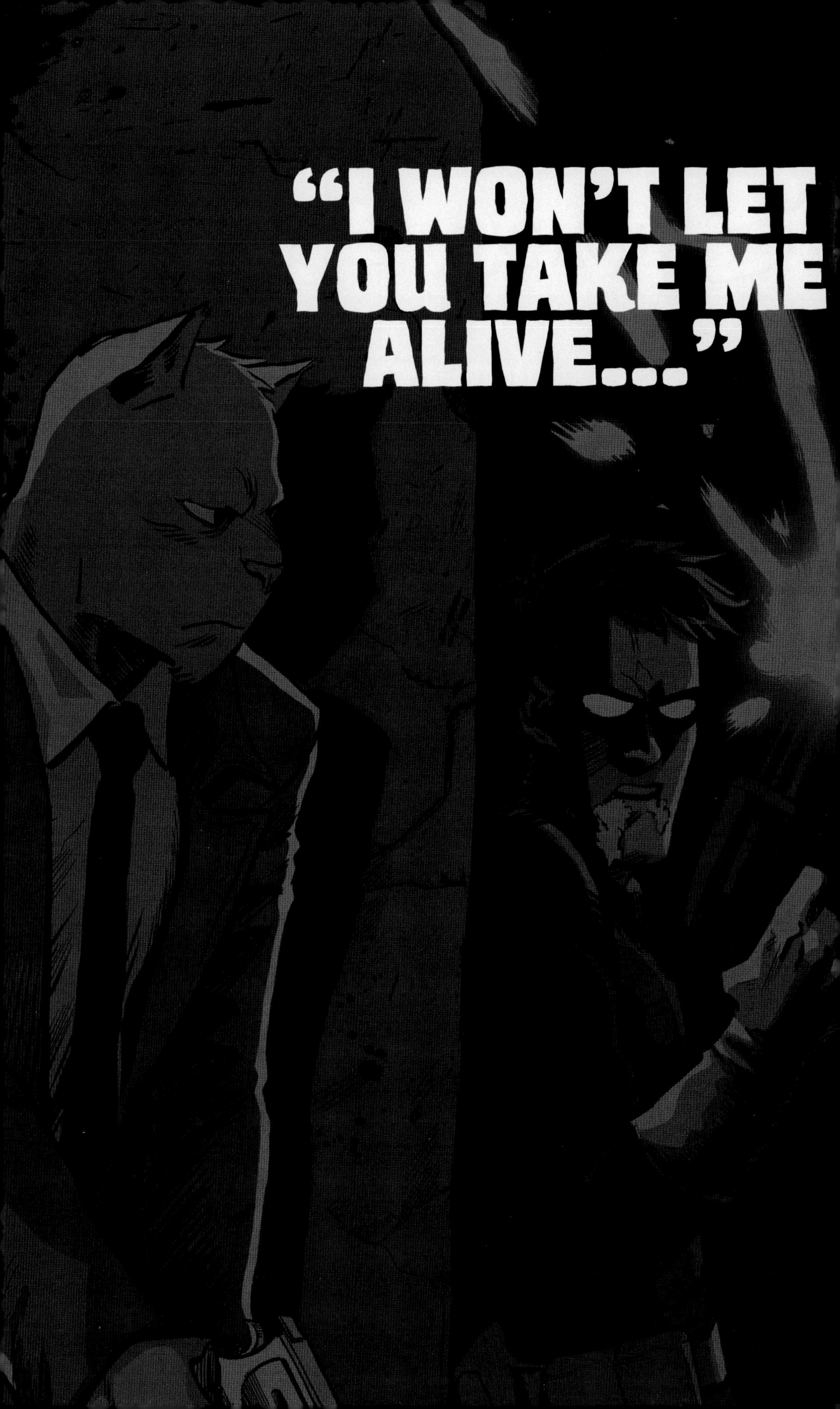
"I WON'T LET YOU TAKE ME ALIVE..."

Spencer & LOCKE ③

WRITTEN BY
DAVID PEPOSE

ART BY
JORGE SANTIAGO, JR.

COLORS BY
JASEN SMITH

LETTERS BY
COLIN BELL

JASON MARTIN: PUBLISHER • SHAWN GABBORIN: EDITOR IN CHIEF • NICOLE D'ANDRIA: MARKETING DIRECTOR/EDITOR
JIM DIETZ: SOCIAL MEDIA MANAGER • DANIELLE DAVISON: EXECUTIVE ADMINISTRATOR • BRYAN SEATON: CEO • SHAWN PRYOR: PRESIDENT OF CREATOR RELATIONS

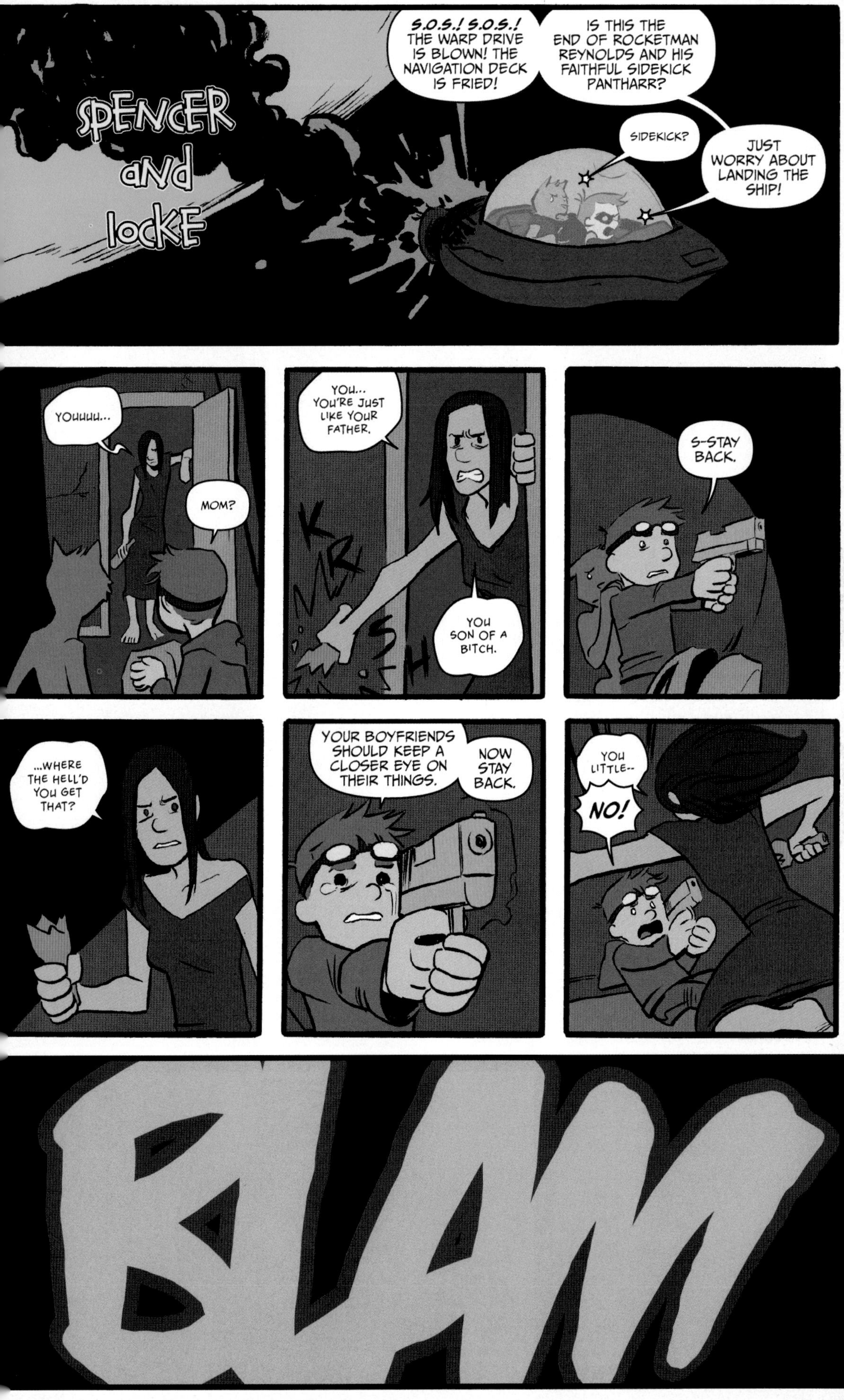
SPENCER and locke
S.O.S.! S.O.S.! THE WARP DRIVE IS BLOWN! THE NAVIGATION DECK IS FRIED!
IS THIS THE END OF ROCKETMAN REYNOLDS AND HIS FAITHFUL SIDEKICK PANTHARR?
SIDEKICK?
JUST WORRY ABOUT LANDING THE SHIP!
YOUuuu...
MOM?
YOU... YOU'RE JUST LIKE YOUR FATHER.
KRASH
YOU SON OF A BITCH.
S-STAY BACK.
...WHERE THE HELL'D YOU GET THAT?
YOUR BOYFRIENDS SHOULD KEEP A CLOSER EYE ON THEIR THINGS.
NOW STAY BACK.
YOU LITTLE--
NO!
BLAM

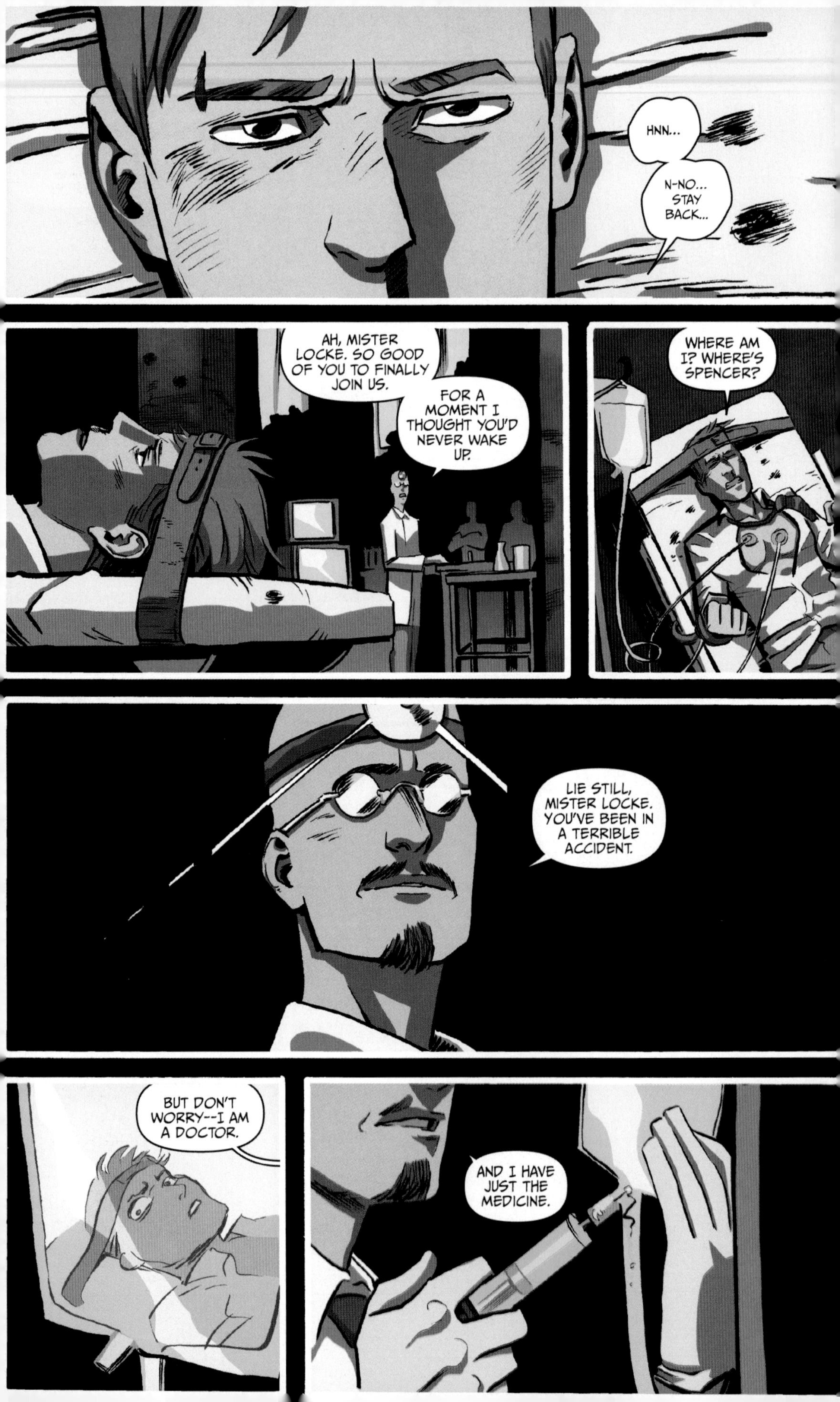
HNN...
N-NO... STAY BACK...
AH, MISTER LOCKE. SO GOOD OF YOU TO FINALLY JOIN US.
FOR A MOMENT I THOUGHT YOU'D NEVER WAKE UP.
WHERE AM I? WHERE'S SPENCER?
LIE STILL, MISTER LOCKE. YOU'VE BEEN IN A TERRIBLE ACCIDENT.
BUT DON'T WORRY--I AM A DOCTOR.
AND I HAVE JUST THE MEDICINE.

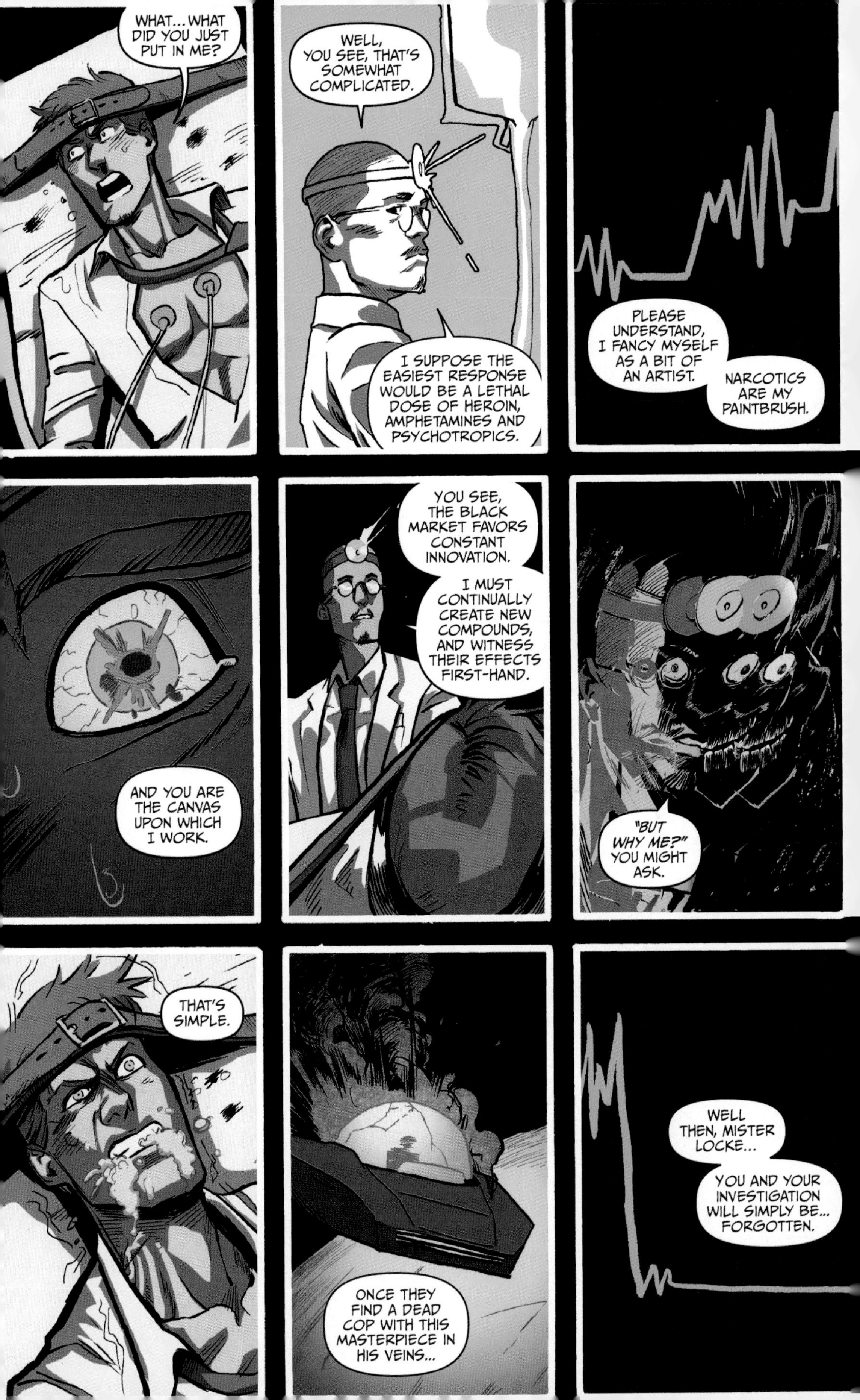
WHAT... WHAT DID YOU JUST PUT IN ME?
WELL, YOU SEE, THAT'S SOMEWHAT COMPLICATED.
I SUPPOSE THE EASIEST RESPONSE WOULD BE A LETHAL DOSE OF HEROIN, AMPHETAMINES AND PSYCHOTROPICS.
PLEASE UNDERSTAND, I FANCY MYSELF AS A BIT OF AN ARTIST.
NARCOTICS ARE MY PAINTBRUSH.
AND YOU ARE THE CANVAS UPON WHICH I WORK.
YOU SEE, THE BLACK MARKET FAVORS CONSTANT INNOVATION.
I MUST CONTINUALLY CREATE NEW COMPOUNDS, AND WITNESS THEIR EFFECTS FIRST-HAND.
"BUT WHY ME?" YOU MIGHT ASK.
THAT'S SIMPLE.
ONCE THEY FIND A DEAD COP WITH THIS MASTERPIECE IN HIS VEINS...
WELL THEN, MISTER LOCKE...
YOU AND YOUR INVESTIGATION WILL SIMPLY BE... FORGOTTEN.

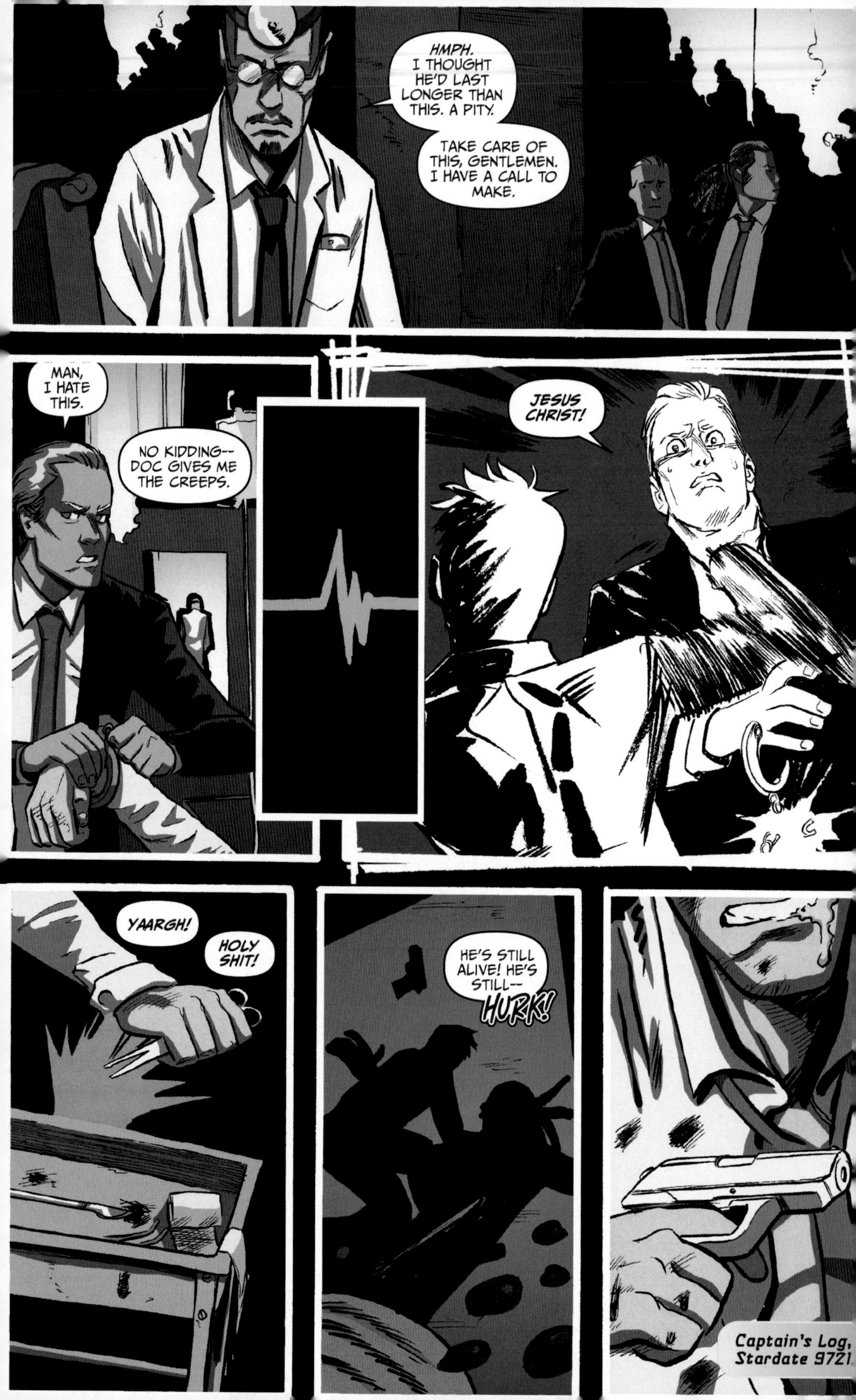
HMPH. I THOUGHT HE'D LAST LONGER THAN THIS. A PITY.
TAKE CARE OF THIS, GENTLEMEN. I HAVE A CALL TO MAKE.
MAN, I HATE THIS.
NO KIDDING-- DOC GIVES ME THE CREEPS.
JESUS CHRIST!
YAARGH!
HOLY SHIT!
HE'S STILL ALIVE! HE'S STILL--
HURK!
Captain's Log, Stardate 9721

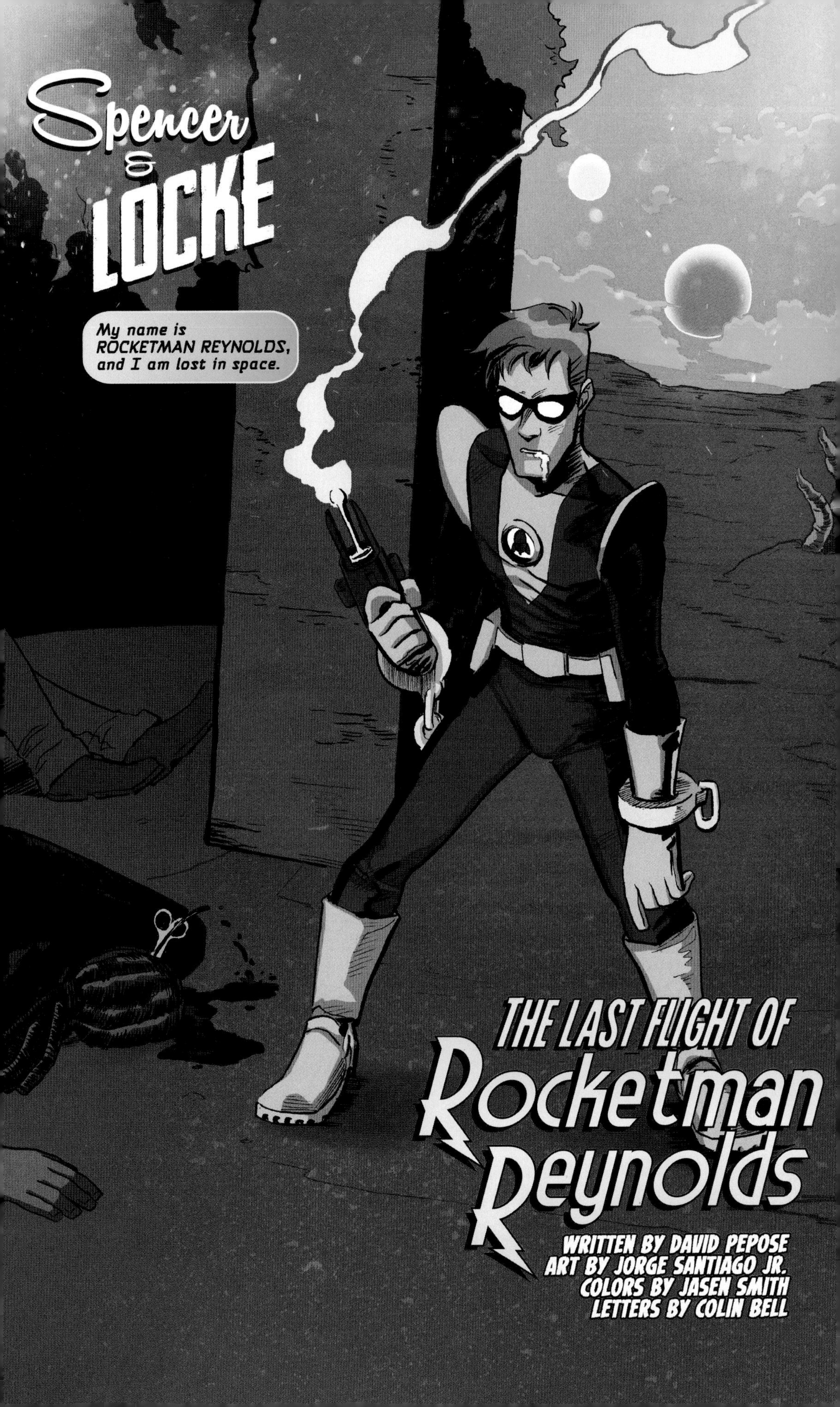
Spencer & LOCKE
My name is ROCKETMAN REYNOLDS, and I am lost in space.
THE LAST FLIGHT OF Rocketman Reynolds
WRITTEN BY DAVID PEPOSE
ART BY JORGE SANTIAGO JR.
COLORS BY JASEN SMITH
LETTERS BY COLIN BELL

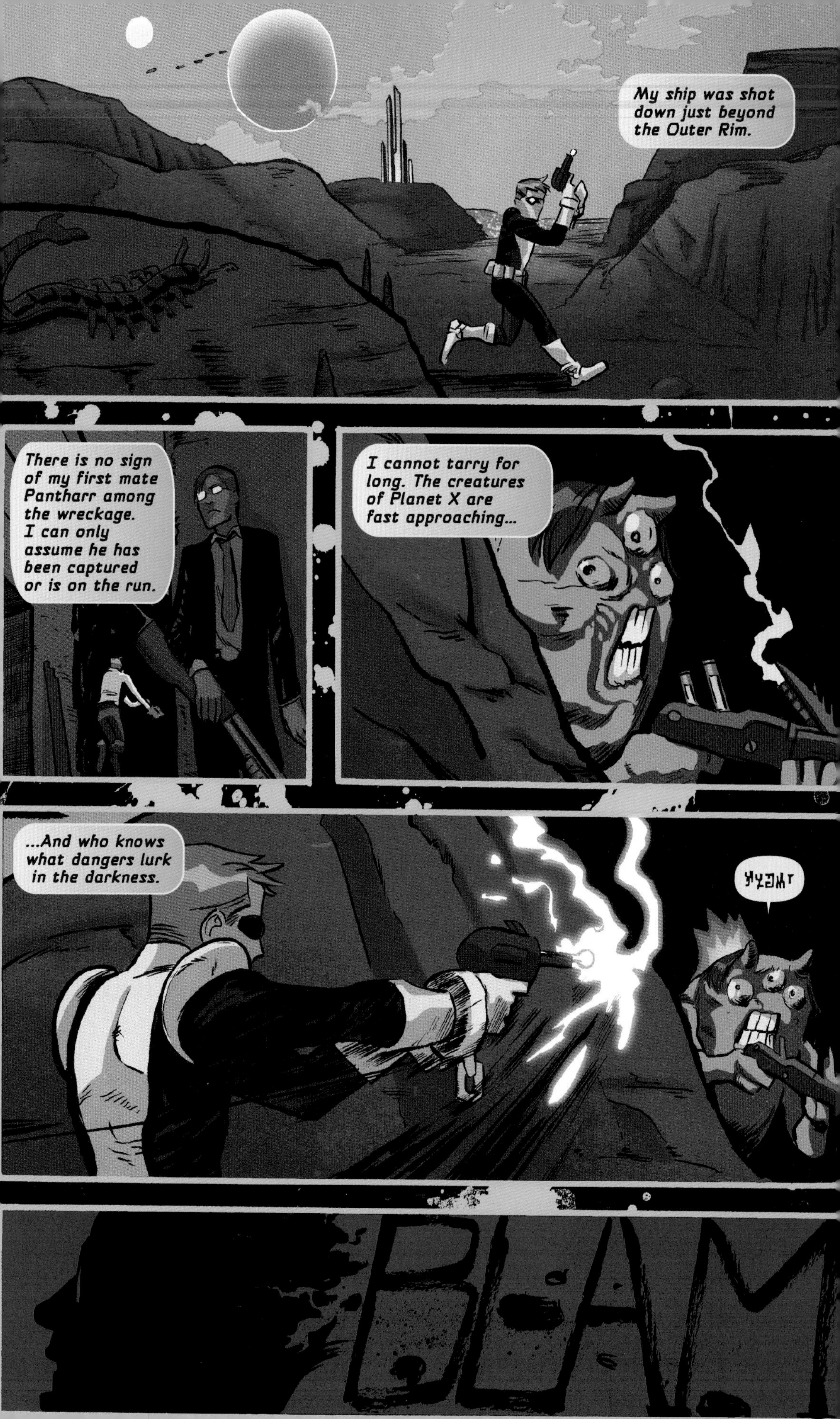
My ship was shot down just beyond the Outer Rim.
There is no sign of my first mate Pantharr among the wreckage. I can only assume he has been captured or is on the run.
I cannot tarry for long. The creatures of Planet X are fast approaching...
...And who knows what dangers lurk in the darkness.
BEAM

This is bad.

I was supposed to be watching him. I was supposed to have his back.

How could I have lost him?

Stop beating yourself up, Spence-- focus on the clues.

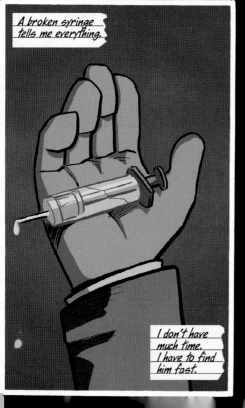

A broken syringe tells me everything.

I don't have much time. I have to find him fast.

Because with this stuff pumping through his system...

...Locke's one step away from a heart attack.

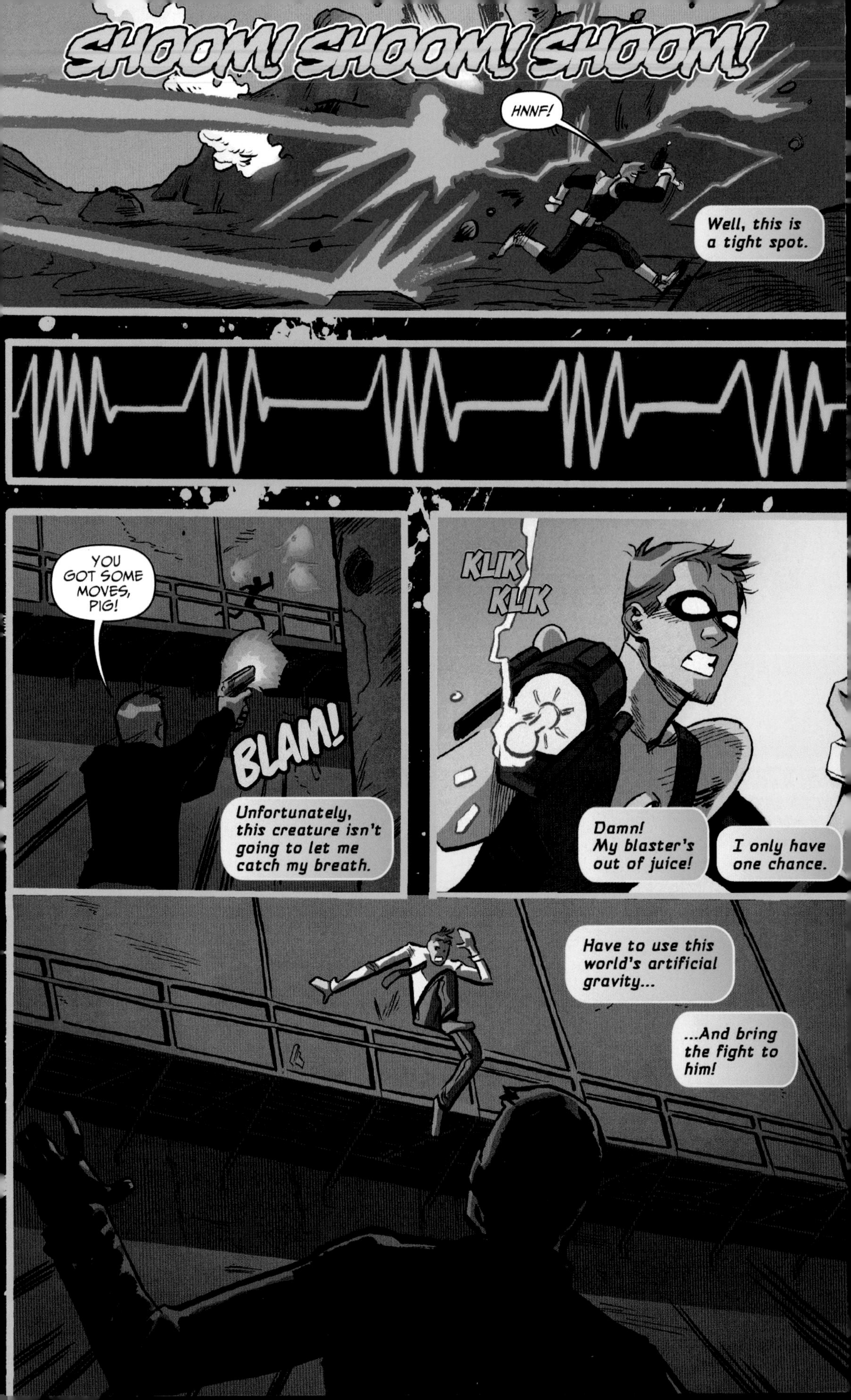
SHOOM! SHOOM! SHOOM!
HNNF!
Well, this is a tight spot.
YOU GOT SOME MOVES, PIG!
BLAM!
Unfortunately, this creature isn't going to let me catch my breath.
KLIK KLIK
Damn! My blaster's out of juice!
I only have one chance.
Have to use this world's artificial gravity...
...And bring the fight to him!

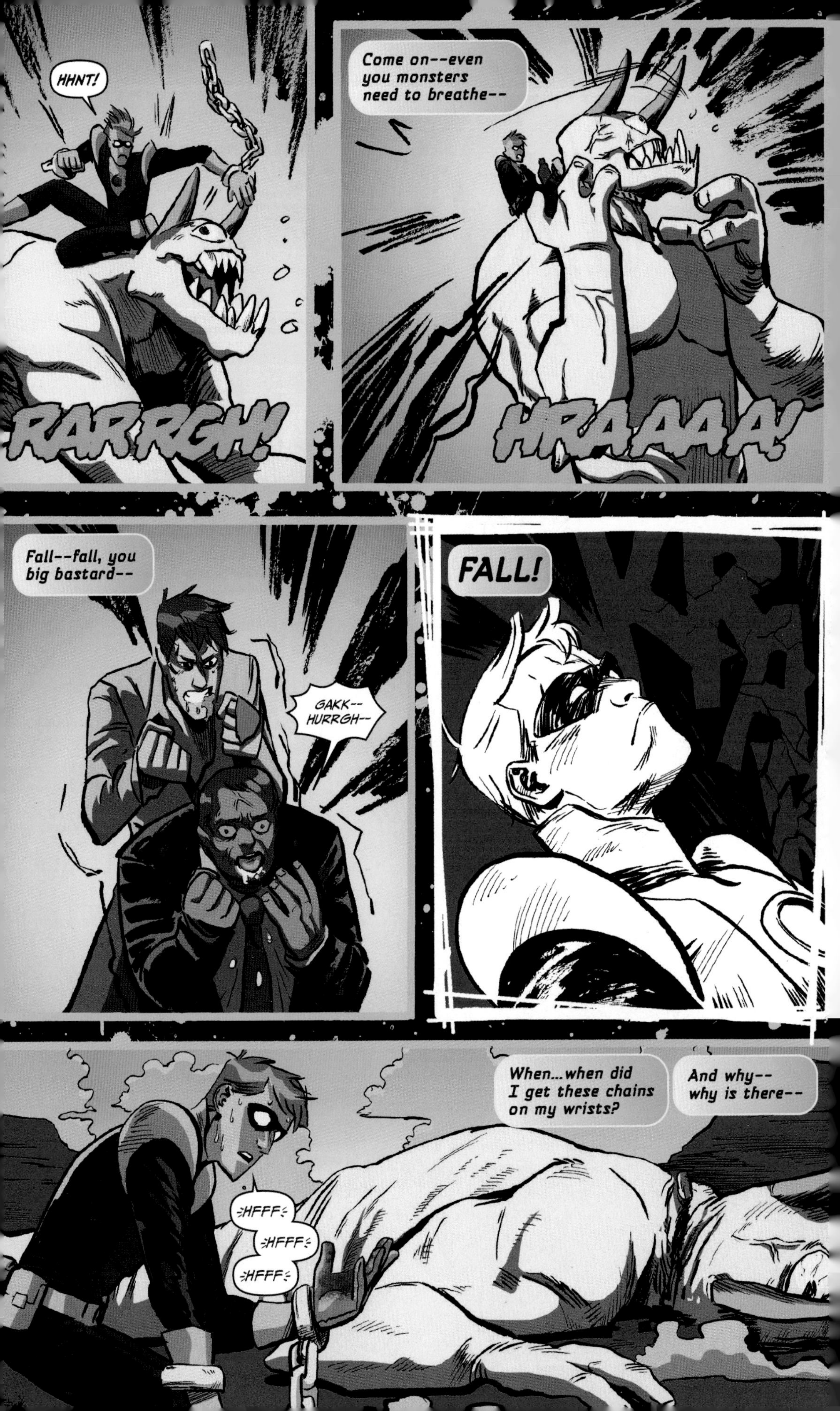
HHNT!
RARRGH!
Come on--even you monsters need to breathe--
HRAAAA!
Fall--fall, you big bastard--
GAKK-- HURRGH--
FALL!
When...when did I get these chains on my wrists?
And why-- why is there--
HFFF
HFFF
HFFF

--SO MUCH BLOOD--

My lungs burn-- heart wants to explode inside my chest--

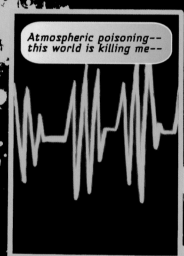

Atmospheric poisoning-- this world is killing me--

C'mon, Reynolds... get up...

You made a promise...

No matter how much it hurts...no matter what it costs you...

You can't give in to this place.

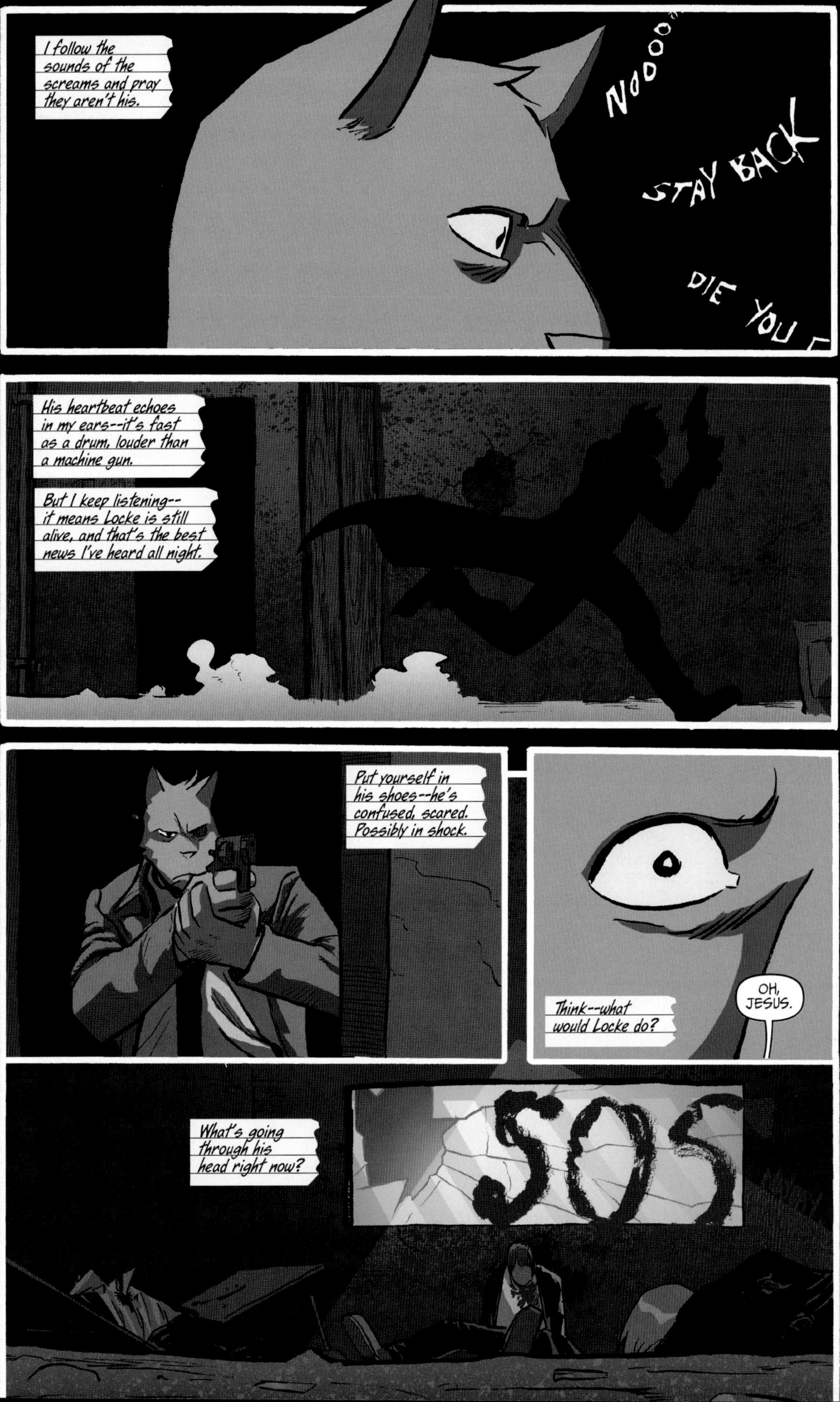
I follow the sounds of the screams and pray they aren't his.
NOOOO
STAY BACK
DIE YOU
His heartbeat echoes in my ears--it's fast as a drum, louder than a machine gun.
But I keep listening--it means Locke is still alive, and that's the best news I've heard all night.
Put yourself in his shoes--he's confused, scared. Possibly in shock.
Think--what would Locke do?
OH, JESUS.
What's going through his head right now?
SOS

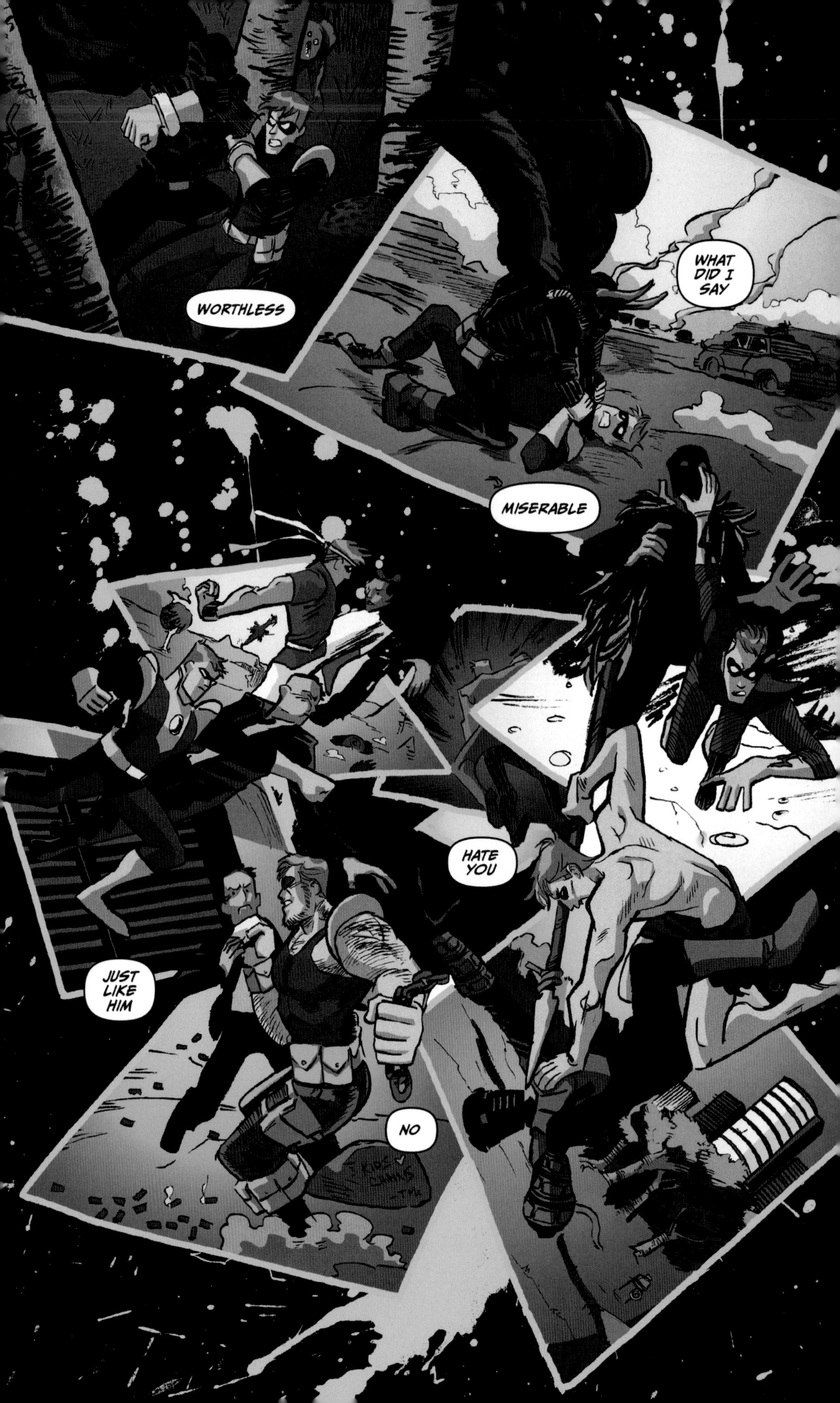
WORTHLESS
WHAT DID I SAY
MISERABLE
HATE YOU
JUST LIKE HIM
NO

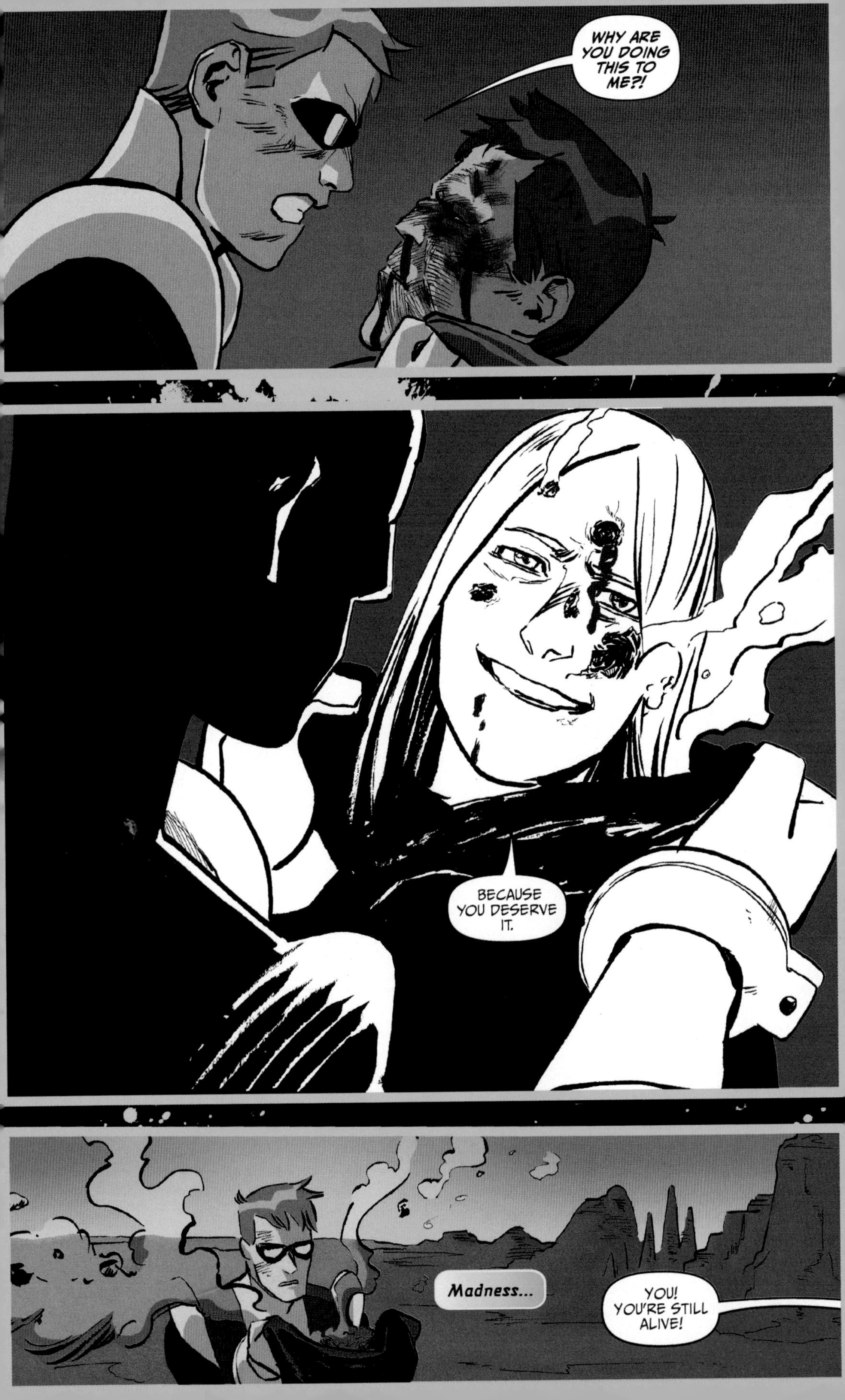
WHY ARE YOU DOING THIS TO ME?!
BECAUSE YOU DESERVE IT.
Madness...
YOU! YOU'RE STILL ALIVE!

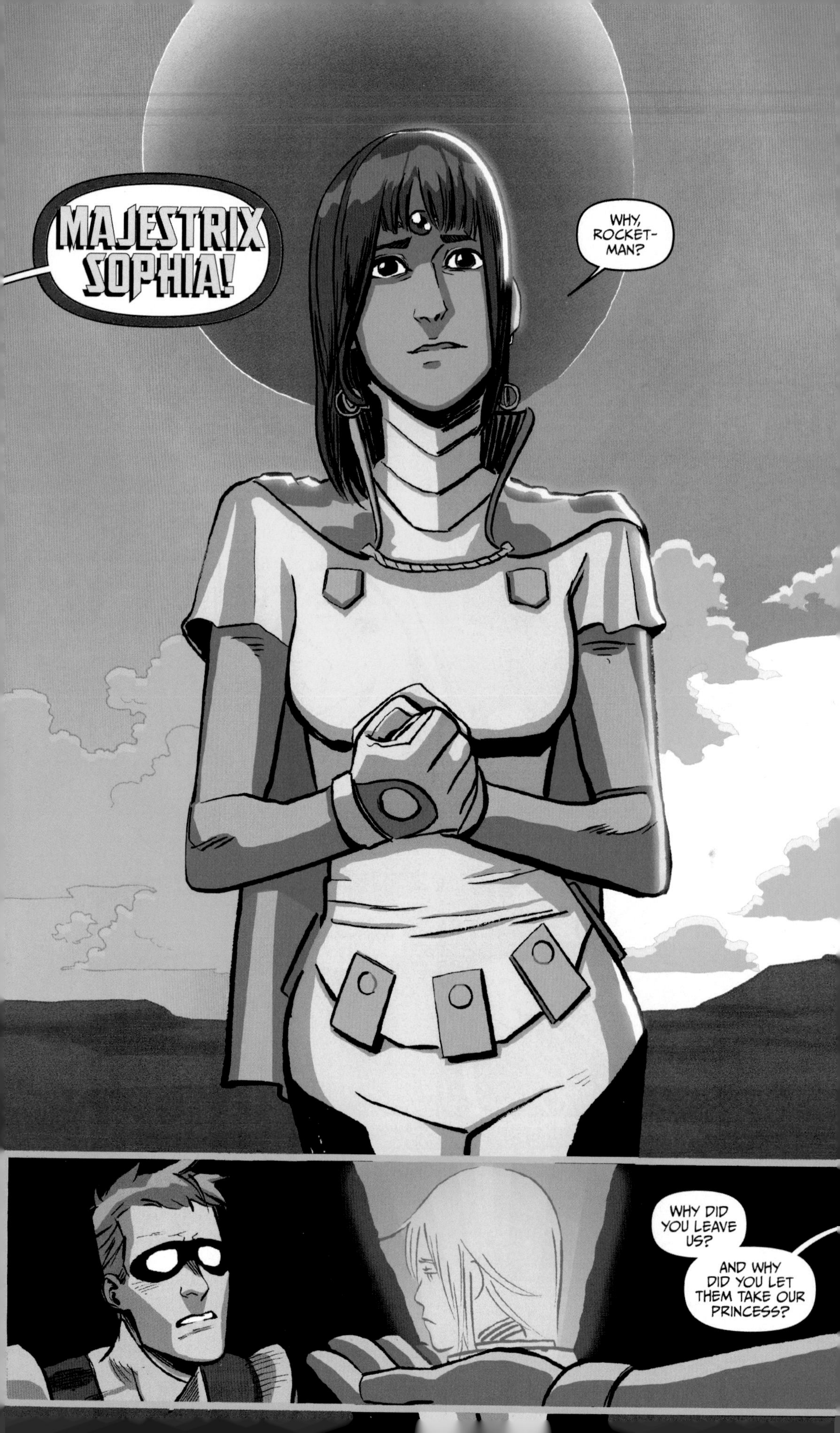
MAJESTRIX SOPHIA!
WHY, ROCKET-MAN?
WHY DID YOU LEAVE US?
AND WHY DID YOU LET THEM TAKE OUR PRINCESS?

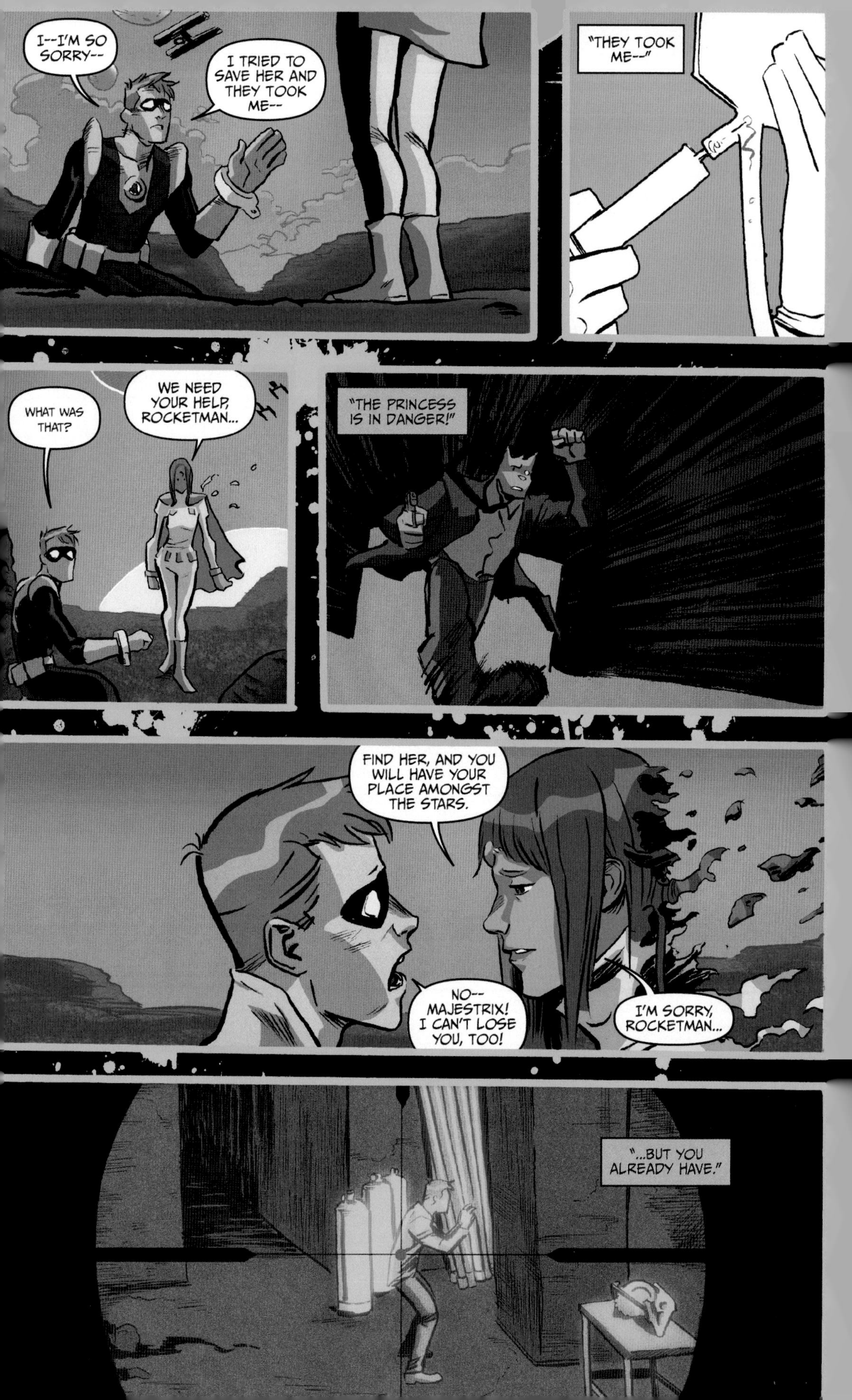
I--I'M SO SORRY--
I TRIED TO SAVE HER AND THEY TOOK ME--
"THEY TOOK ME--"
WHAT WAS THAT?
WE NEED YOUR HELP, ROCKETMAN...
"THE PRINCESS IS IN DANGER!"
FIND HER, AND YOU WILL HAVE YOUR PLACE AMONGST THE STARS.
NO-- MAJESTRIX! I CAN'T LOSE YOU, TOO!
I'M SORRY, ROCKETMAN...
"...BUT YOU ALREADY HAVE."

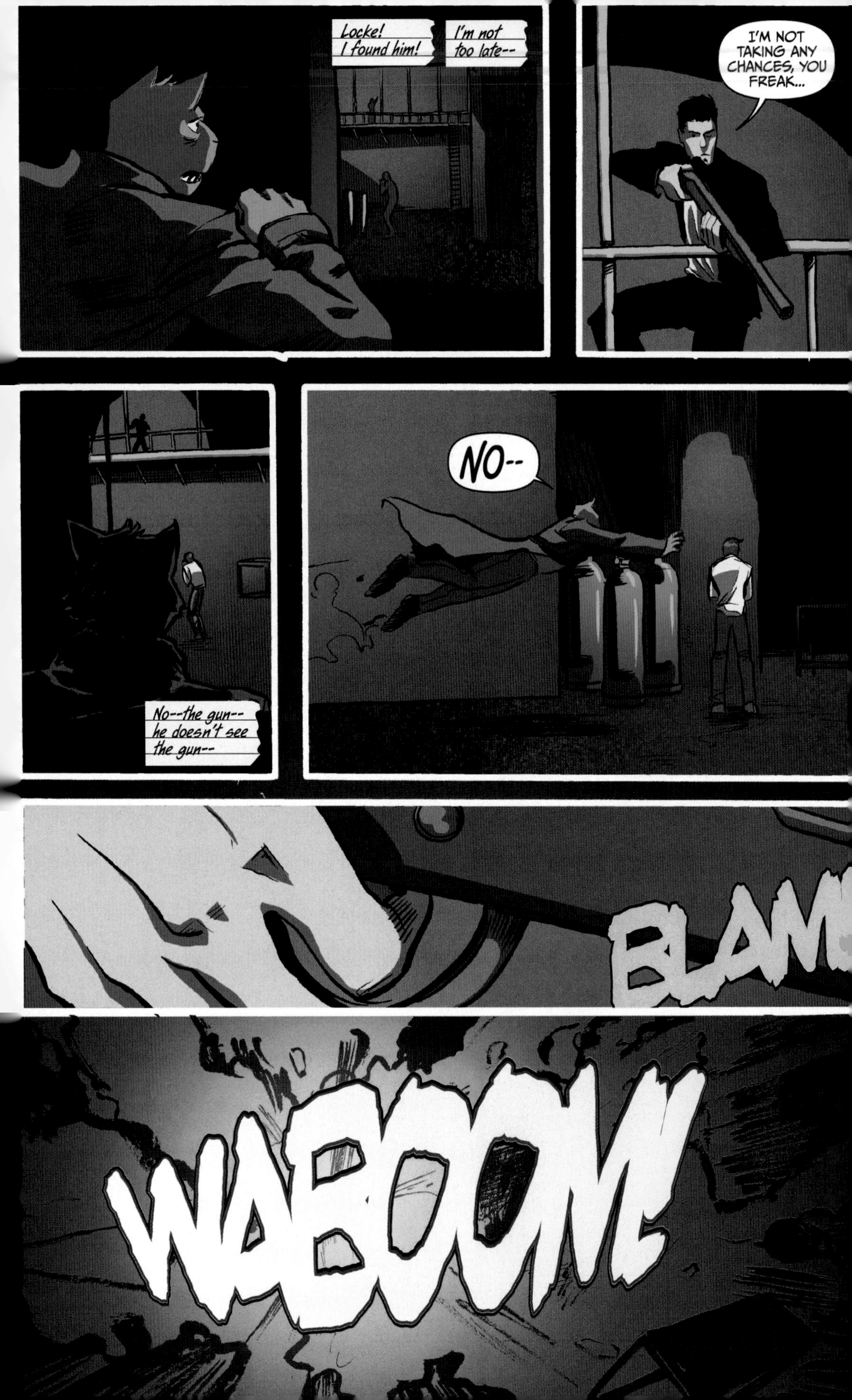
Locke!
I found him!
I'm not
too late--
I'M NOT TAKING ANY CHANCES, YOU FREAK...
No--the gun--
he doesn't see
the gun--
NO--
BLAM
WABOOM!

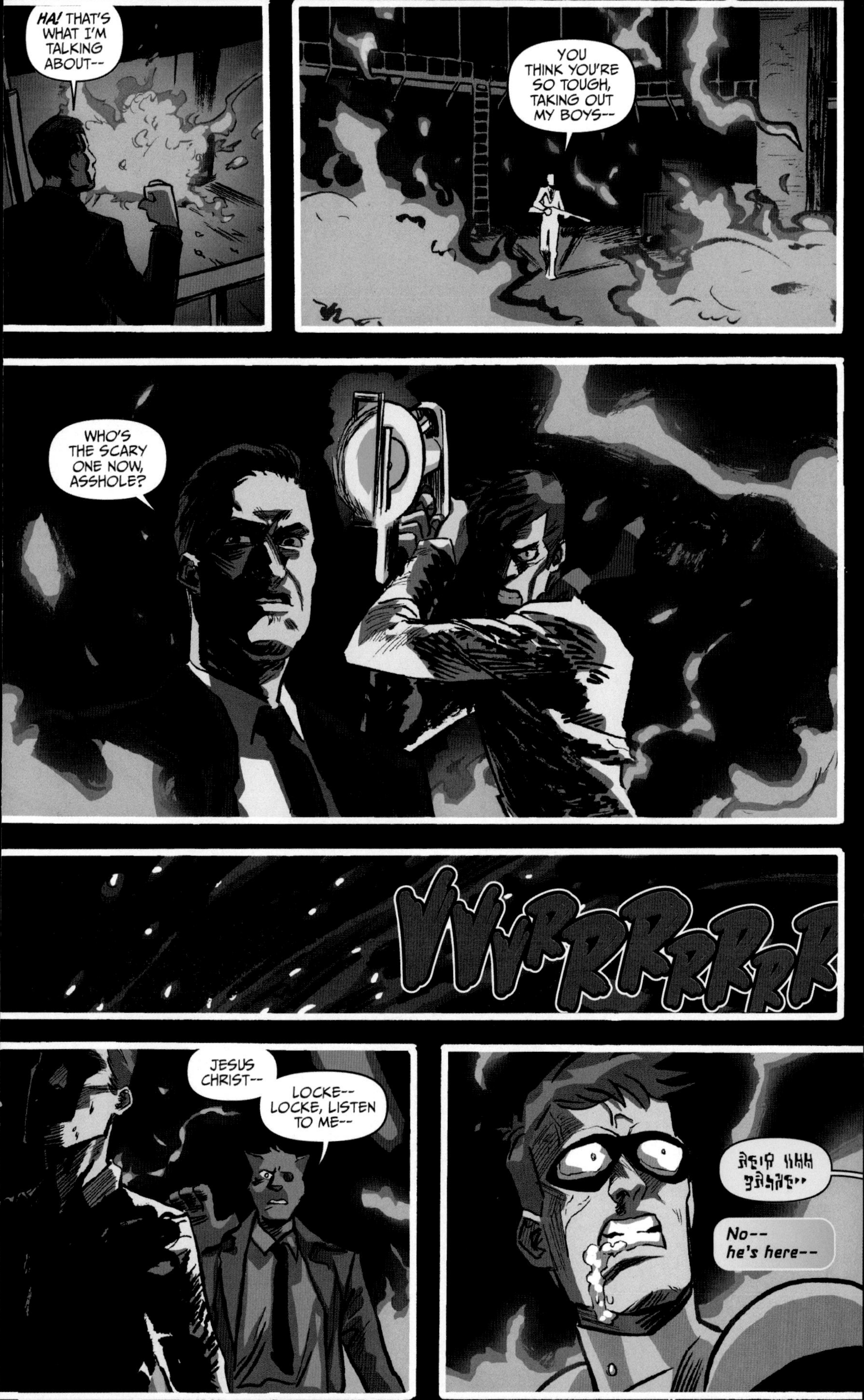
HA! THAT'S WHAT I'M TALKING ABOUT--
YOU THINK YOU'RE SO TOUGH, TAKING OUT MY BOYS--
WHO'S THE SCARY ONE NOW, ASSHOLE?
VVVRRRRRRR
JESUS CHRIST--
LOCKE-- LOCKE, LISTEN TO ME--
No-- he's here--

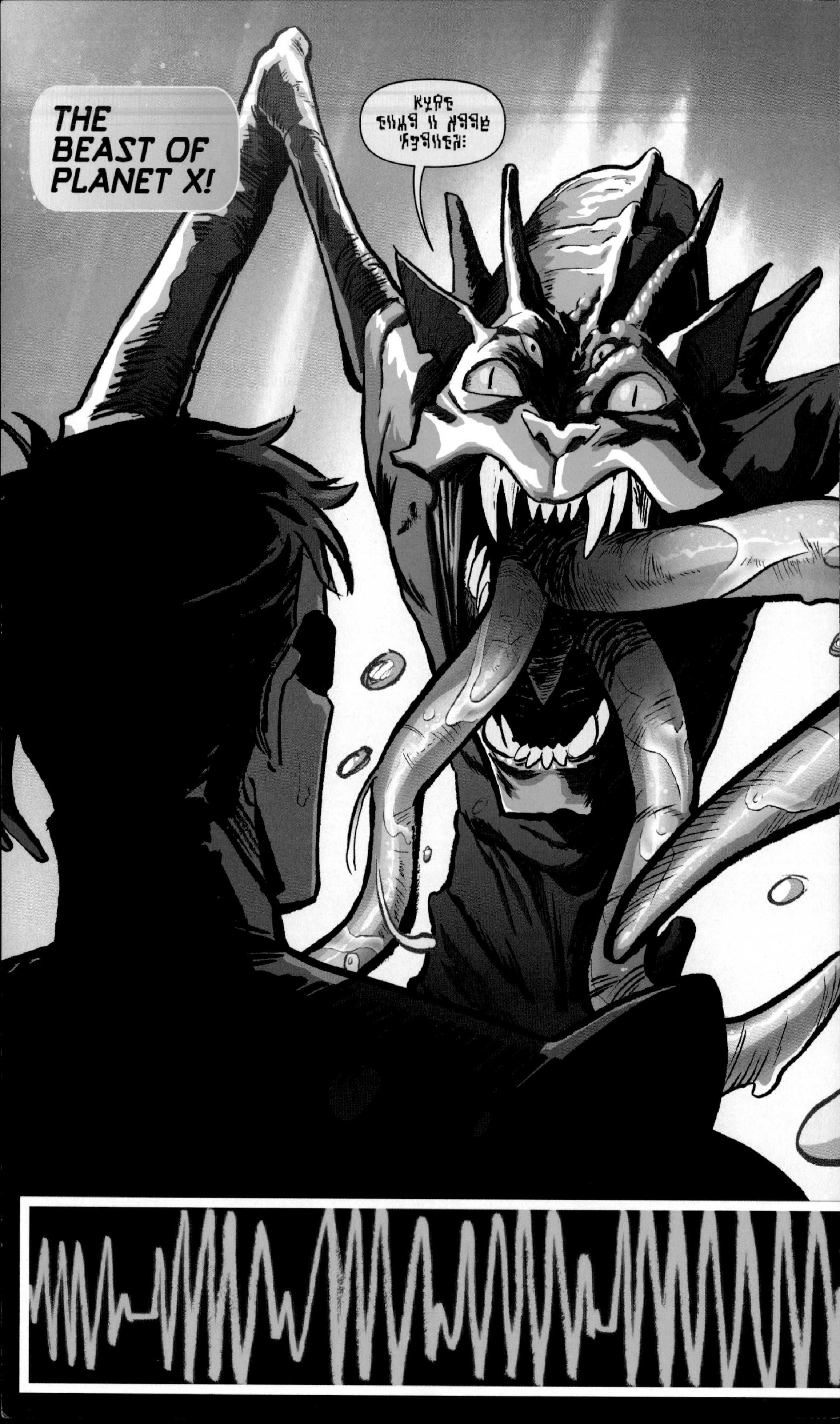
THE BEAST OF PLANET X!

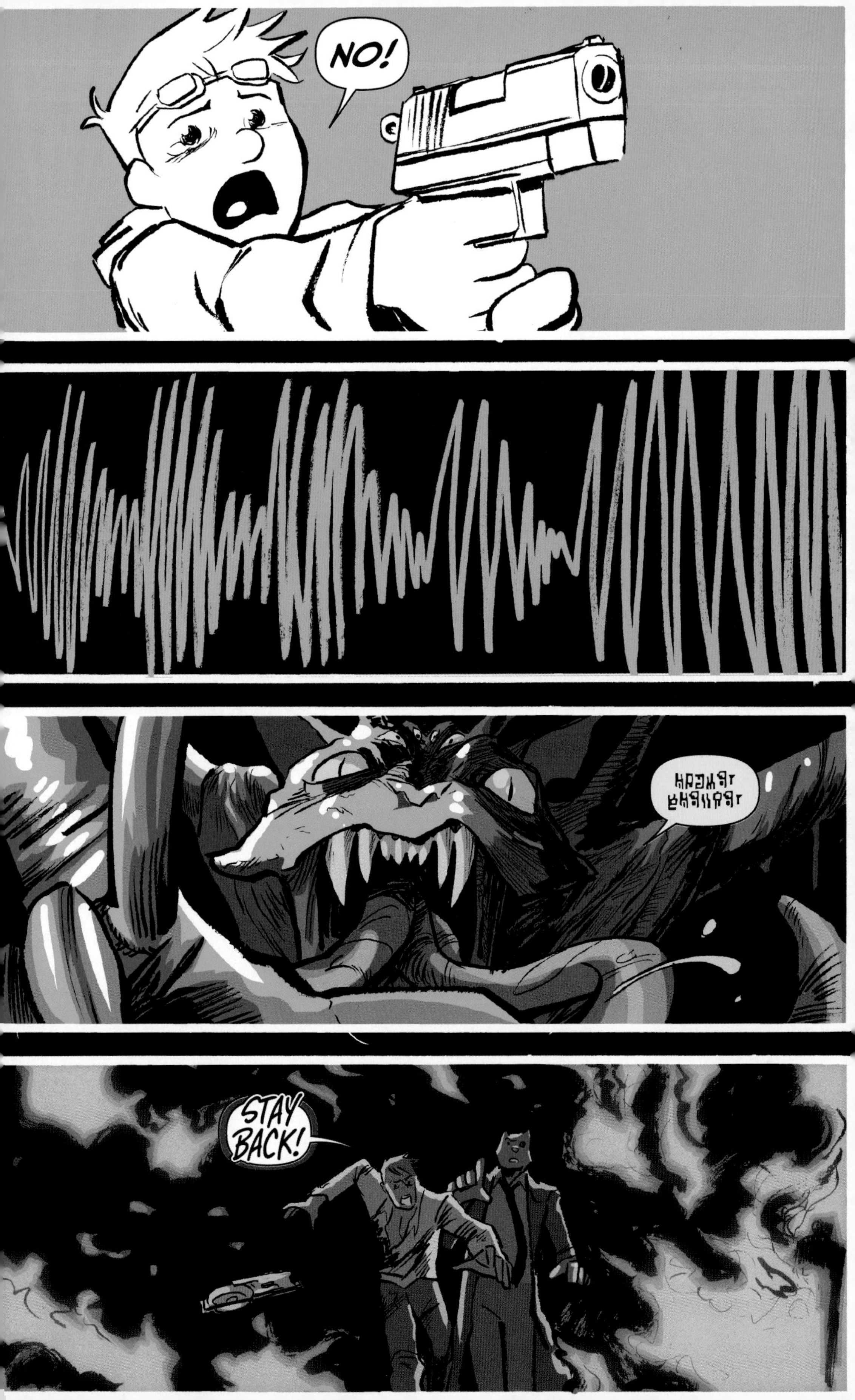
NO!
STAY BACK!

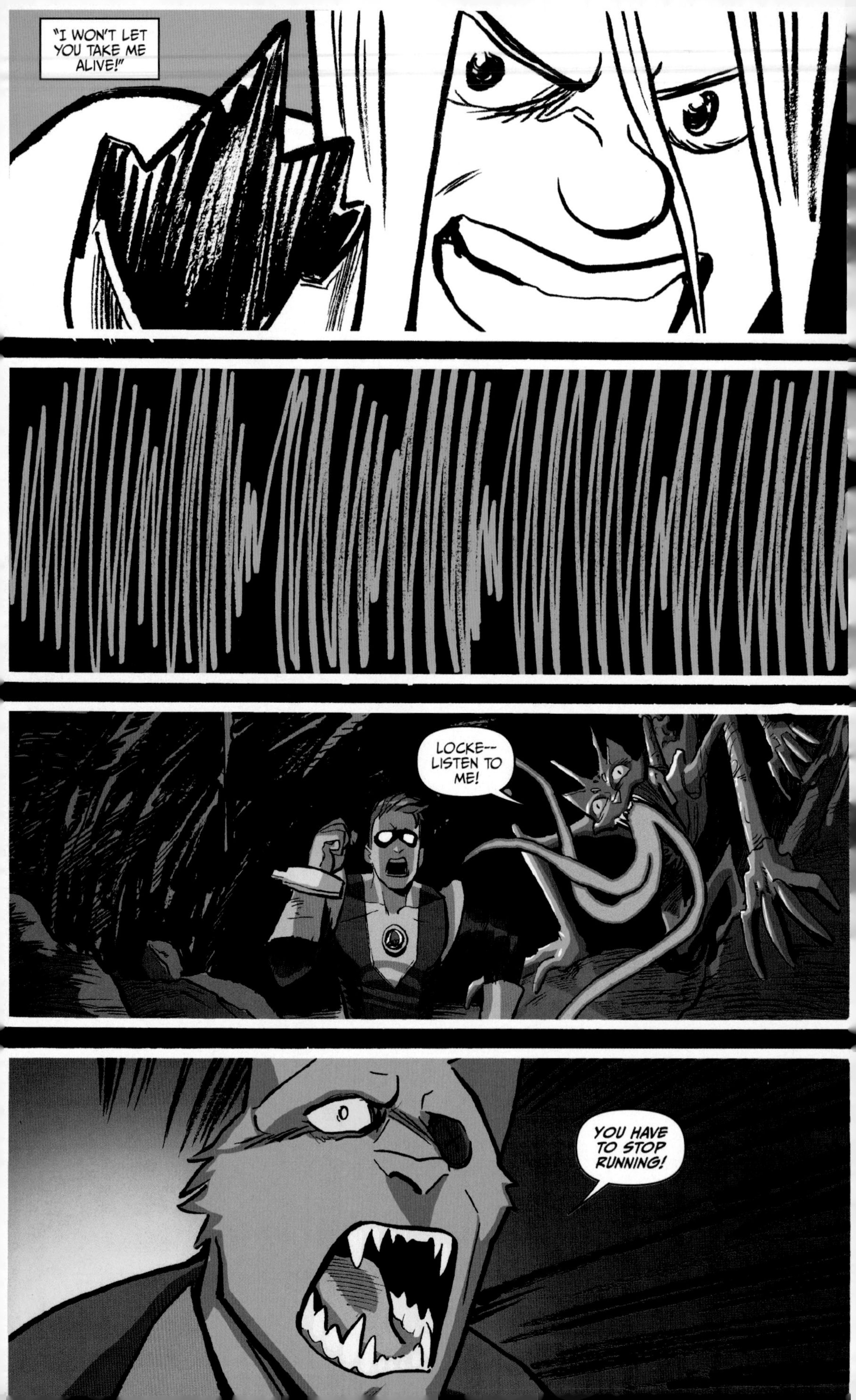
"I WON'T LET YOU TAKE ME ALIVE!"
LOCKE-- LISTEN TO ME!
YOU HAVE TO STOP RUNNING!

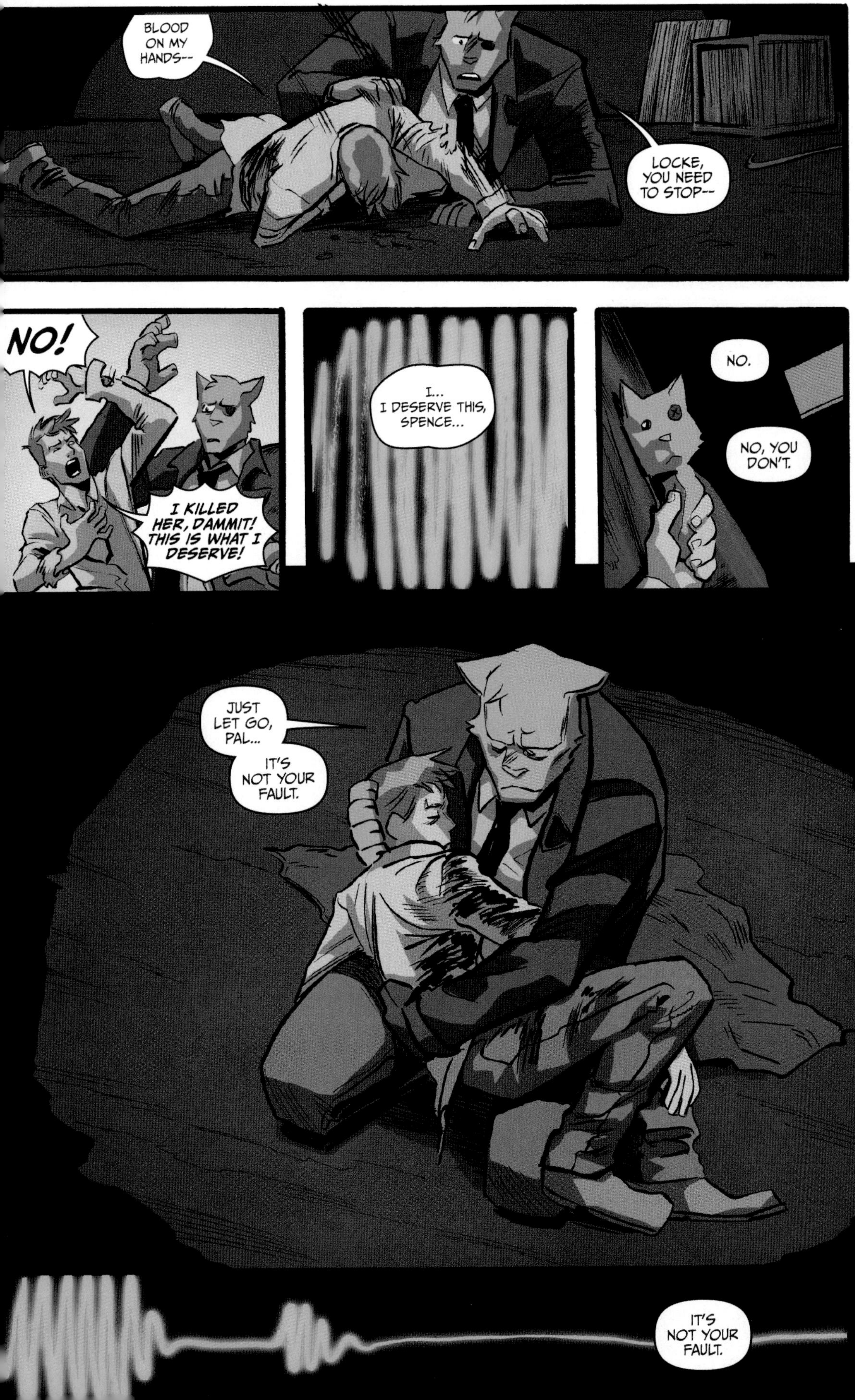
BLOOD ON MY HANDS--
LOCKE, YOU NEED TO STOP--
NO!
I KILLED HER, DAMMIT! THIS IS WHAT I DESERVE!
I... I DESERVE THIS, SPENCE...
NO.
NO, YOU DON'T.
JUST LET GO, PAL...
IT'S NOT YOUR FAULT.
IT'S NOT YOUR FAULT.

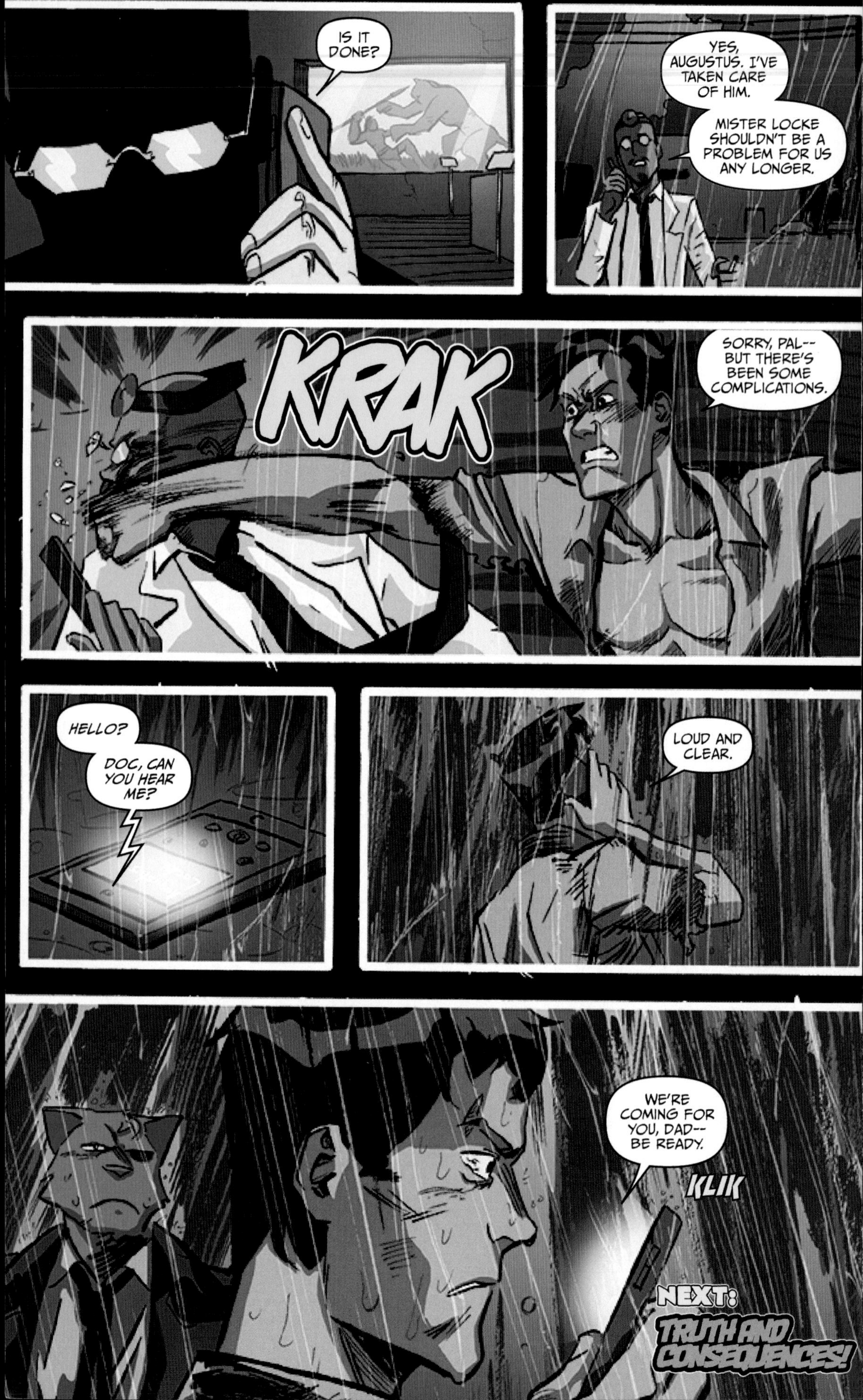
IS IT DONE?
YES, AUGUSTUS. I'VE TAKEN CARE OF HIM.
MISTER LOCKE SHOULDN'T BE A PROBLEM FOR US ANY LONGER.
KRAK
SORRY, PAL-- BUT THERE'S BEEN SOME COMPLICATIONS.
HELLO?
DOC, CAN YOU HEAR ME?
LOUD AND CLEAR.
WE'RE COMING FOR YOU, DAD-- BE READY.
KLIK
NEXT:
TRUTH AND CONSEQUENCES!

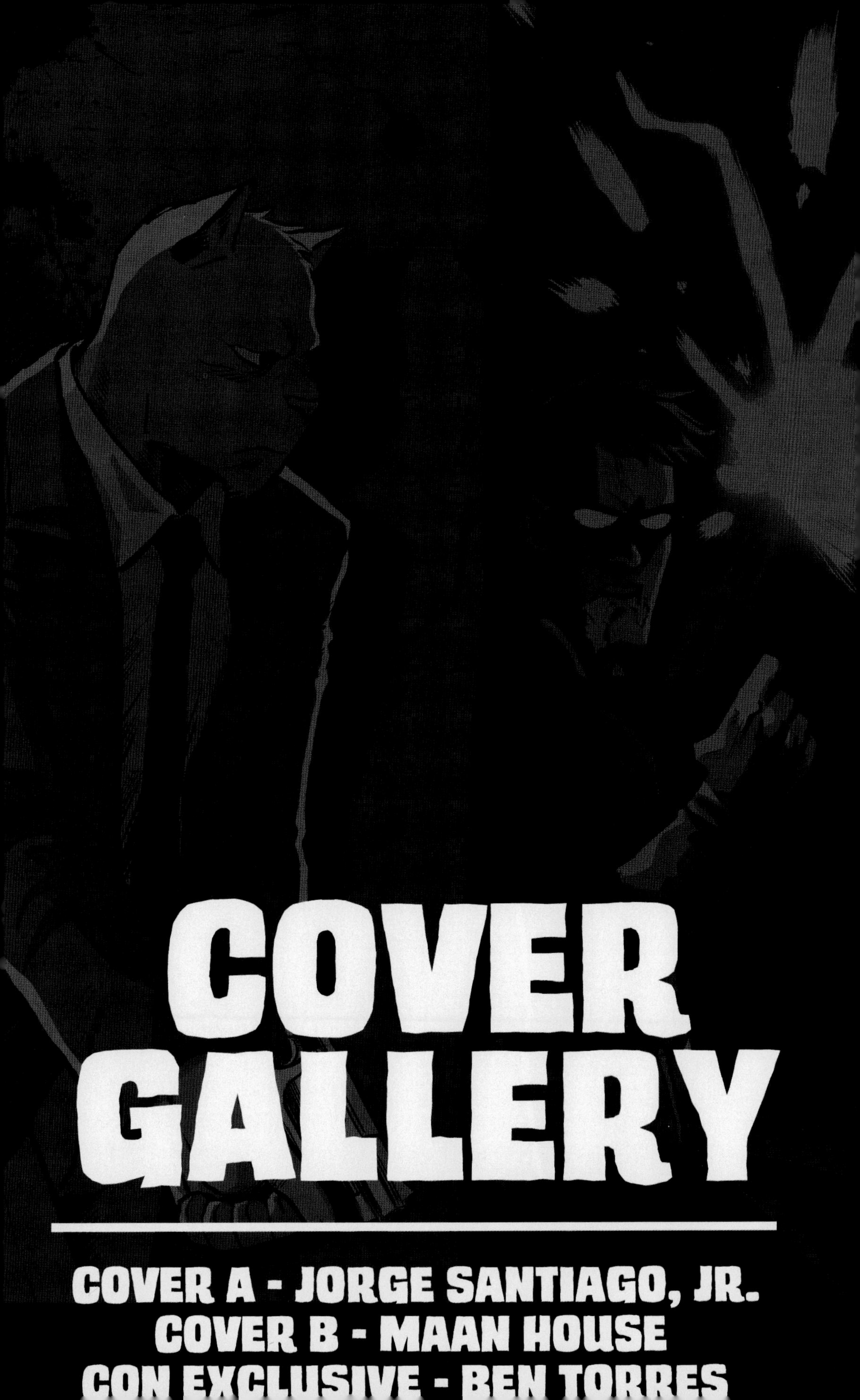

COVER GALLERY

COVER A - JORGE SANTIAGO, JR.
COVER B - MAAN HOUSE
CON EXCLUSIVE - BEN TORRES

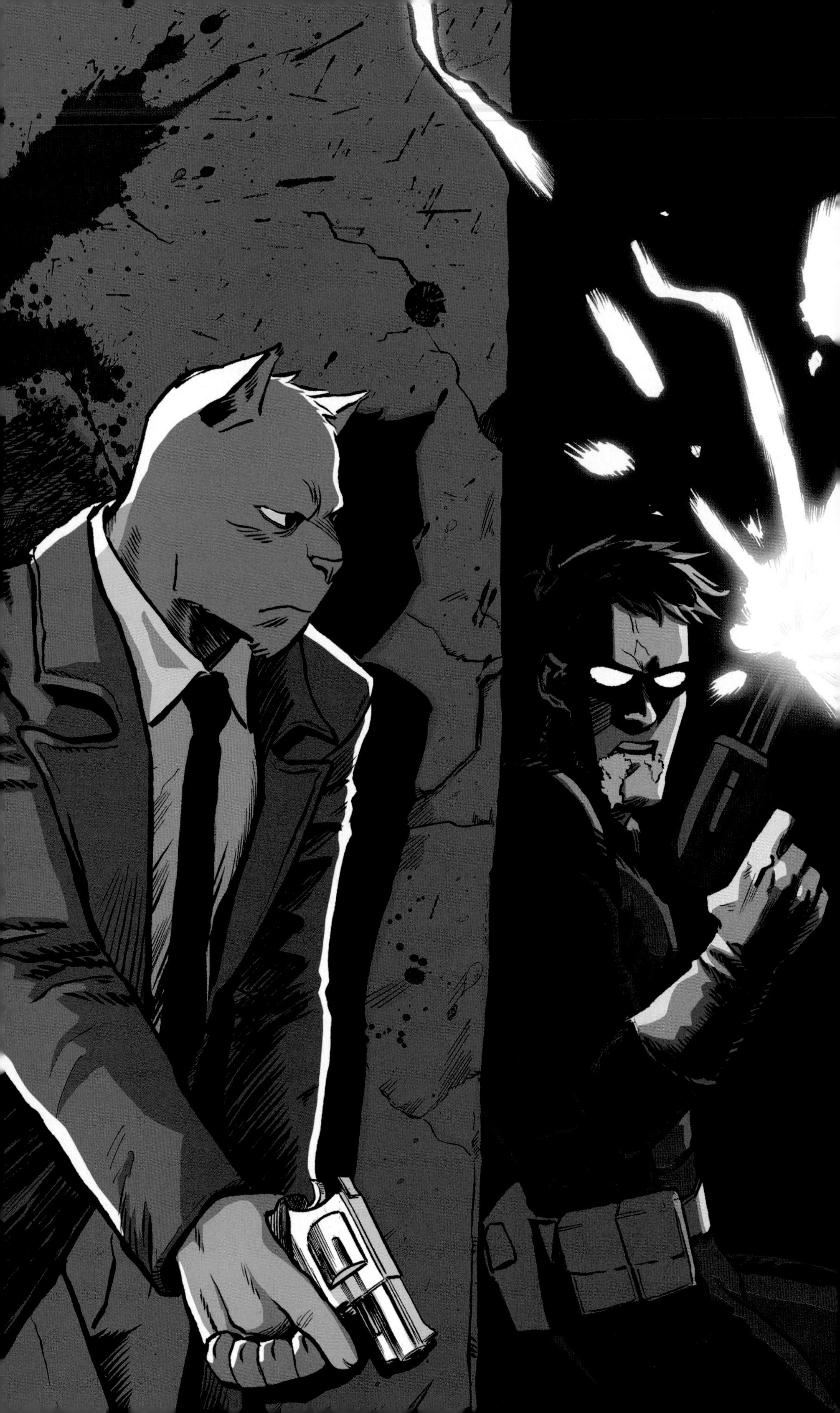

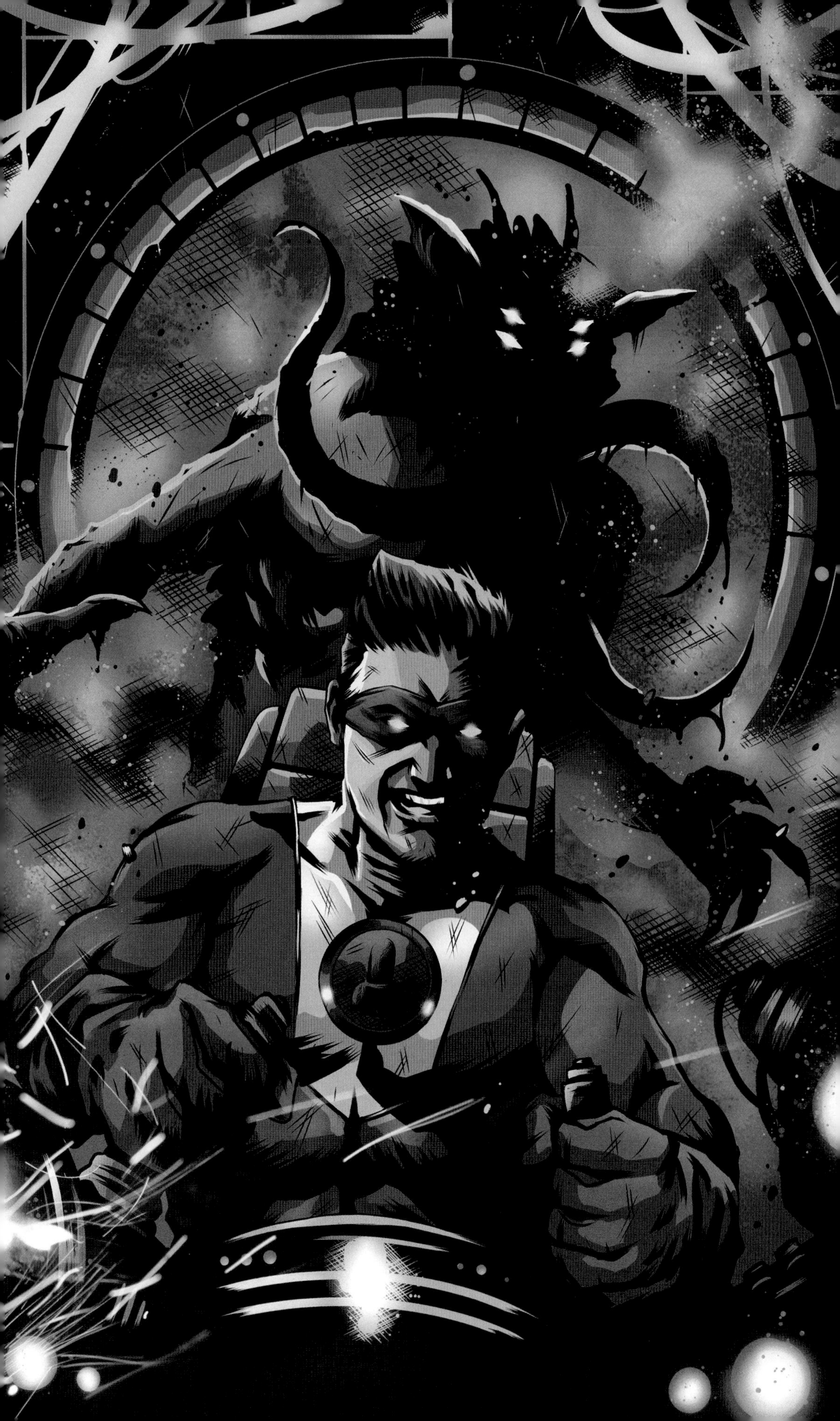

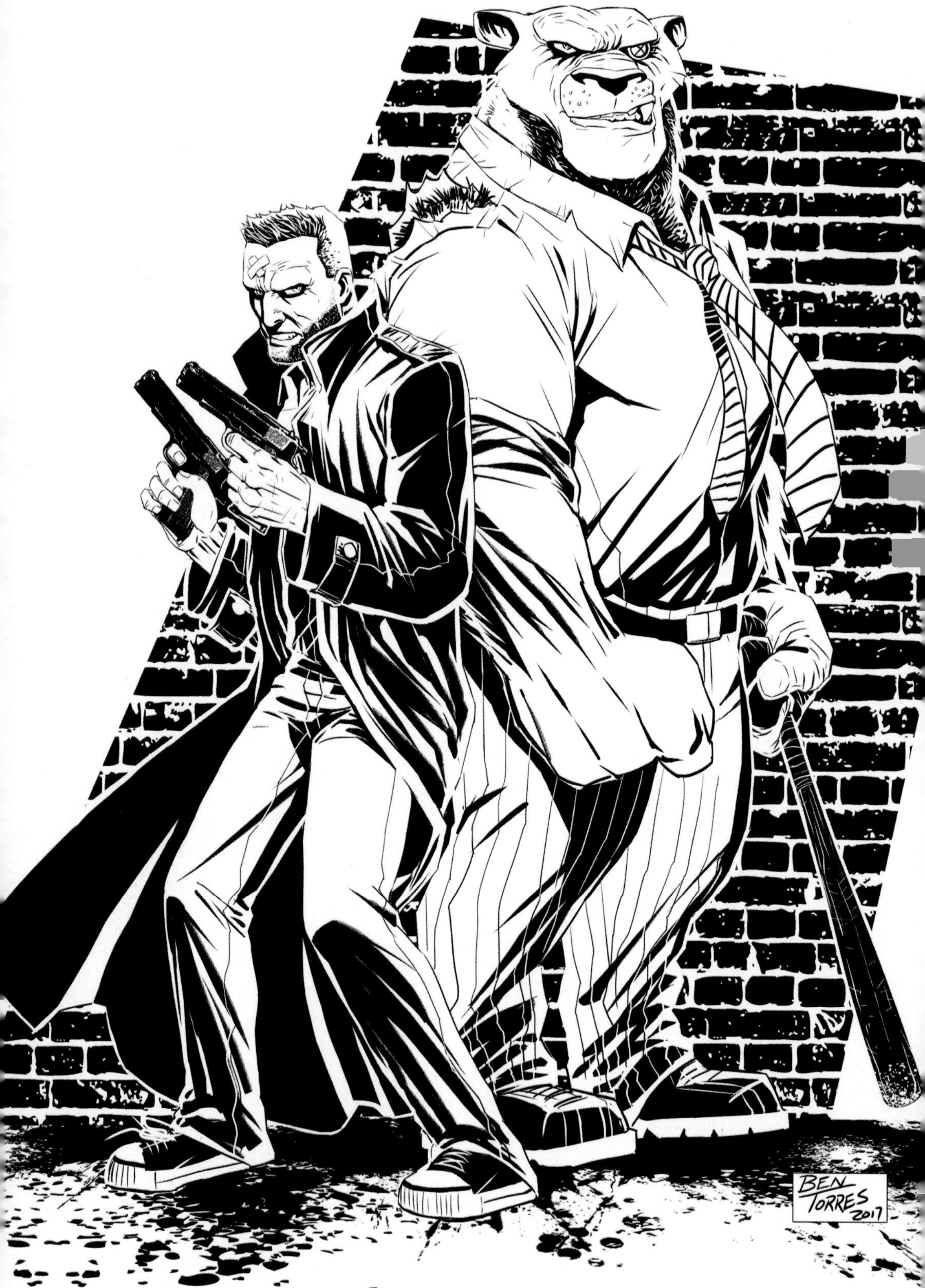
BEN
TORRES
2017

PAGE 12 PENCILS
BY JORGE SANTIAGO, JR.

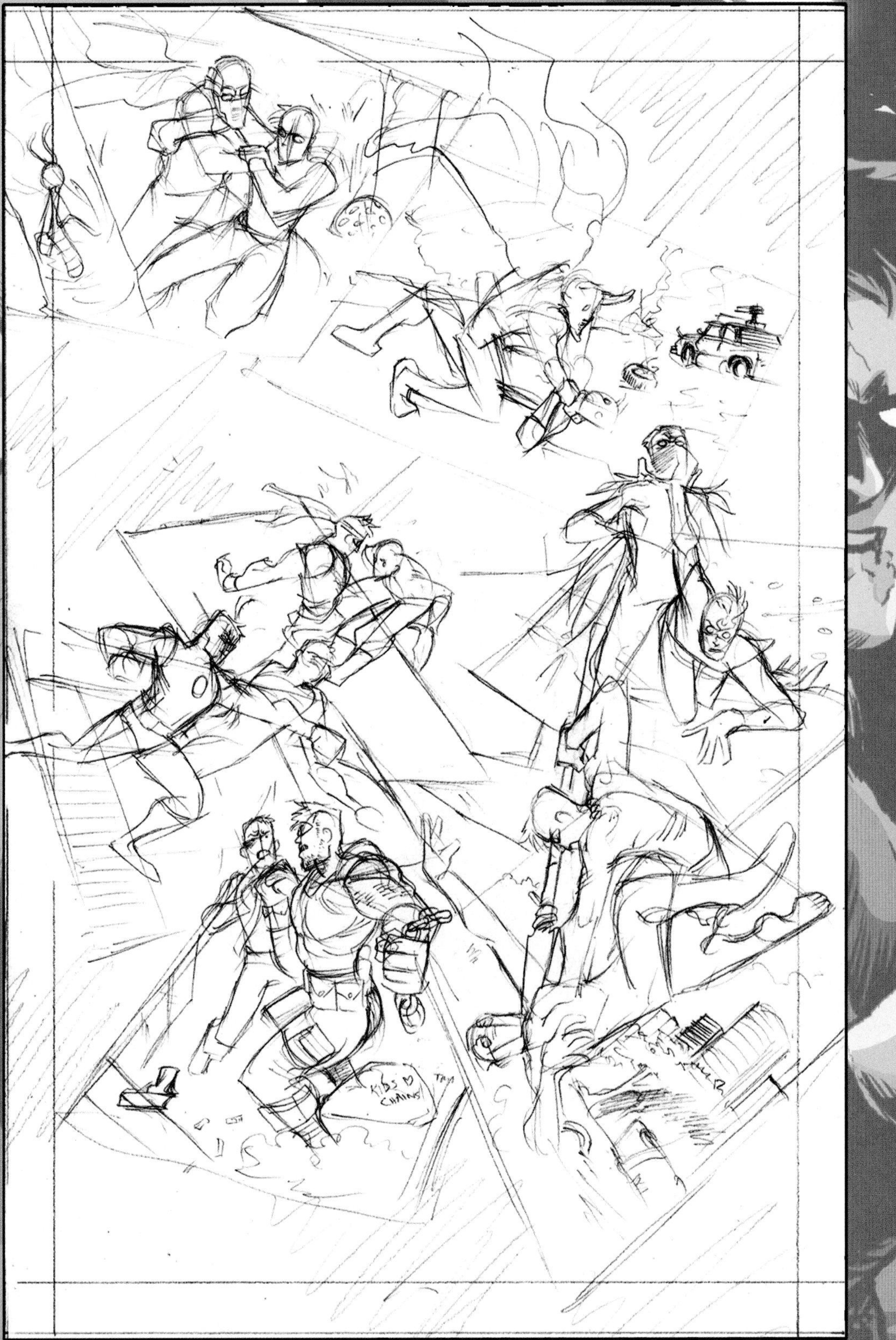
KIDS ♡ CHAINS

PAGE 12 INKS
BY JORGE SANTIAGO, JR.

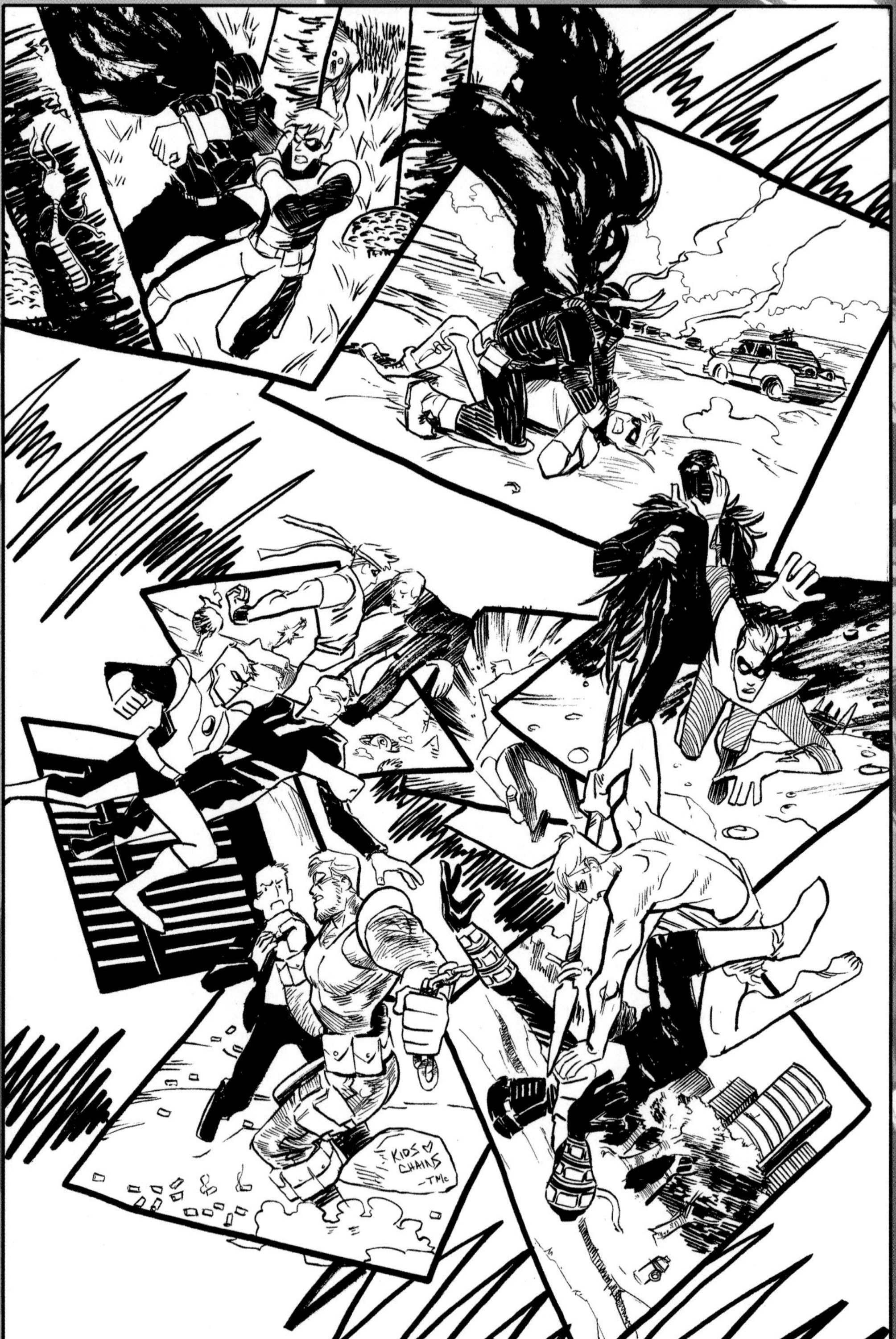
KIDS ♡ CHAINS -TMc

PAGE 12 COLORS
BY JASEN SMITH

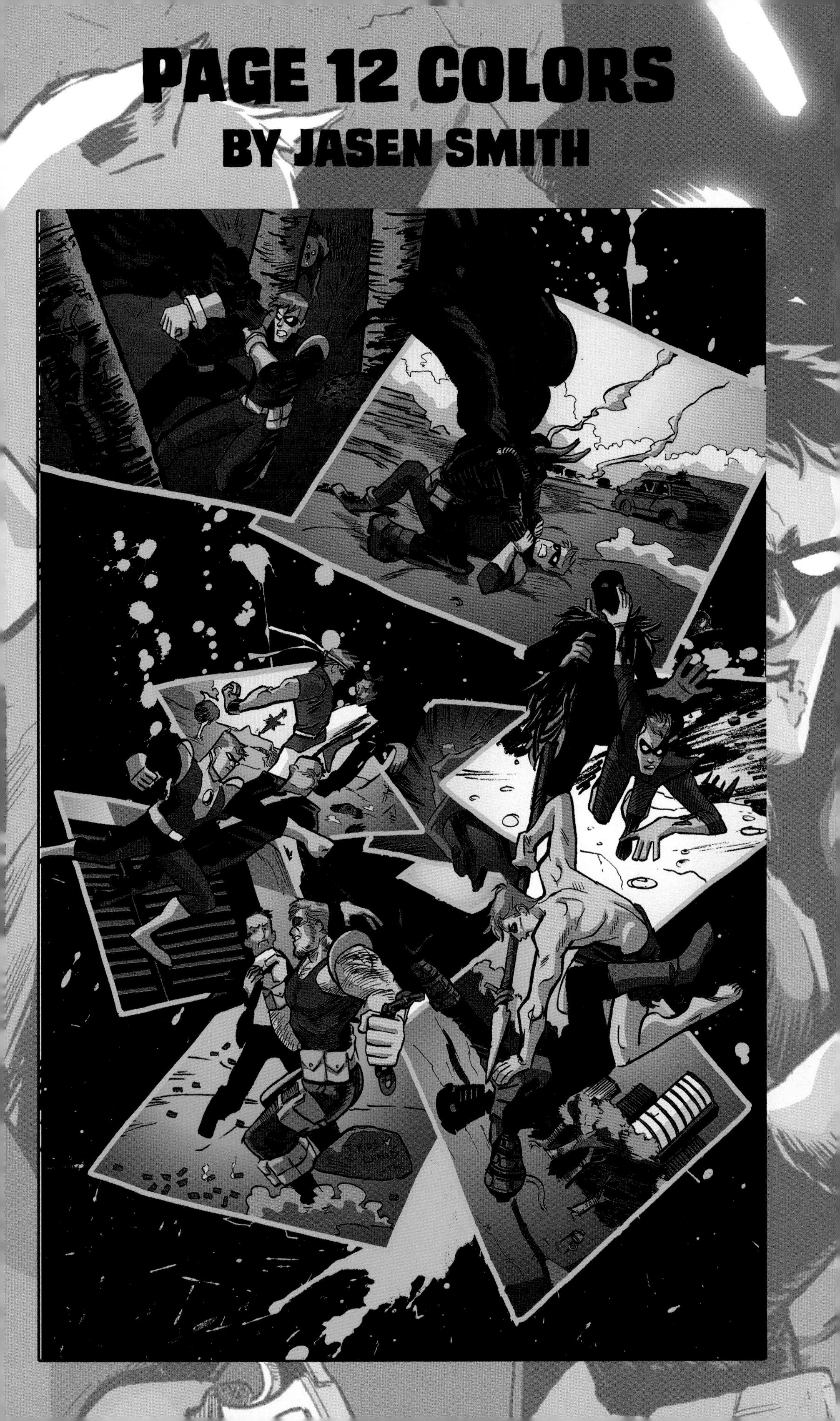

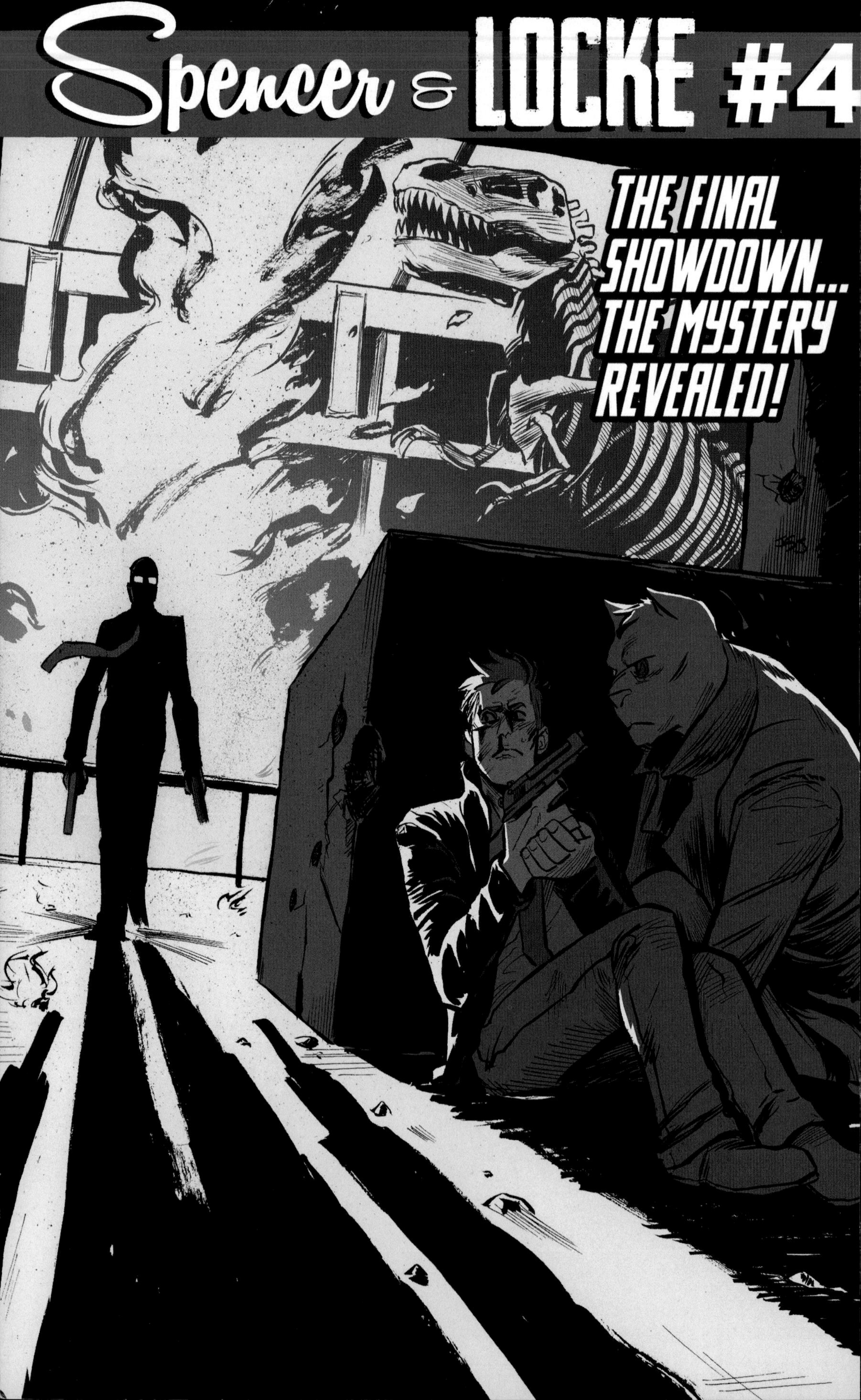
Spencer & LOCKE #4
THE FINAL SHOWDOWN... THE MYSTERY REVEALED!

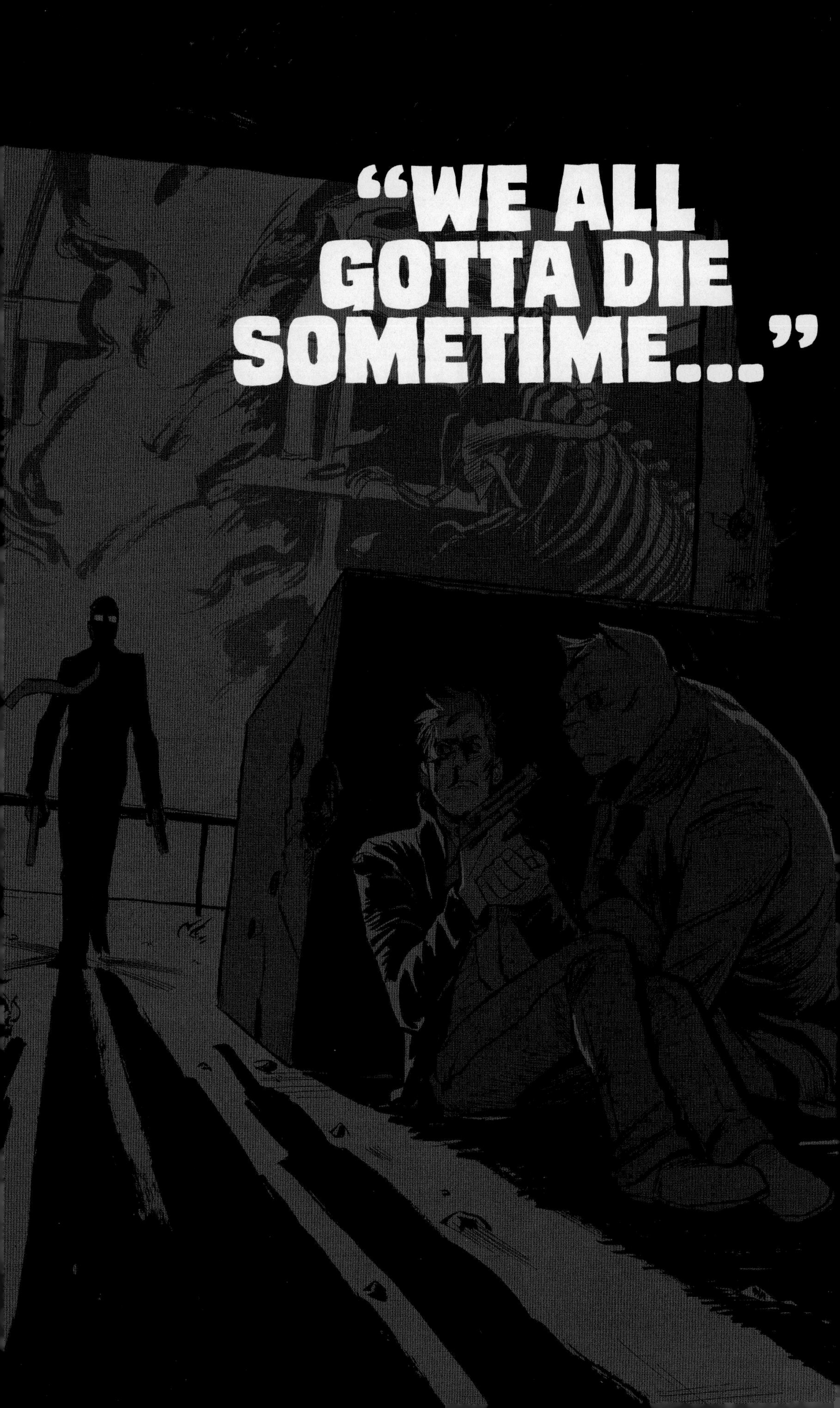
"WE ALL GOTTA DIE SOMETIME...."

Spencer & LOCKE 4

WRITTEN BY
DAVID PEPOSE

ART BY
JORGE SANTIAGO, JR.

COLORS BY
JASEN SMITH

LETTERS BY
COLIN BELL

JASON MARTIN: PUBLISHER • SHAWN GABBORIN: EDITOR IN CHIEF • NICOLE D'ANDRIA: MARKETING DIRECTOR/EDITOR
JIM DIETZ: SOCIAL MEDIA MANAGER • DANIELLE DAVISON: EXECUTIVE ADMINISTRATOR • BRYAN SEATON: CEO • SHAWN PRYOR: PRESIDENT OF CREATOR RELATIONS

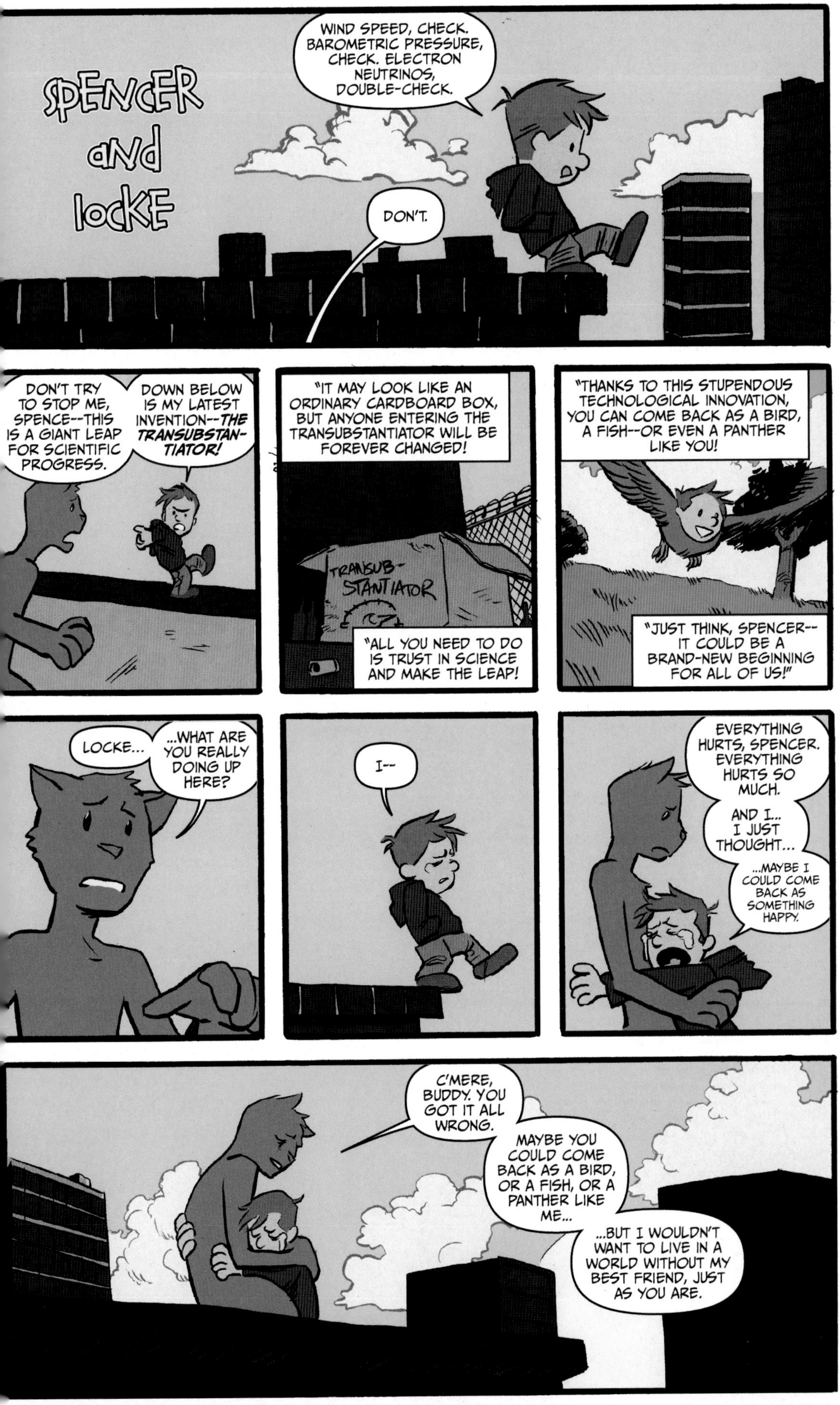
SPENCER and LOCKE
WIND SPEED, CHECK. BAROMETRIC PRESSURE, CHECK. ELECTRON NEUTRINOS, DOUBLE-CHECK.
DON'T.
DON'T TRY TO STOP ME, SPENCE--THIS IS A GIANT LEAP FOR SCIENTIFIC PROGRESS.
DOWN BELOW IS MY LATEST INVENTION--THE TRANSUBSTANTIATOR!
"IT MAY LOOK LIKE AN ORDINARY CARDBOARD BOX, BUT ANYONE ENTERING THE TRANSUBSTANTIATOR WILL BE FOREVER CHANGED!
TRANSUB-STANTIATOR
"ALL YOU NEED TO DO IS TRUST IN SCIENCE AND MAKE THE LEAP!
"THANKS TO THIS STUPENDOUS TECHNOLOGICAL INNOVATION, YOU CAN COME BACK AS A BIRD, A FISH--OR EVEN A PANTHER LIKE YOU!
"JUST THINK, SPENCER--IT COULD BE A BRAND-NEW BEGINNING FOR ALL OF US!"
LOCKE...
...WHAT ARE YOU REALLY DOING UP HERE?
I--
EVERYTHING HURTS, SPENCER. EVERYTHING HURTS SO MUCH.
AND I... I JUST THOUGHT...
...MAYBE I COULD COME BACK AS SOMETHING HAPPY.
C'MERE, BUDDY. YOU GOT IT ALL WRONG.
MAYBE YOU COULD COME BACK AS A BIRD, OR A FISH, OR A PANTHER LIKE ME...
...BUT I WOULDN'T WANT TO LIVE IN A WORLD WITHOUT MY BEST FRIEND, JUST AS YOU ARE.

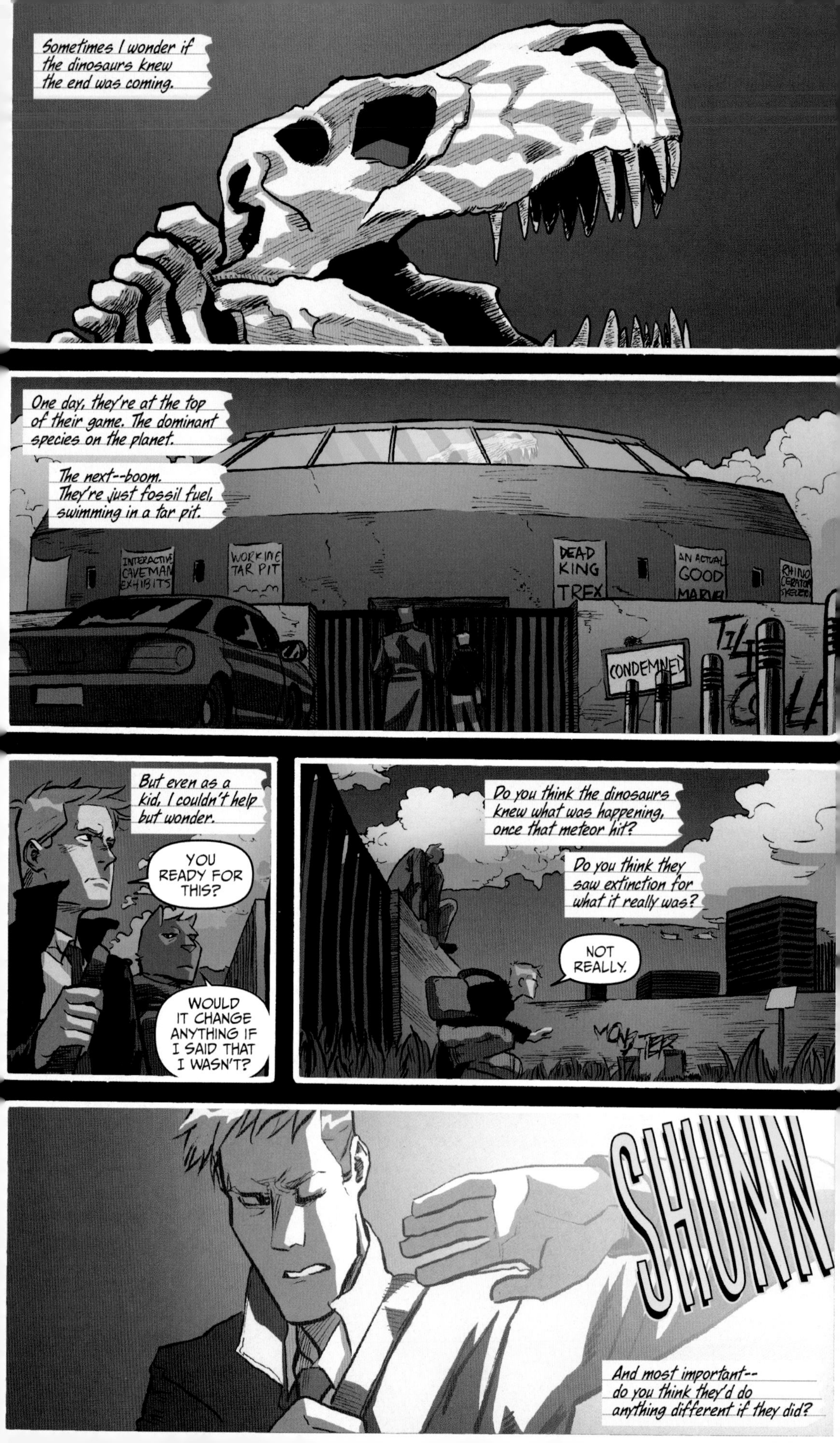
Sometimes I wonder if the dinosaurs knew the end was coming.
One day, they're at the top of their game. The dominant species on the planet.
The next--boom. They're just fossil fuel, swimming in a tar pit.
INTERACTIVE CAVEMAN EXHIBITS
WORKING TAR PIT
DEAD KING TREX
CONDEMNED
But even as a kid, I couldn't help but wonder.
YOU READY FOR THIS?
WOULD IT CHANGE ANYTHING IF I SAID THAT I WASN'T?
Do you think the dinosaurs knew what was happening, once that meteor hit?
Do you think they saw extinction for what it really was?
NOT REALLY.
SHUNN
And most important-- do you think they'd do anything different if they did?

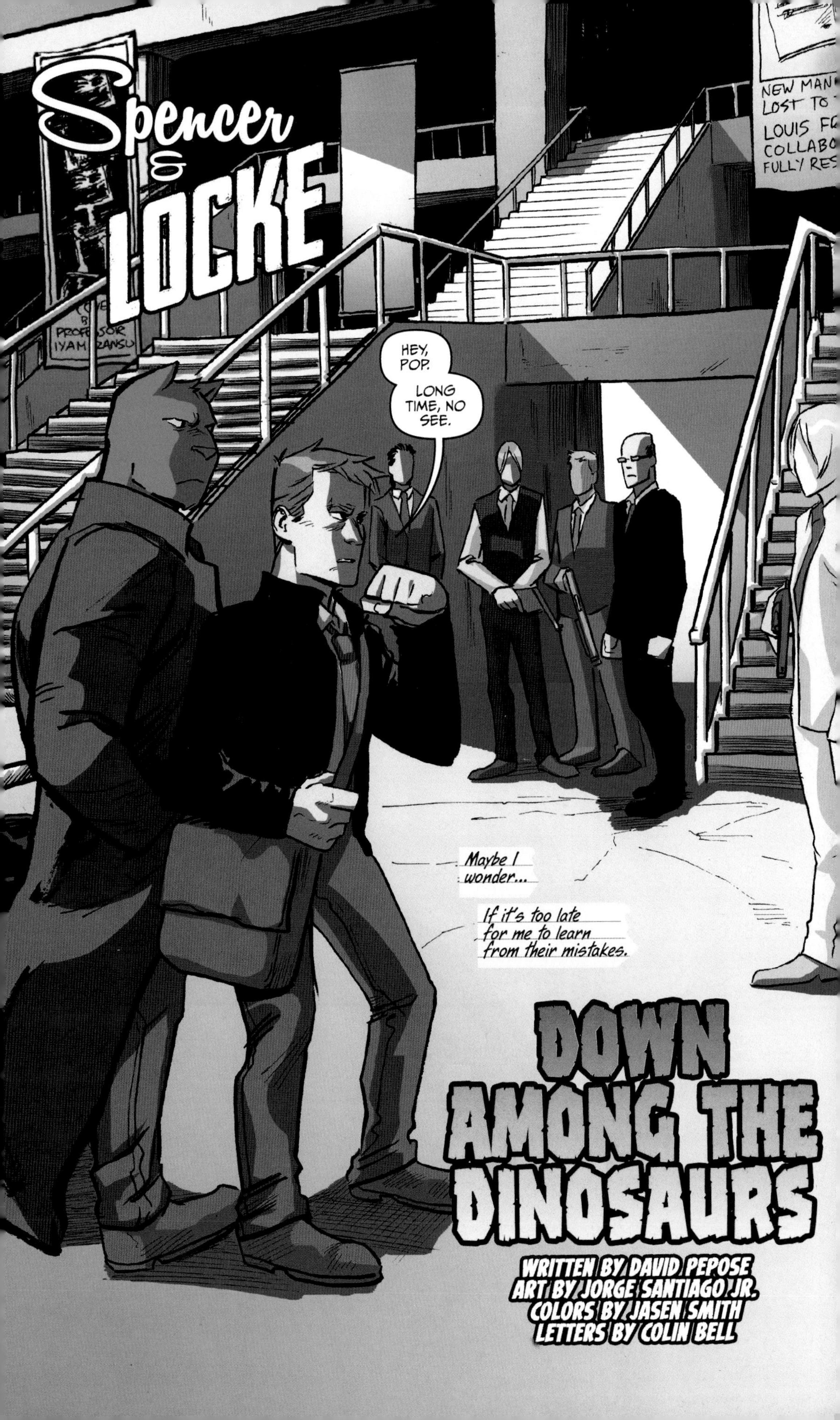
Spencer & LOCKE
NEW MAN
LOST TO
LOUIS F
COLLABO
FULLY RES
PROFESSOR
IYAM
HEY, POP.
LONG TIME, NO SEE.
Maybe I wonder...
If it's too late for me to learn from their mistakes.
DOWN AMONG THE DINOSAURS
WRITTEN BY DAVID PEPOSE
ART BY JORGE SANTIAGO JR.
COLORS BY JASEN SMITH
LETTERS BY COLIN BELL

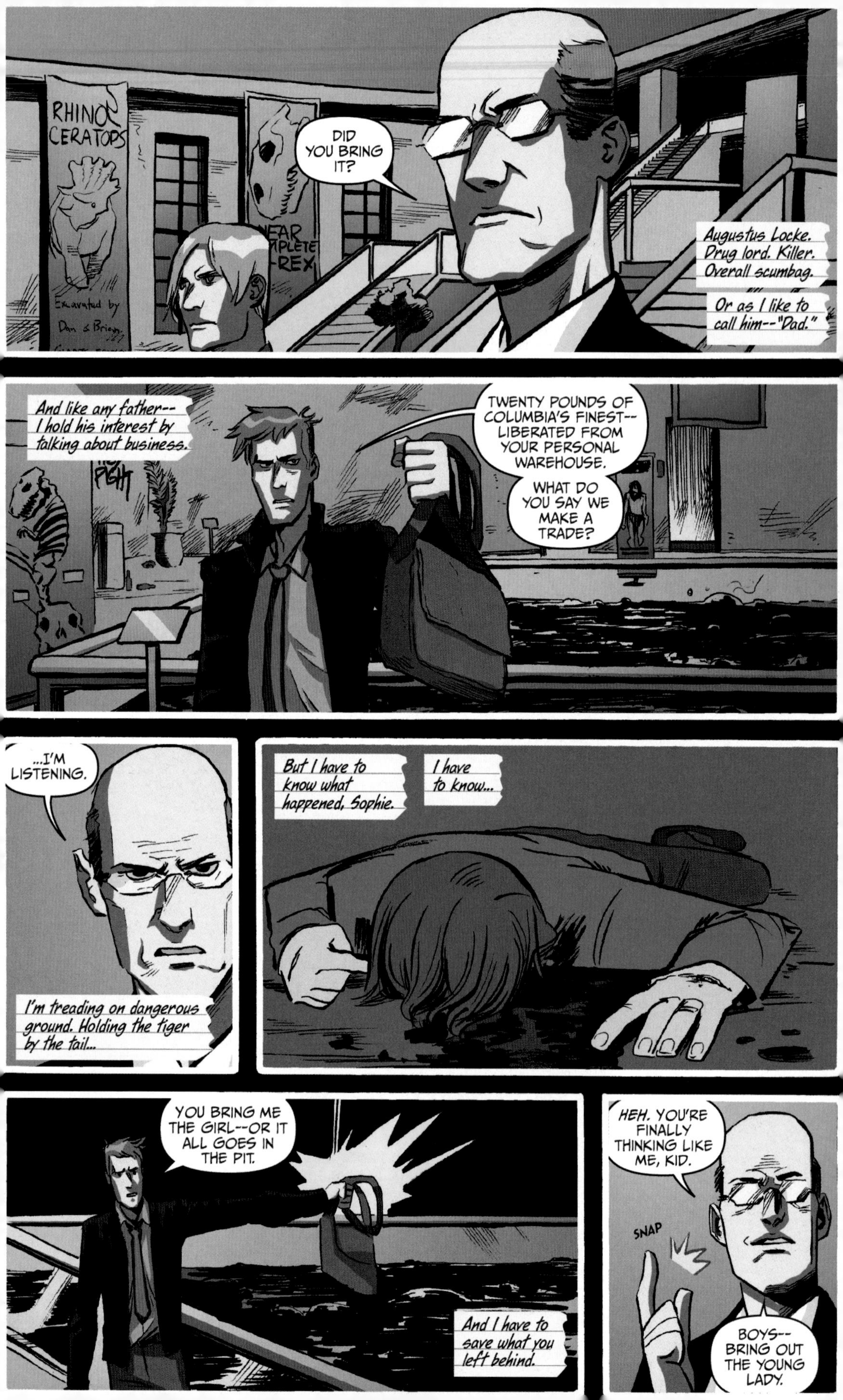
RHINOCERATOPS
Excavated by Dan & Brian
NEAR COMPLETE T-REX
DID YOU BRING IT?
Augustus Locke. Drug lord. Killer. Overall scumbag.
Or as I like to call him--"Dad."
And like any father-- I hold his interest by talking about business.
TWENTY POUNDS OF COLUMBIA'S FINEST-- LIBERATED FROM YOUR PERSONAL WAREHOUSE.
WHAT DO YOU SAY WE MAKE A TRADE?
...I'M LISTENING.
I'm treading on dangerous ground. Holding the tiger by the tail...
But I have to know what happened, Sophie.
I have to know...
YOU BRING ME THE GIRL--OR IT ALL GOES IN THE PIT.
And I have to save what you left behind.
HEH. YOU'RE FINALLY THINKING LIKE ME, KID.
SNAP
BOYS-- BRING OUT THE YOUNG LADY.

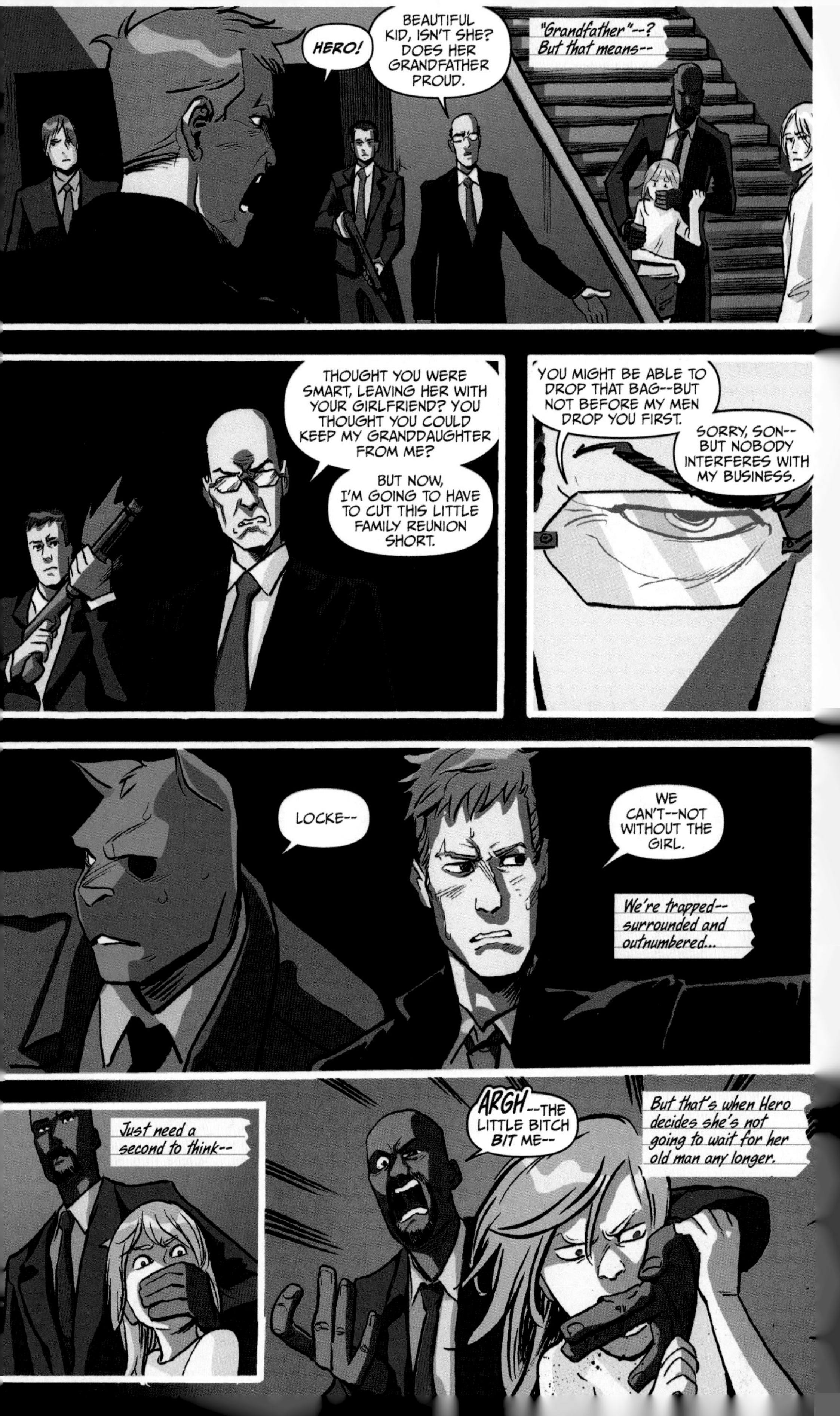
HERO!
BEAUTIFUL KID, ISN'T SHE? DOES HER GRANDFATHER PROUD.
"Grandfather"--? But that means--
THOUGHT YOU WERE SMART, LEAVING HER WITH YOUR GIRLFRIEND? YOU THOUGHT YOU COULD KEEP MY GRANDDAUGHTER FROM ME?
BUT NOW, I'M GOING TO HAVE TO CUT THIS LITTLE FAMILY REUNION SHORT.
YOU MIGHT BE ABLE TO DROP THAT BAG--BUT NOT BEFORE MY MEN DROP YOU FIRST.
SORRY, SON--BUT NOBODY INTERFERES WITH MY BUSINESS.
LOCKE--
WE CAN'T--NOT WITHOUT THE GIRL.
We're trapped--surrounded and outnumbered...
Just need a second to think--
ARGH--THE LITTLE BITCH BIT ME--
But that's when Hero decides she's not going to wait for her old man any longer.

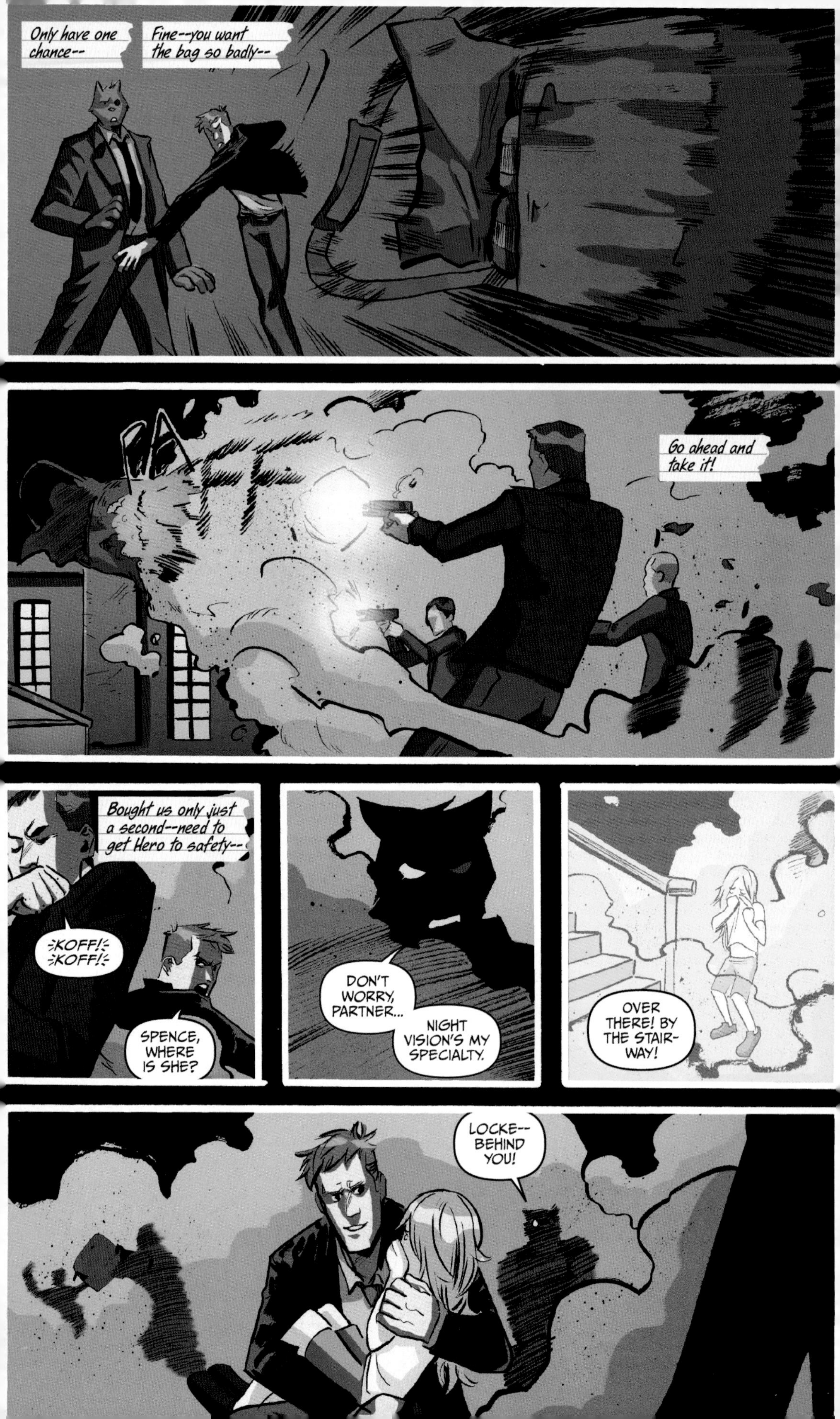
Only have one chance--
Fine--you want the bag so badly--
Go ahead and take it!
Bought us only just a second--need to get Hero to safety--
KOFF! KOFF!
SPENCE, WHERE IS SHE?
DON'T WORRY, PARTNER...
NIGHT VISION'S MY SPECIALTY.
OVER THERE! BY THE STAIR-WAY!
LOCKE--BEHIND YOU!

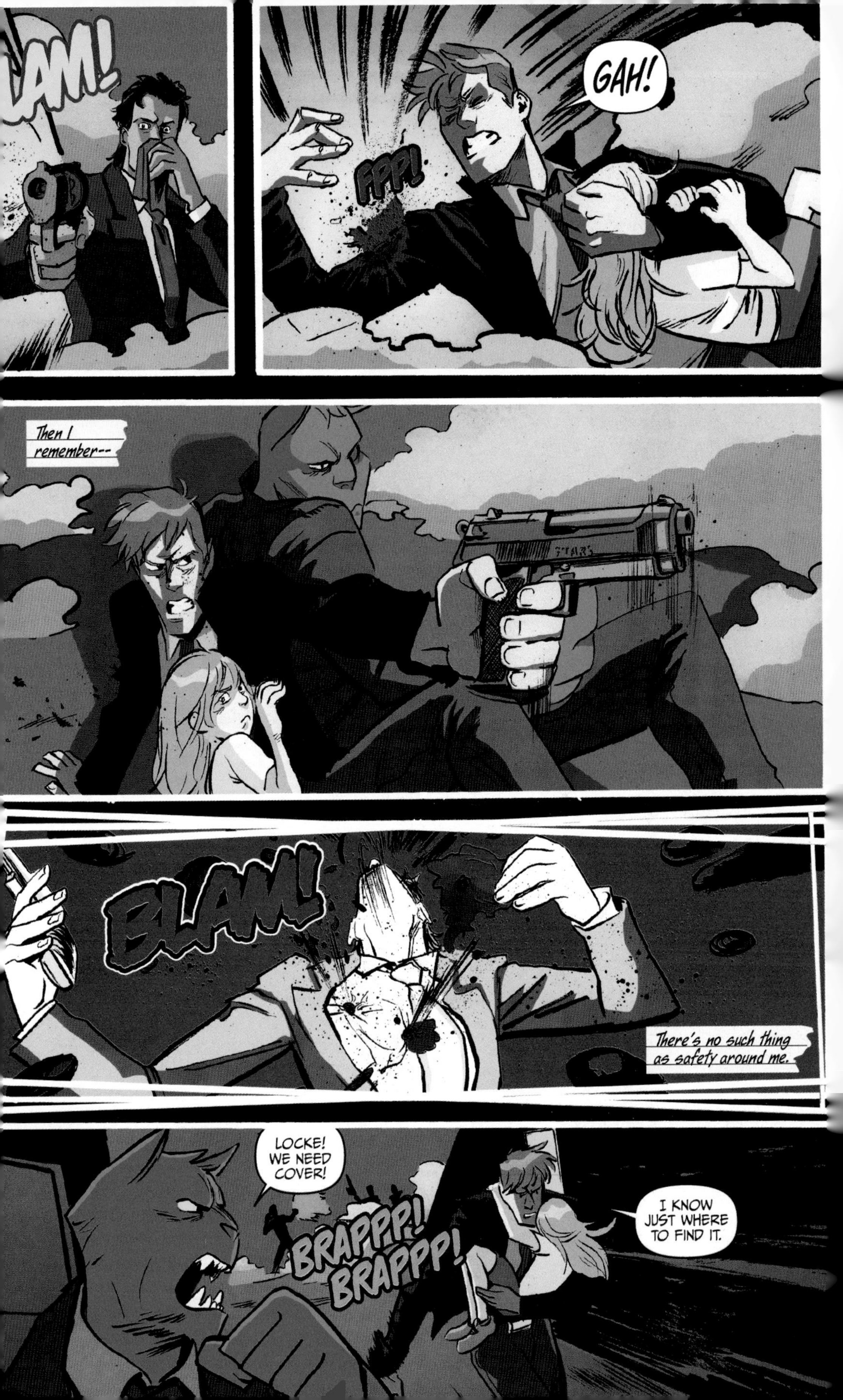
BLAM!
GAH!
FFPP!
Then I remember--
BLAM!
There's no such thing as safety around me.
LOCKE! WE NEED COVER!
BRAPPP! BRAPPP!
I KNOW JUST WHERE TO FIND IT.

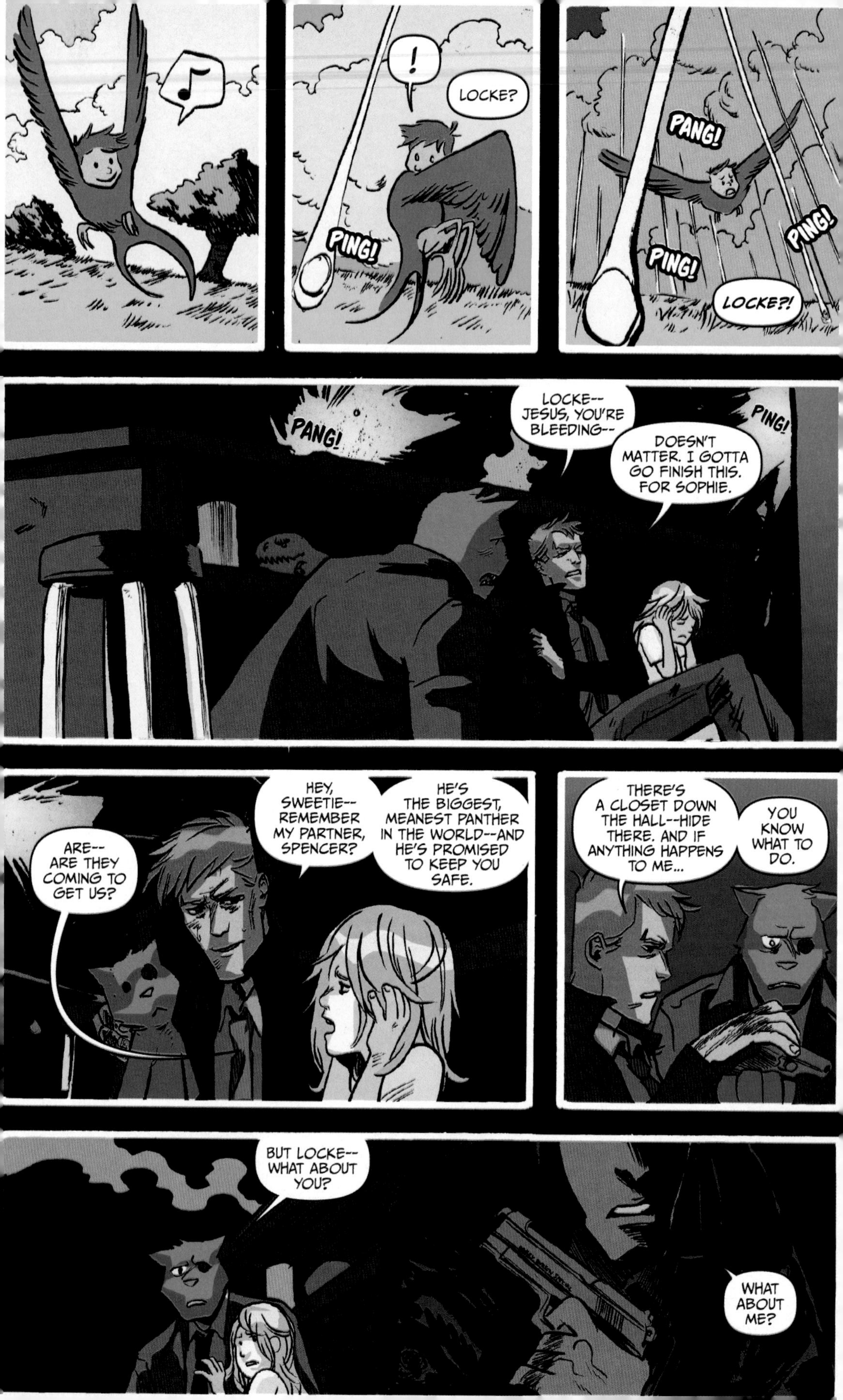

!
LOCKE?
PING!
PANG!
PING!
PING!
LOCKE?!
PANG!
LOCKE-- JESUS, YOU'RE BLEEDING--
PING!
DOESN'T MATTER. I GOTTA GO FINISH THIS. FOR SOPHIE.
ARE-- ARE THEY COMING TO GET US?
HEY, SWEETIE-- REMEMBER MY PARTNER, SPENCER?
HE'S THE BIGGEST, MEANEST PANTHER IN THE WORLD--AND HE'S PROMISED TO KEEP YOU SAFE.
THERE'S A CLOSET DOWN THE HALL--HIDE THERE. AND IF ANYTHING HAPPENS TO ME...
YOU KNOW WHAT TO DO.
BUT LOCKE-- WHAT ABOUT YOU?
WHAT ABOUT ME?

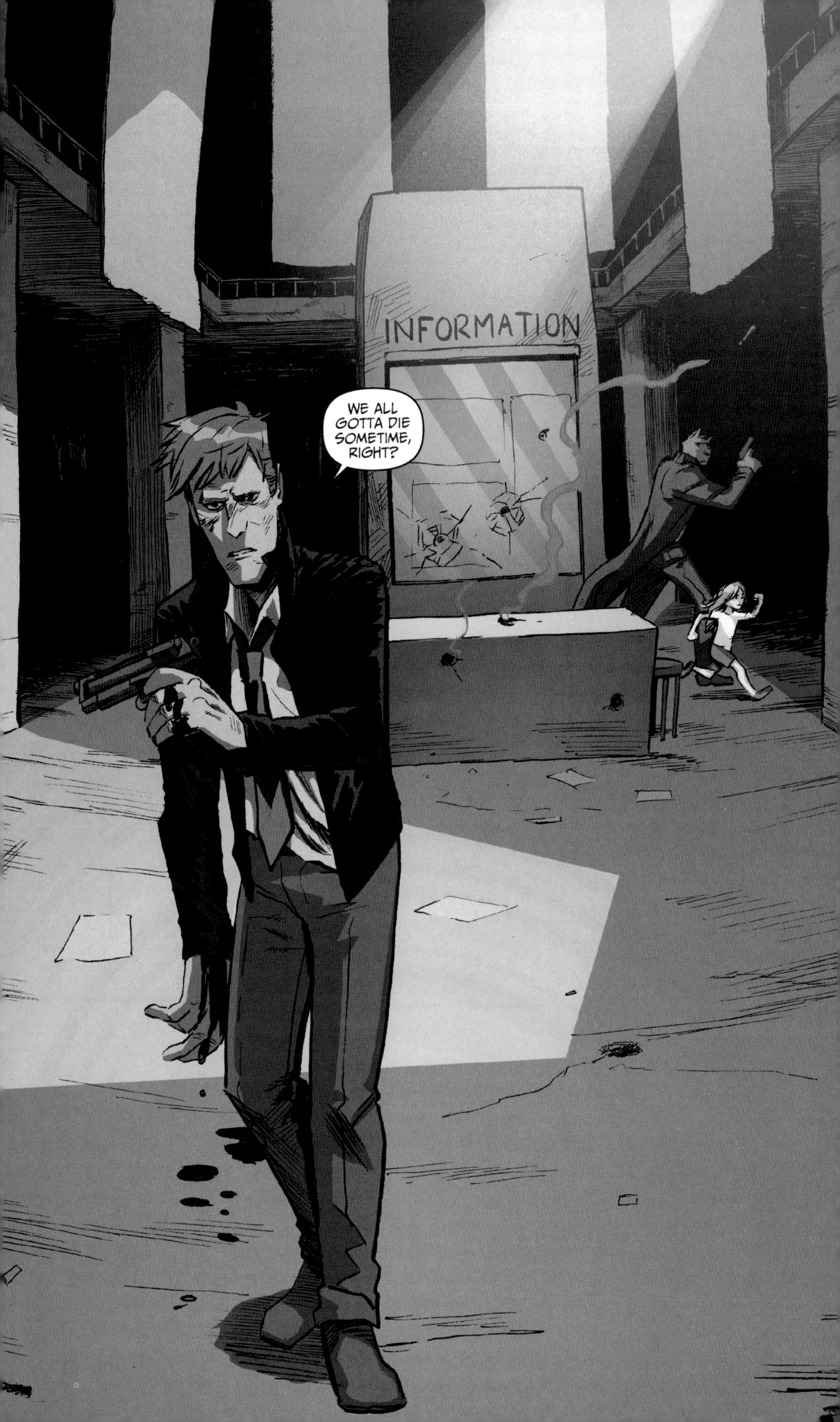
INFORMATION
WE ALL GOTTA DIE SOMETIME, RIGHT?

KREAK

BLAM BLA

BLAM

BLAM

WELL, NOW--EITHER MY EARS ARE DECEIVING ME...

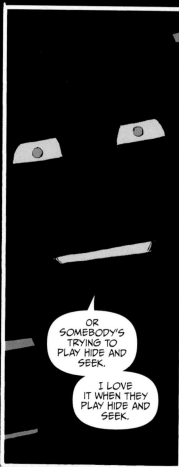

OR SOMEBODY'S TRYING TO PLAY HIDE AND SEEK.

I LOVE IT WHEN THEY PLAY HIDE AND SEEK.

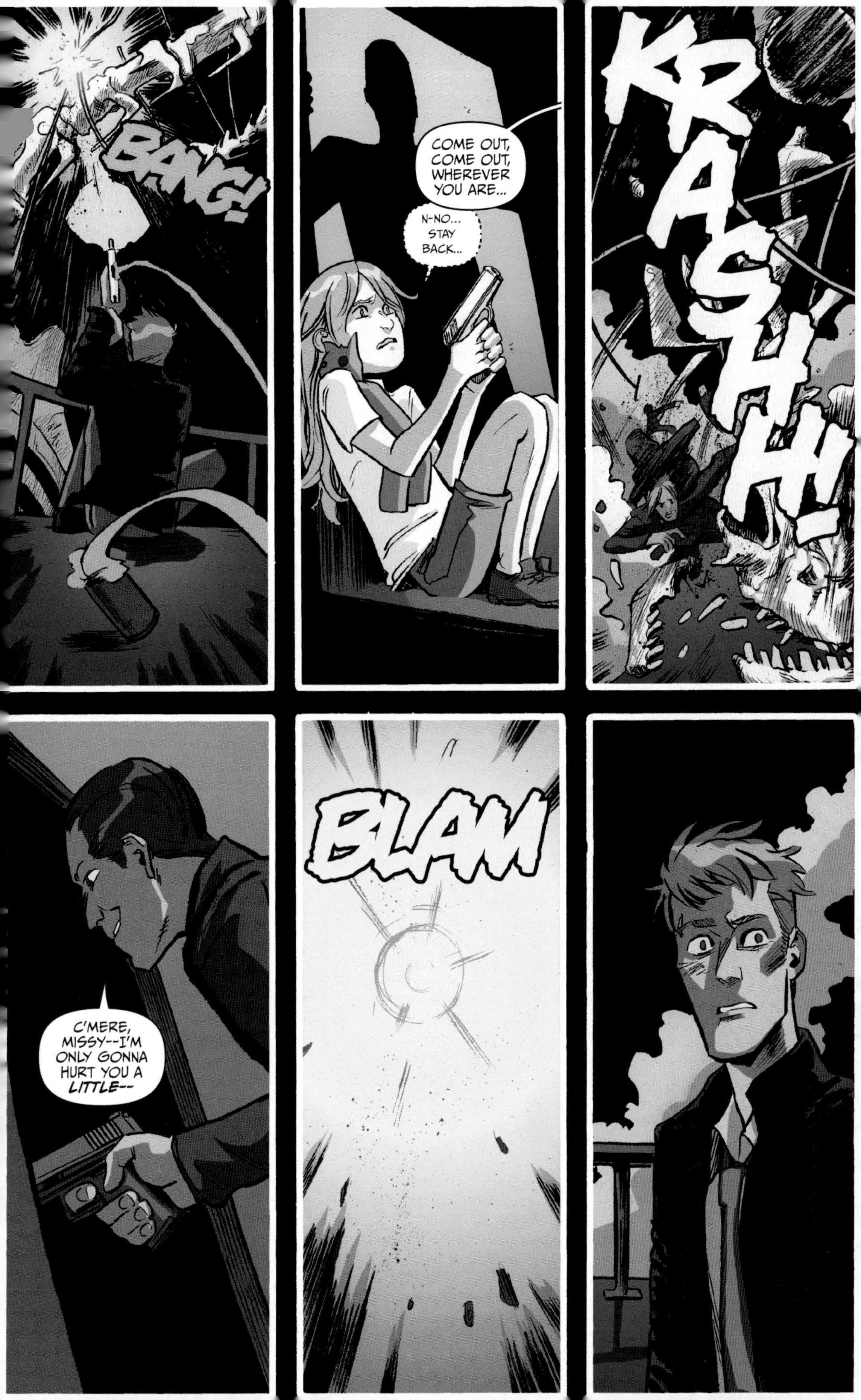
BANG!
COME OUT, COME OUT, WHEREVER YOU ARE...
N-NO... STAY BACK...
KRASH!
C'MERE, MISSY--I'M ONLY GONNA HURT YOU A LITTLE--
BLAM

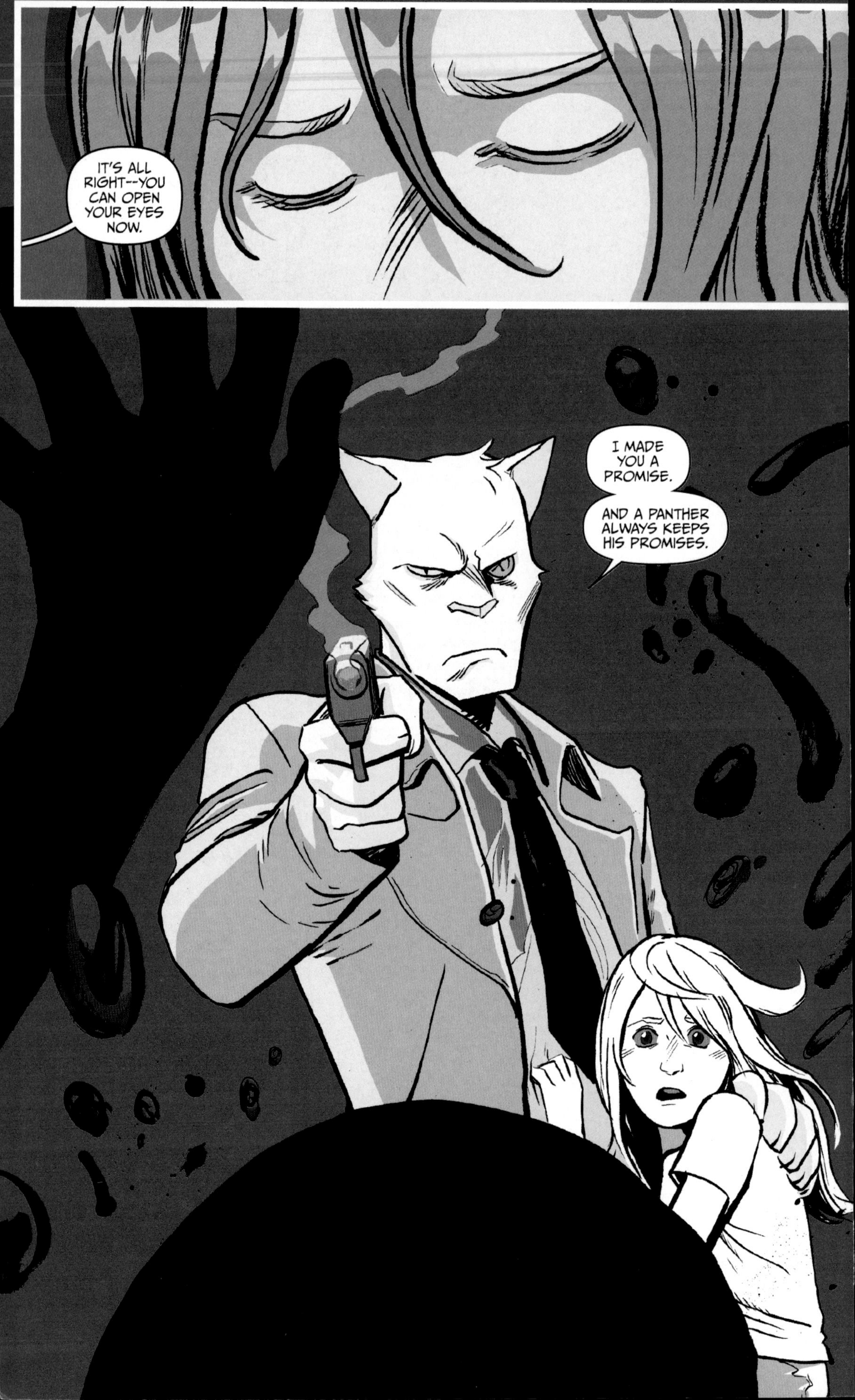
IT'S ALL RIGHT--YOU CAN OPEN YOUR EYES NOW.
I MADE YOU A PROMISE.
AND A PANTHER ALWAYS KEEPS HIS PROMISES.

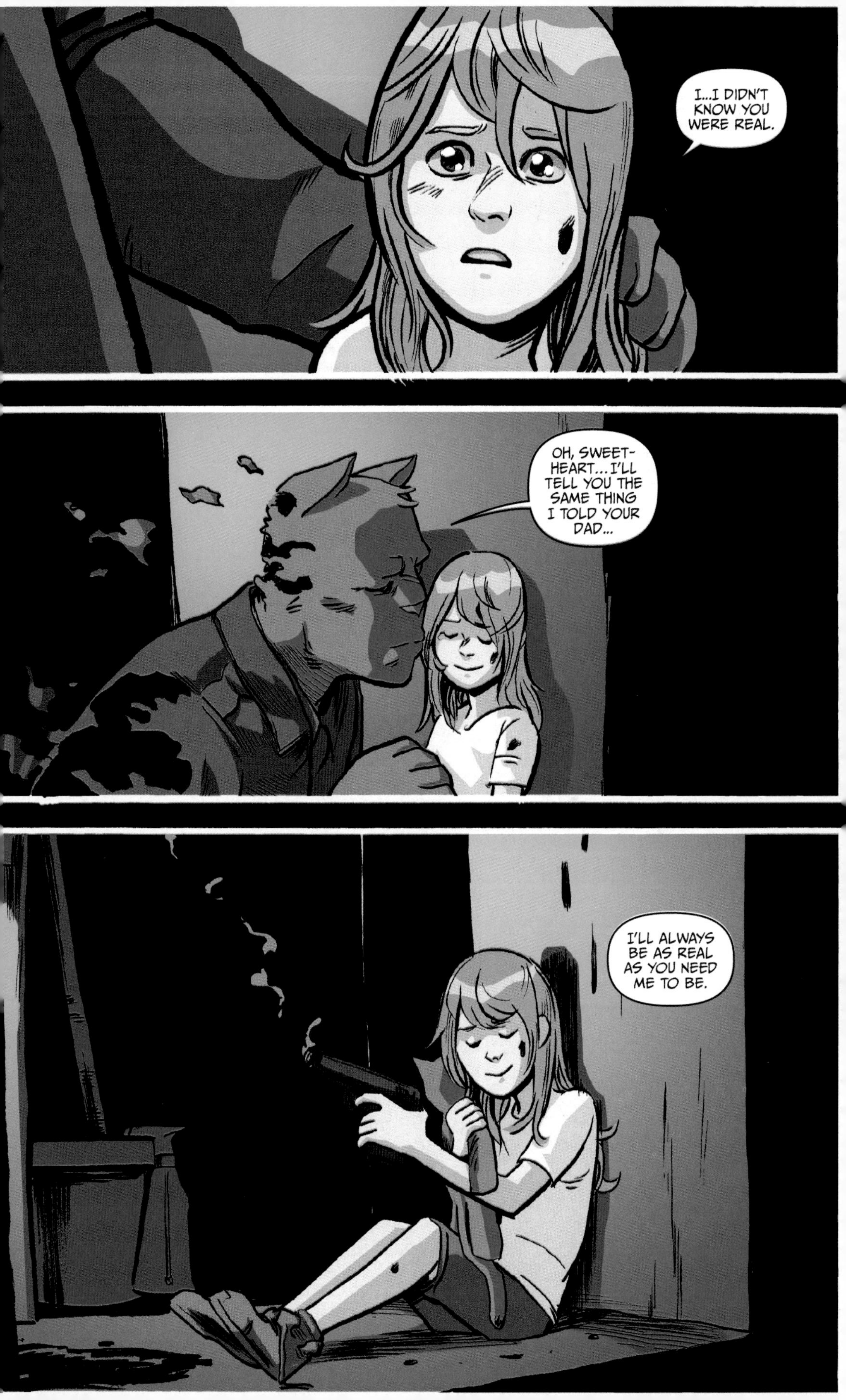
I...I DIDN'T KNOW YOU WERE REAL.
OH, SWEET-HEART... I'LL TELL YOU THE SAME THING I TOLD YOUR DAD...
I'LL ALWAYS BE AS REAL AS YOU NEED ME TO BE.

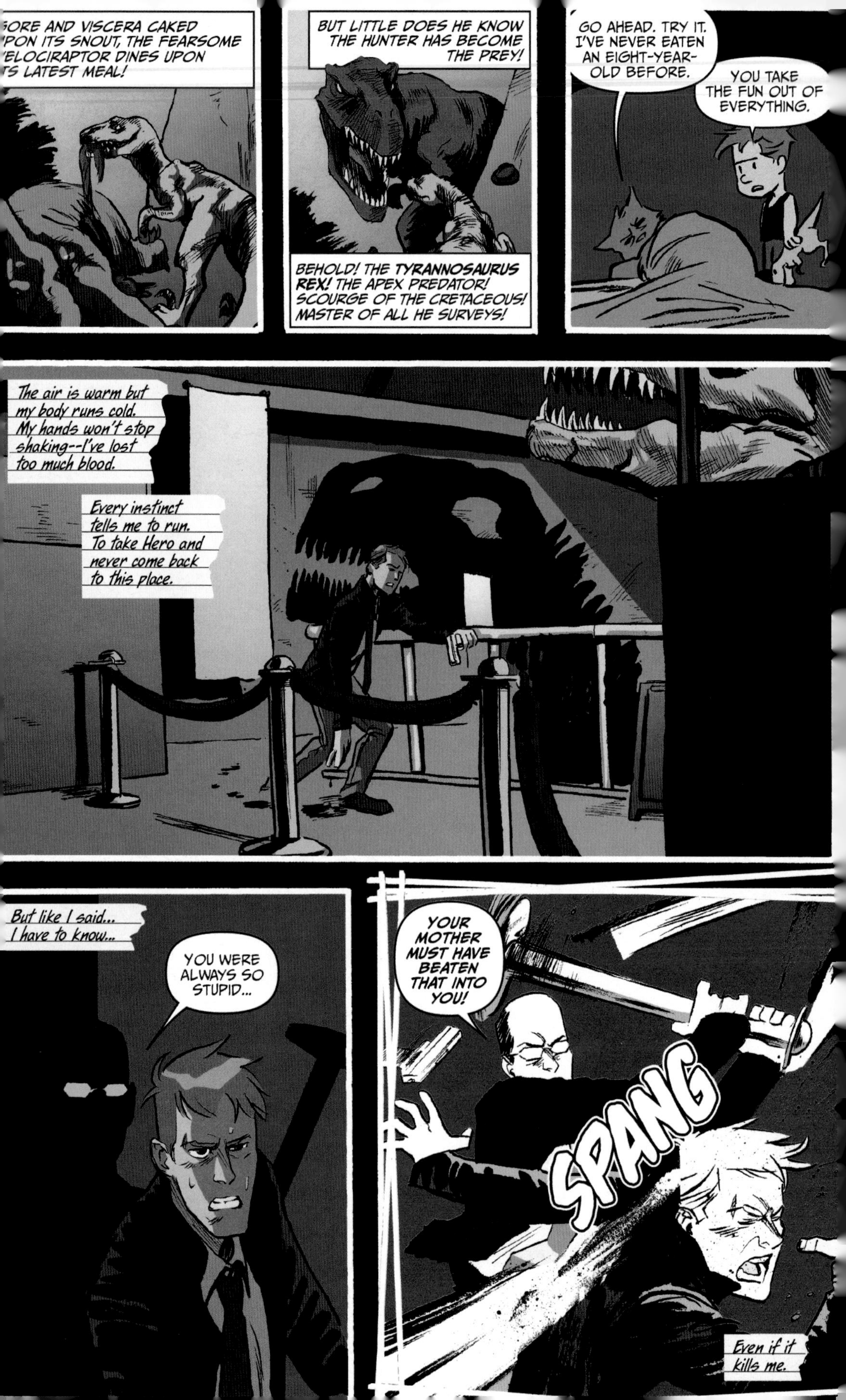
GORE AND VISCERA CAKED UPON ITS SNOUT, THE FEARSOME VELOCIRAPTOR DINES UPON ITS LATEST MEAL!
BUT LITTLE DOES HE KNOW THE HUNTER HAS BECOME THE PREY!
BEHOLD! THE TYRANNOSAURUS REX! THE APEX PREDATOR! SCOURGE OF THE CRETACEOUS! MASTER OF ALL HE SURVEYS!
GO AHEAD. TRY IT. I'VE NEVER EATEN AN EIGHT-YEAR-OLD BEFORE.
YOU TAKE THE FUN OUT OF EVERYTHING.
The air is warm but my body runs cold. My hands won't stop shaking--I've lost too much blood.
Every instinct tells me to run. To take Hero and never come back to this place.
But like I said... I have to know...
YOU WERE ALWAYS SO STUPID...
YOUR MOTHER MUST HAVE BEATEN THAT INTO YOU!
SPANG
Even if it kills me.

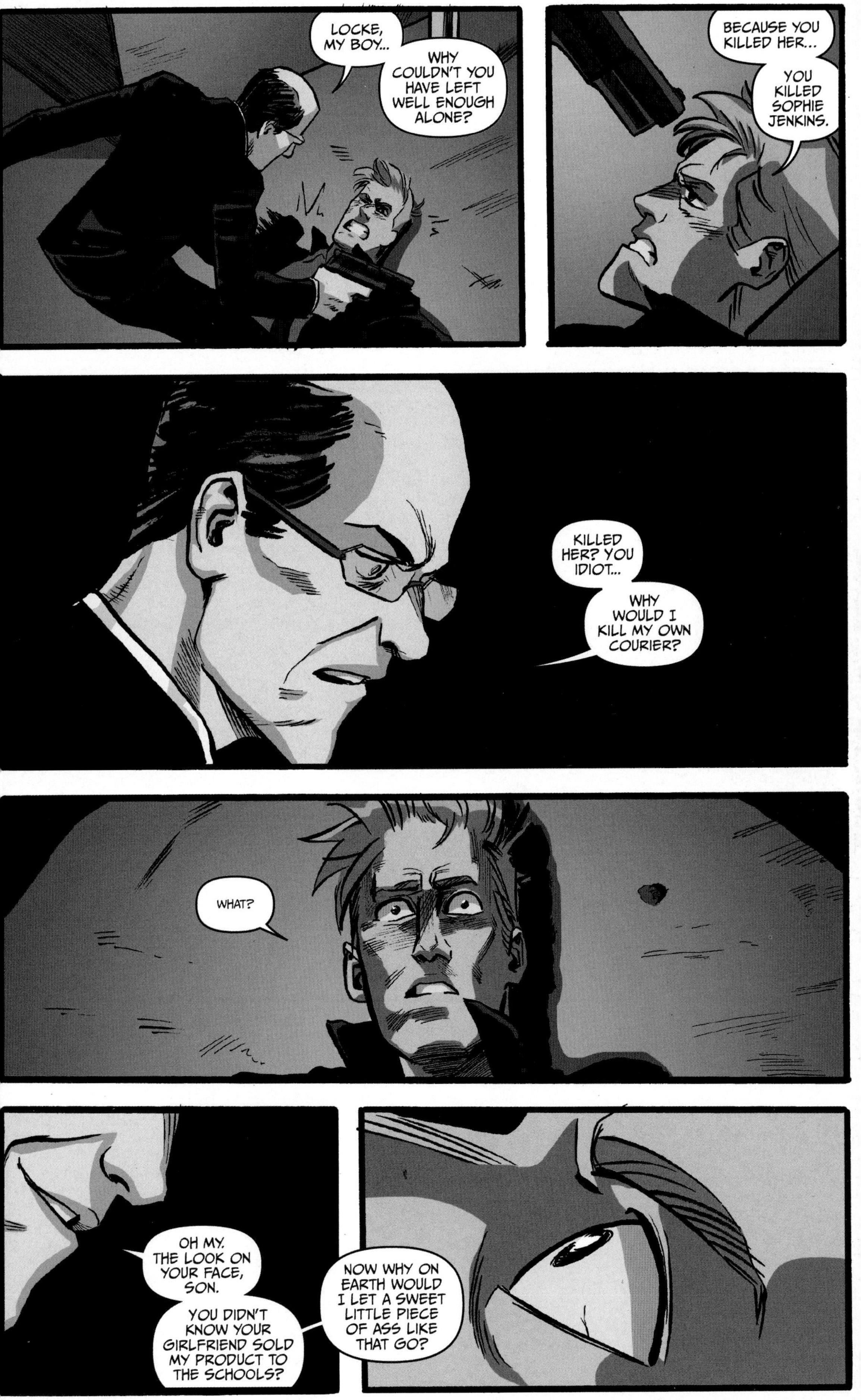
LOCKE, MY BOY...
WHY COULDN'T YOU HAVE LEFT WELL ENOUGH ALONE?
BECAUSE YOU KILLED HER...
YOU KILLED SOPHIE JENKINS.
KILLED HER? YOU IDIOT...
WHY WOULD I KILL MY OWN COURIER?
WHAT?
OH MY. THE LOOK ON YOUR FACE, SON.
YOU DIDN'T KNOW YOUR GIRLFRIEND SOLD MY PRODUCT TO THE SCHOOLS?
NOW WHY ON EARTH WOULD I LET A SWEET LITTLE PIECE OF ASS LIKE THAT GO?

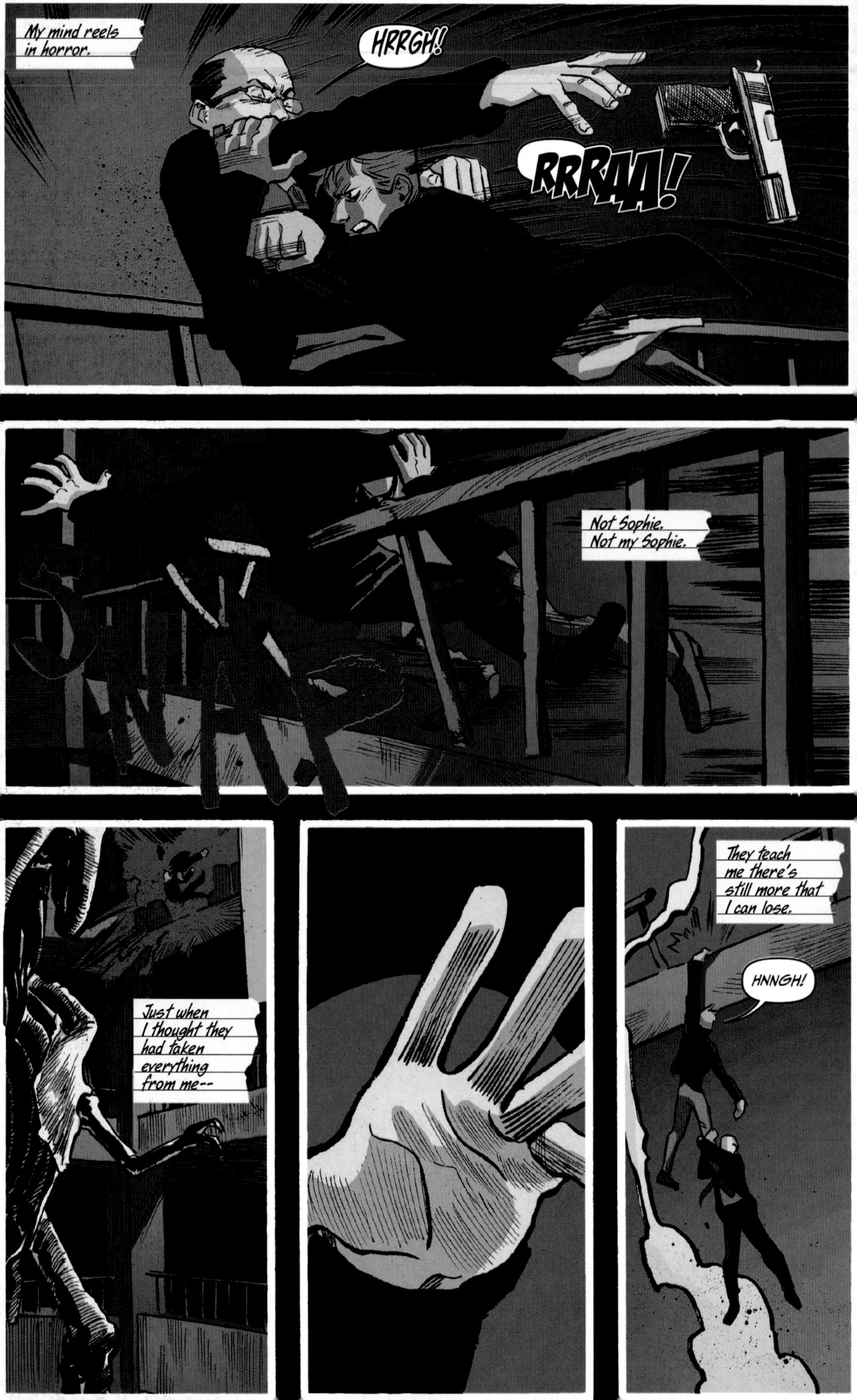
My mind reels in horror.
HRRGH!
RRRAAA!
Not Sophie. Not my Sophie.
Just when I thought they had taken everything from me--
They teach me there's still more that I can lose.
HNNGH!

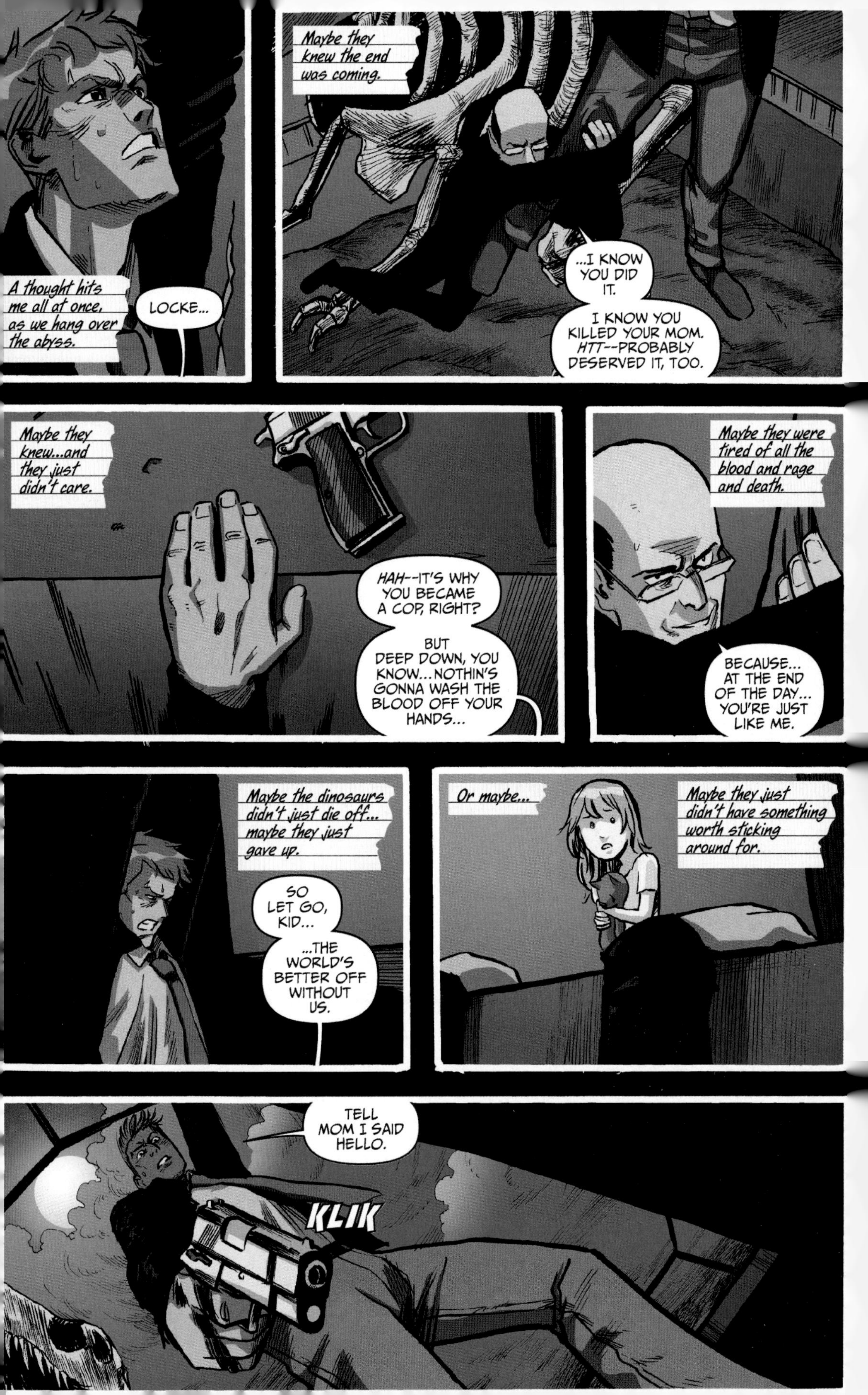

A thought hits me all at once, as we hang over the abyss.
LOCKE...
Maybe they knew the end was coming.
...I KNOW YOU DID IT.
I KNOW YOU KILLED YOUR MOM. HTT--PROBABLY DESERVED IT, TOO.
Maybe they knew...and they just didn't care.
HAH--IT'S WHY YOU BECAME A COP, RIGHT?
BUT DEEP DOWN, YOU KNOW...NOTHIN'S GONNA WASH THE BLOOD OFF YOUR HANDS...
Maybe they were tired of all the blood and rage and death.
BECAUSE... AT THE END OF THE DAY... YOU'RE JUST LIKE ME.
Maybe the dinosaurs didn't just die off... maybe they just gave up.
SO LET GO, KID...
...THE WORLD'S BETTER OFF WITHOUT US.
Or maybe...
Maybe they just didn't have something worth sticking around for.
TELL MOM I SAID HELLO.
KLIK

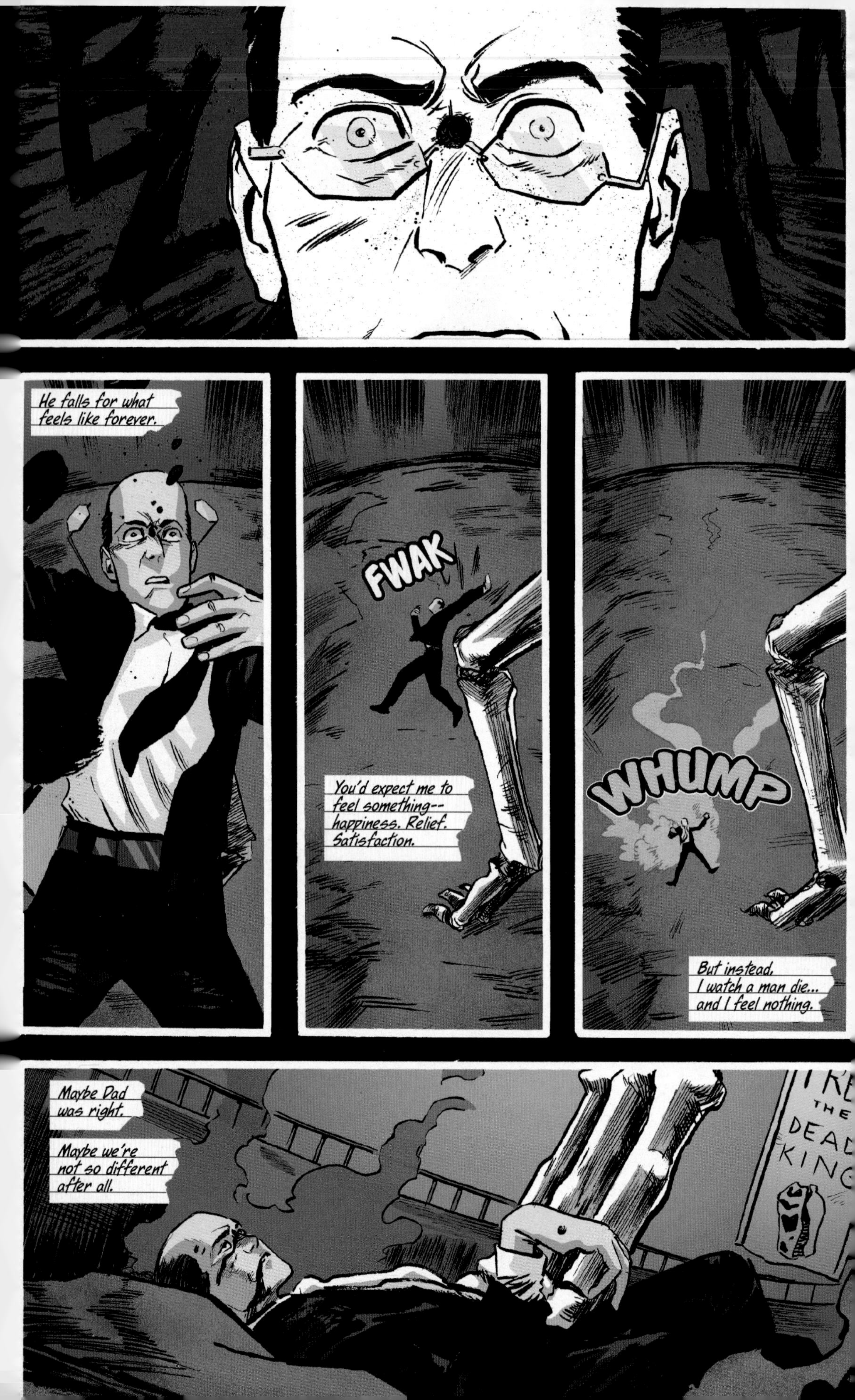
He falls for what feels like forever.
FWAK
You'd expect me to feel something-- happiness. Relief. Satisfaction.
WHUMP
But instead, I watch a man die... and I feel nothing.
Maybe Dad was right.
Maybe we're not so different after all.

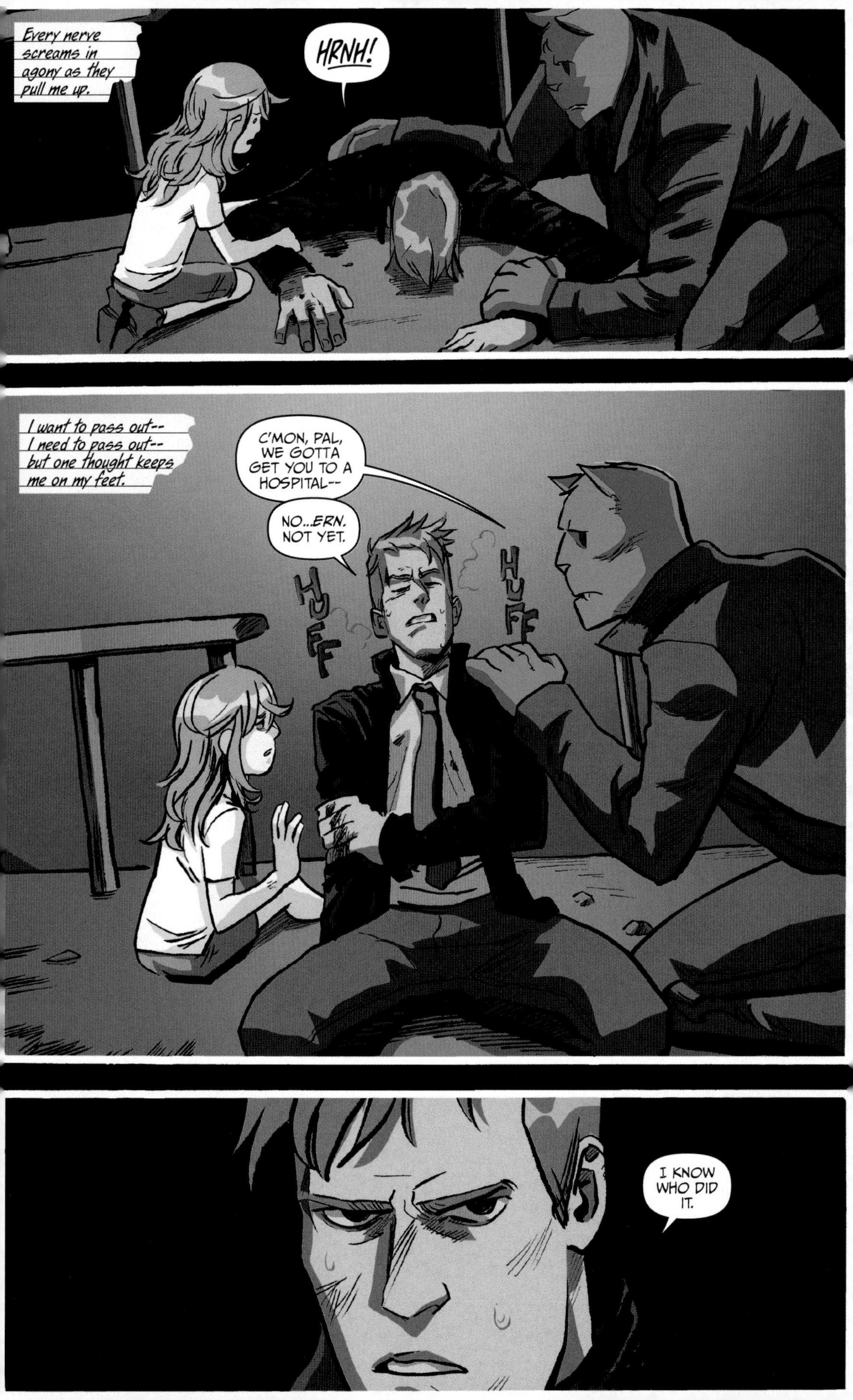
Every nerve screams in agony as they pull me up.
HRNH!
I want to pass out-- I need to pass out-- but one thought keeps me on my feet.
C'MON, PAL, WE GOTTA GET YOU TO A HOSPITAL--
NO...ERN. NOT YET.
HUFF
HUFF
I KNOW WHO DID IT.

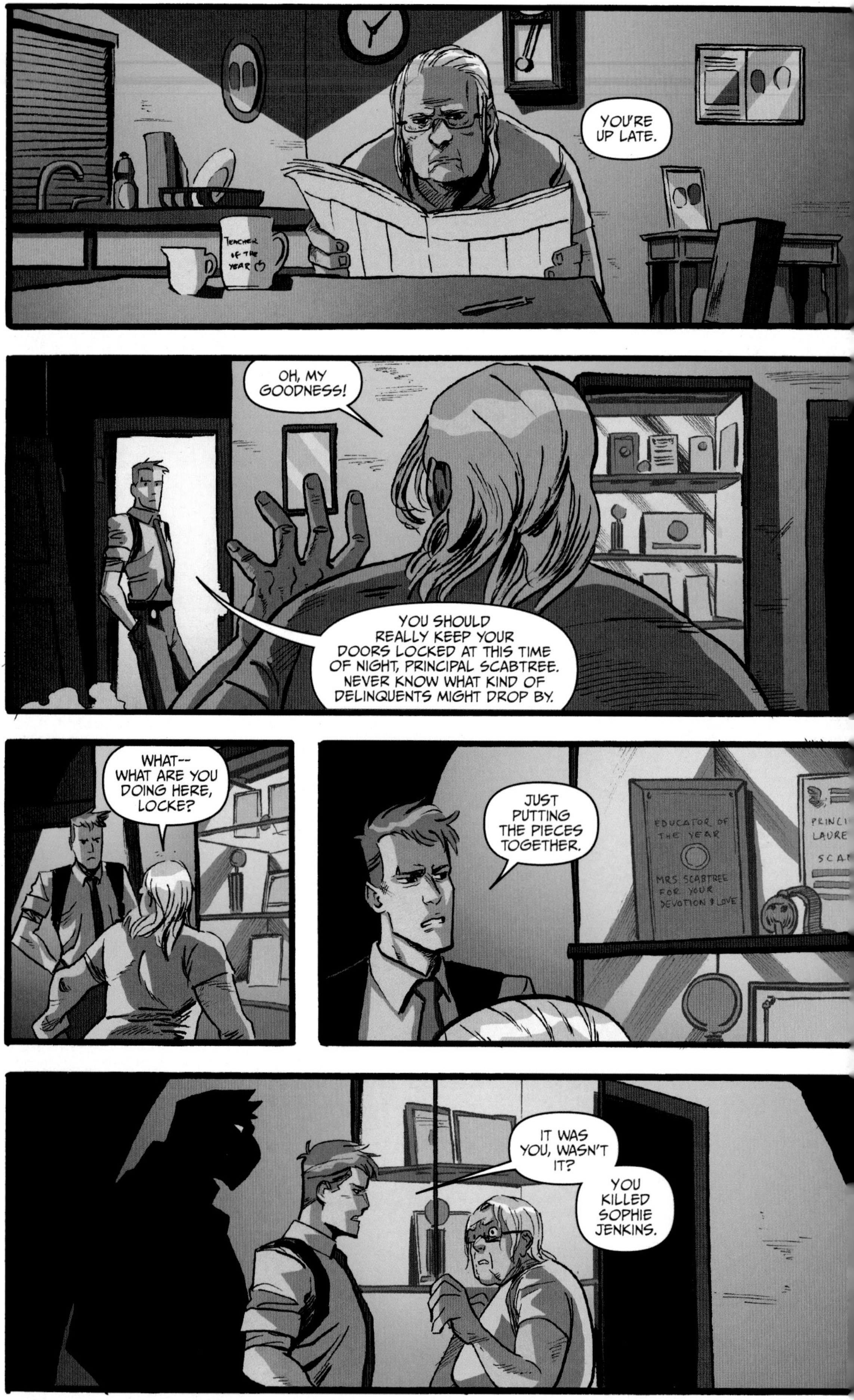
TEACHER OF THE YEAR
YOU'RE UP LATE.
OH, MY GOODNESS!
YOU SHOULD REALLY KEEP YOUR DOORS LOCKED AT THIS TIME OF NIGHT, PRINCIPAL SCABTREE. NEVER KNOW WHAT KIND OF DELINQUENTS MIGHT DROP BY.
WHAT-- WHAT ARE YOU DOING HERE, LOCKE?
JUST PUTTING THE PIECES TOGETHER.
EDUCATOR OF THE YEAR
MRS SCABTREE FOR YOUR DEVOTION & LOVE
IT WAS YOU, WASN'T IT?
YOU KILLED SOPHIE JENKINS.

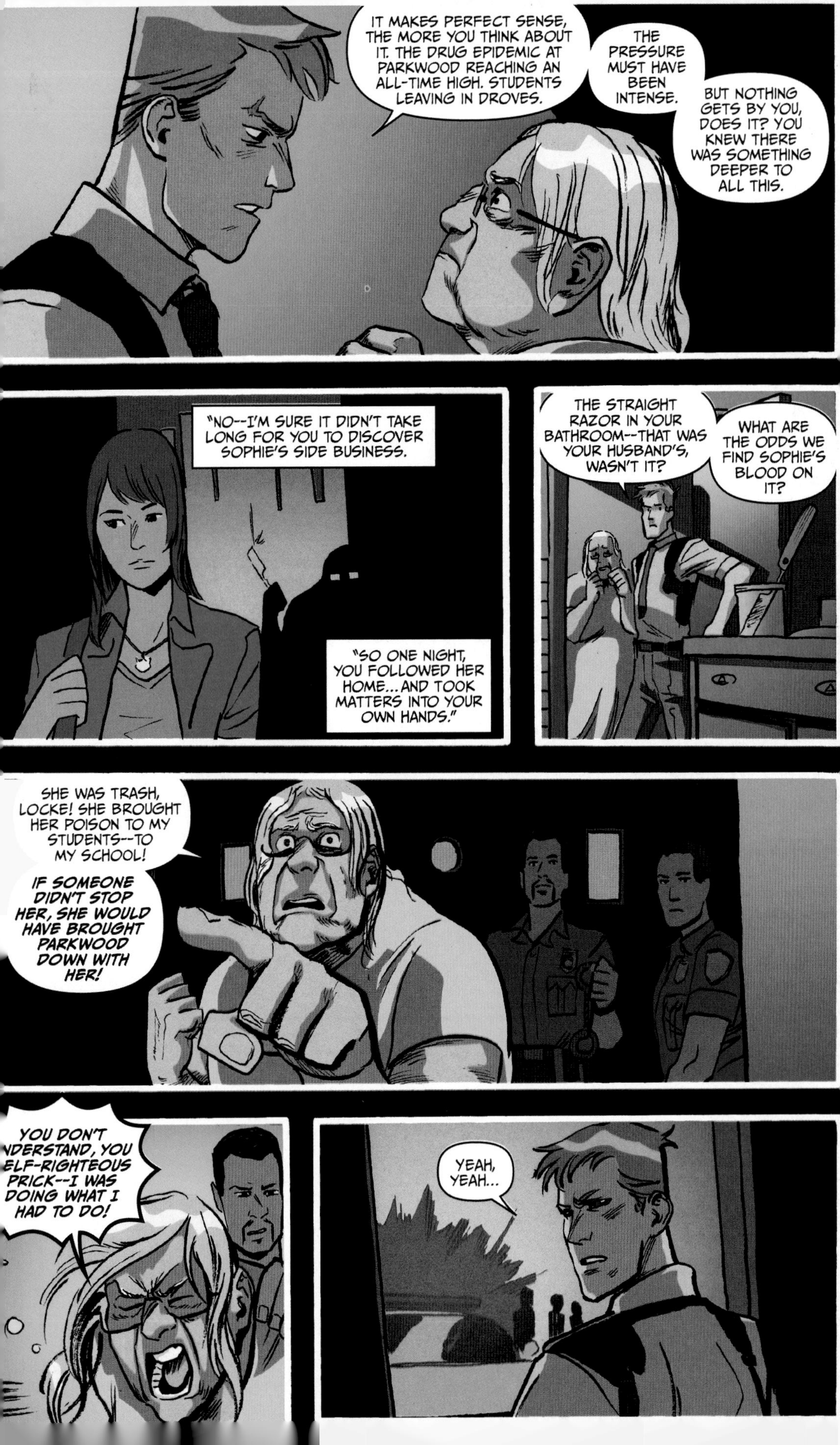
IT MAKES PERFECT SENSE, THE MORE YOU THINK ABOUT IT. THE DRUG EPIDEMIC AT PARKWOOD REACHING AN ALL-TIME HIGH. STUDENTS LEAVING IN DROVES.
THE PRESSURE MUST HAVE BEEN INTENSE.
BUT NOTHING GETS BY YOU, DOES IT? YOU KNEW THERE WAS SOMETHING DEEPER TO ALL THIS.
"NO--I'M SURE IT DIDN'T TAKE LONG FOR YOU TO DISCOVER SOPHIE'S SIDE BUSINESS.
"SO ONE NIGHT, YOU FOLLOWED HER HOME...AND TOOK MATTERS INTO YOUR OWN HANDS."
THE STRAIGHT RAZOR IN YOUR BATHROOM--THAT WAS YOUR HUSBAND'S, WASN'T IT?
WHAT ARE THE ODDS WE FIND SOPHIE'S BLOOD ON IT?
SHE WAS TRASH, LOCKE! SHE BROUGHT HER POISON TO MY STUDENTS--TO MY SCHOOL!
IF SOMEONE DIDN'T STOP HER, SHE WOULD HAVE BROUGHT PARKWOOD DOWN WITH HER!
YOU DON'T NDERSTAND, YOU ELF-RIGHTEOUS PRICK--I WAS DOING WHAT I HAD TO DO!
YEAH, YEAH...

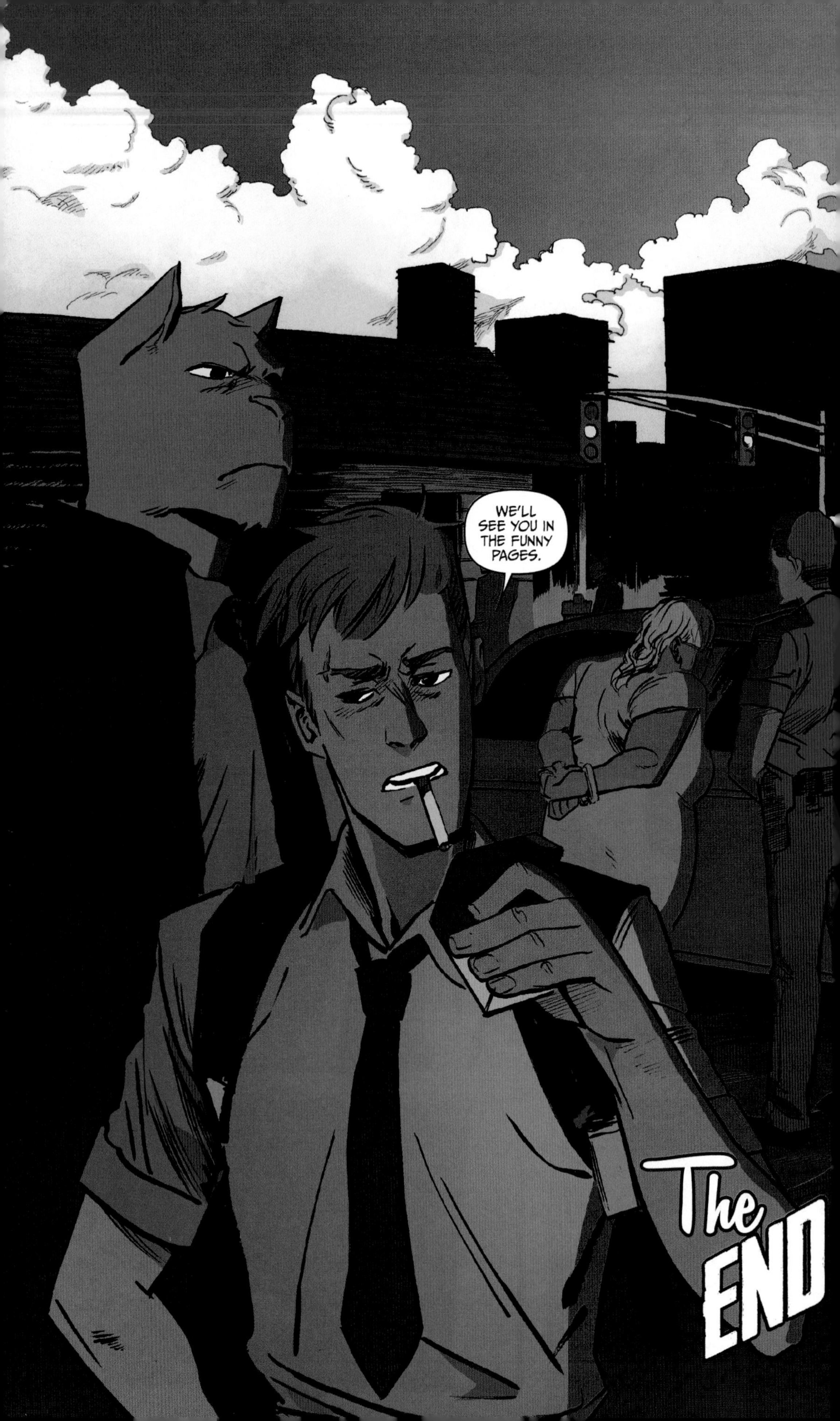
WE'LL SEE YOU IN THE FUNNY PAGES.
The END

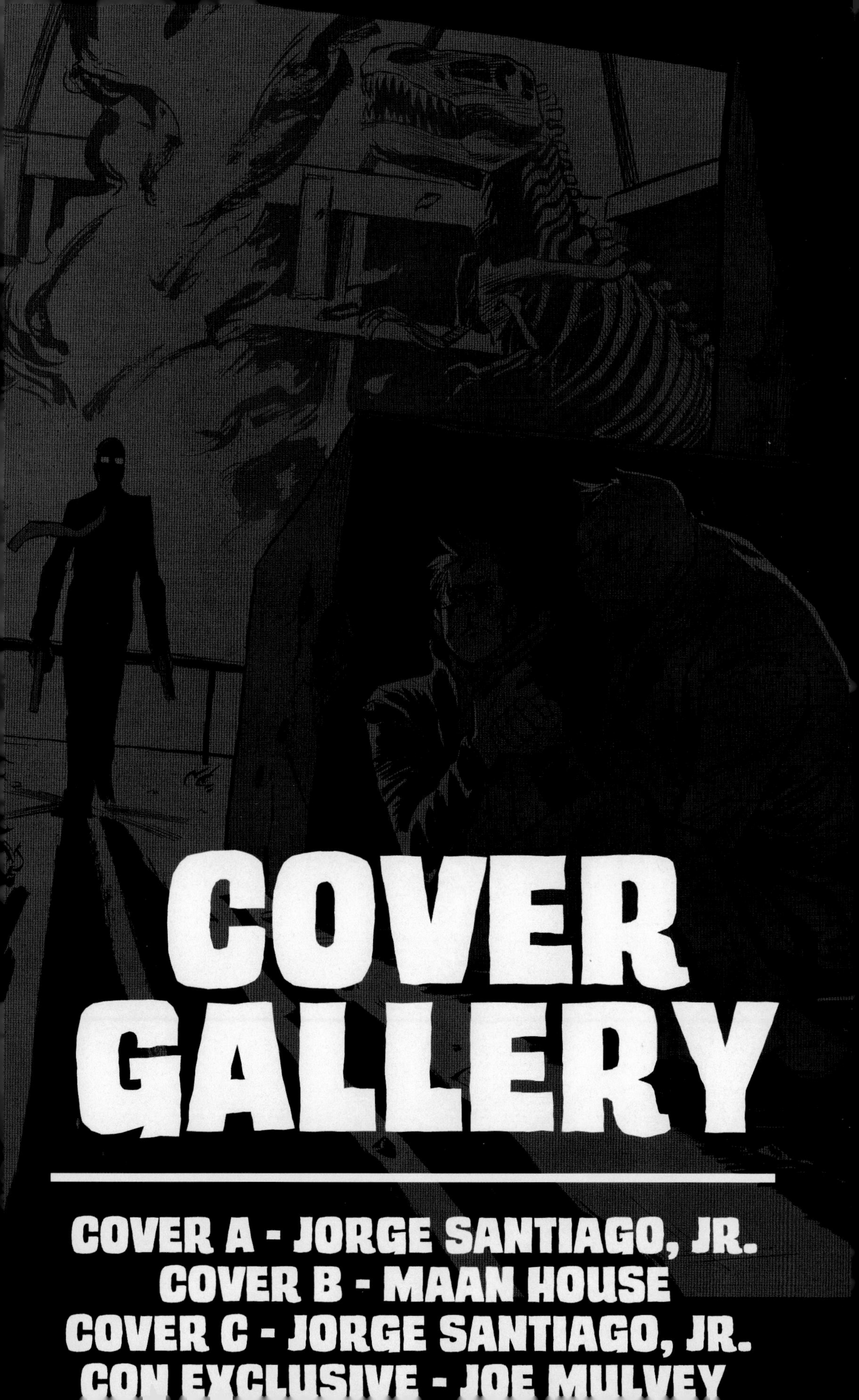

COVER GALLERY

COVER A - JORGE SANTIAGO, JR.
COVER B - MAAN HOUSE
COVER C - JORGE SANTIAGO, JR.
CON EXCLUSIVE - JOE MULVEY

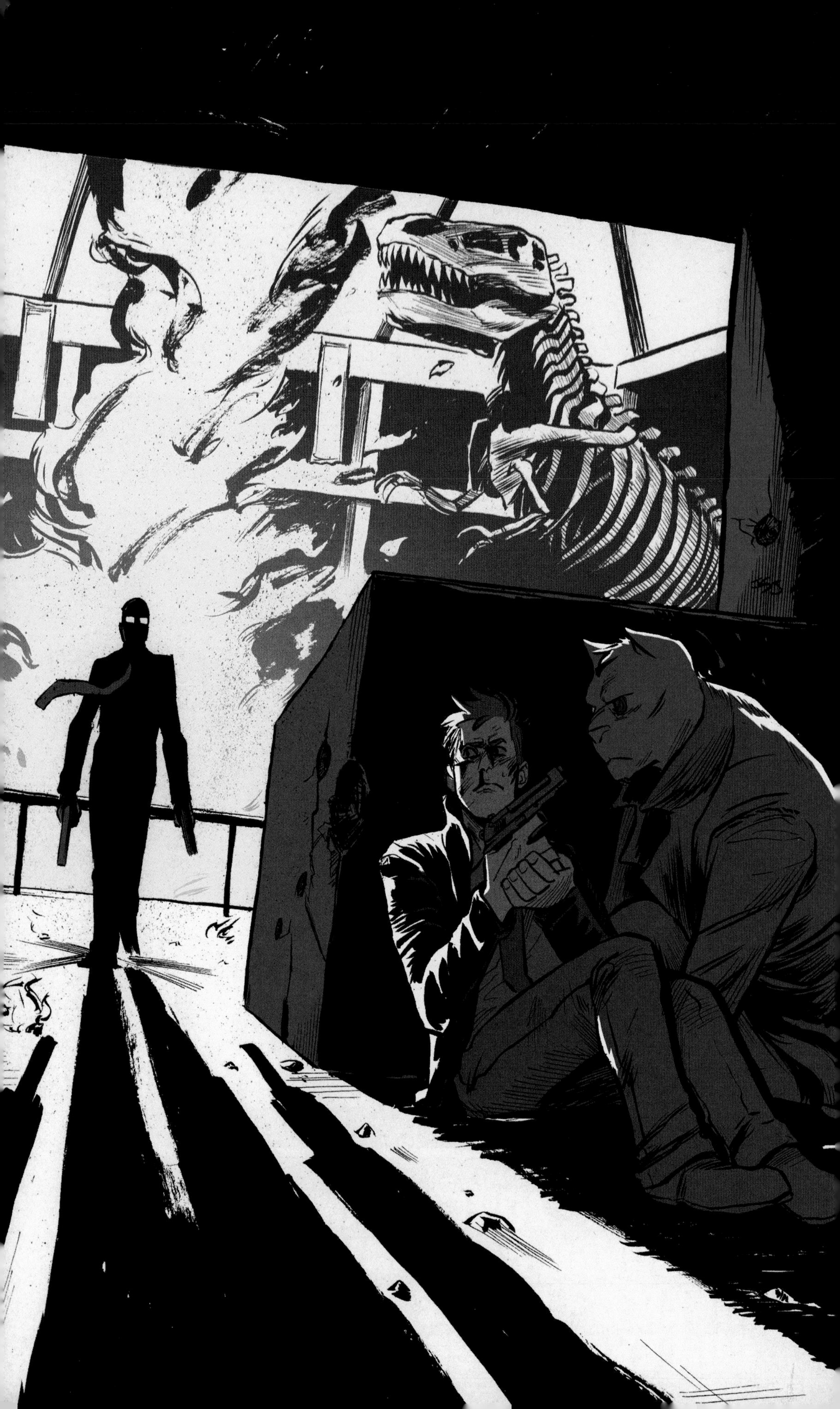

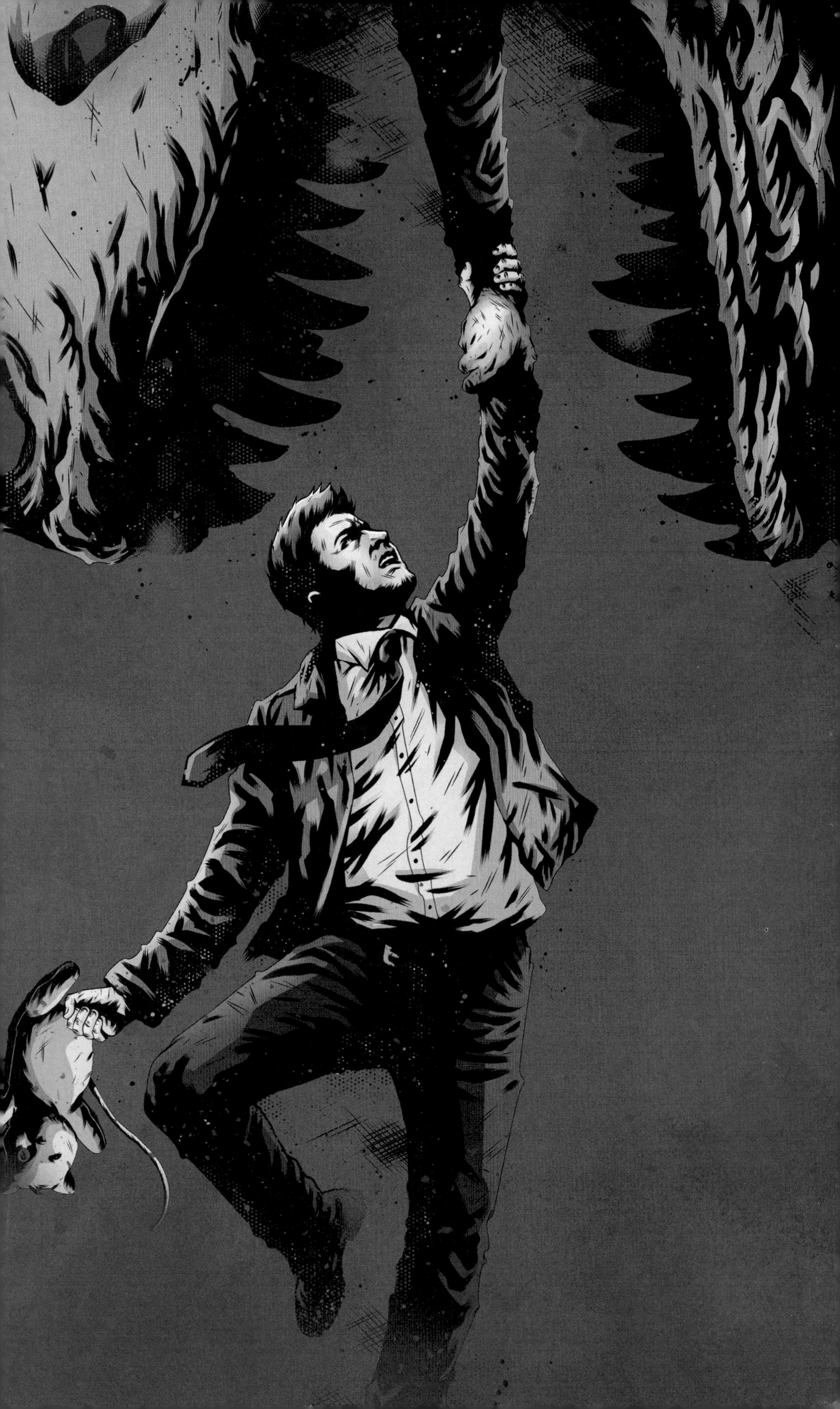

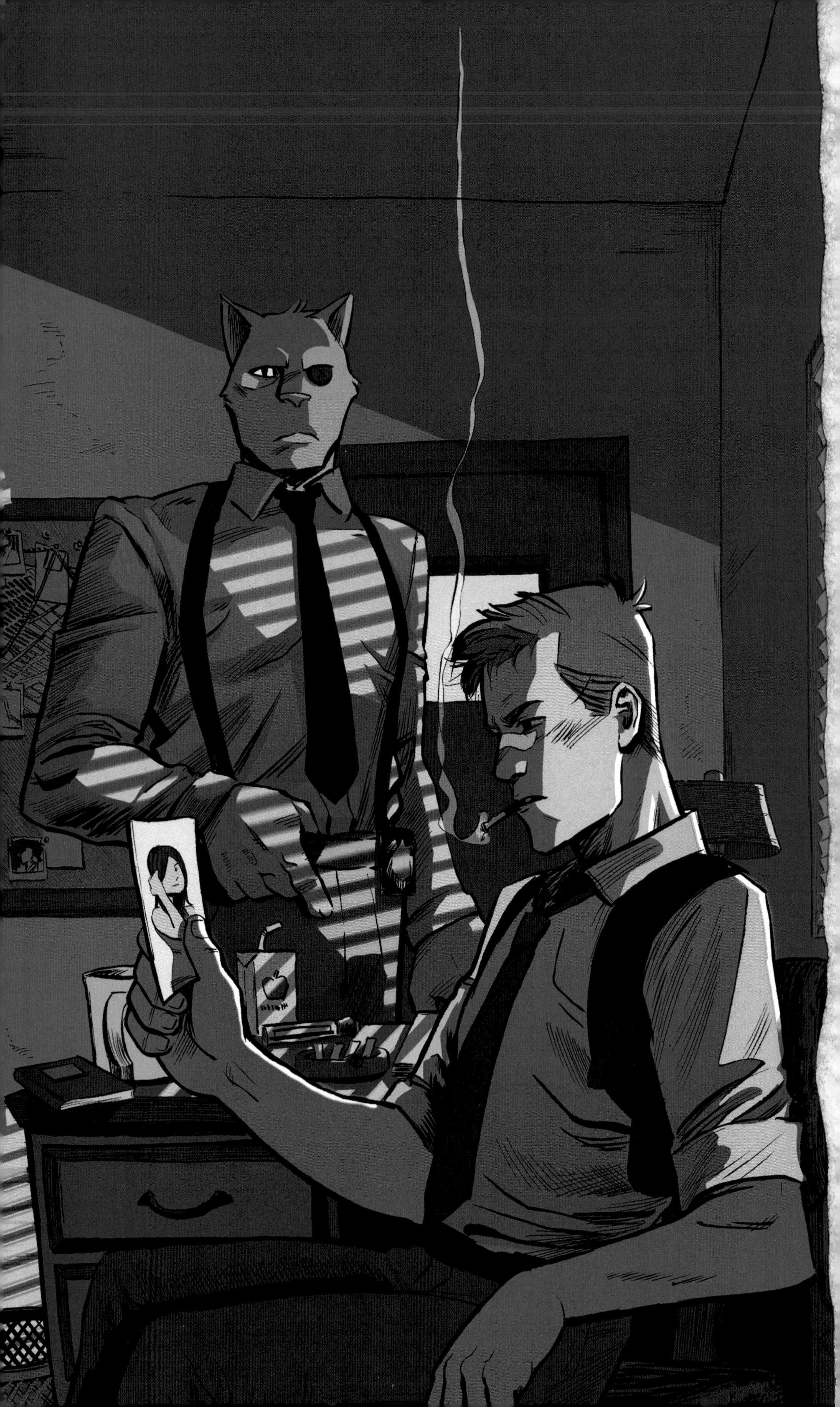

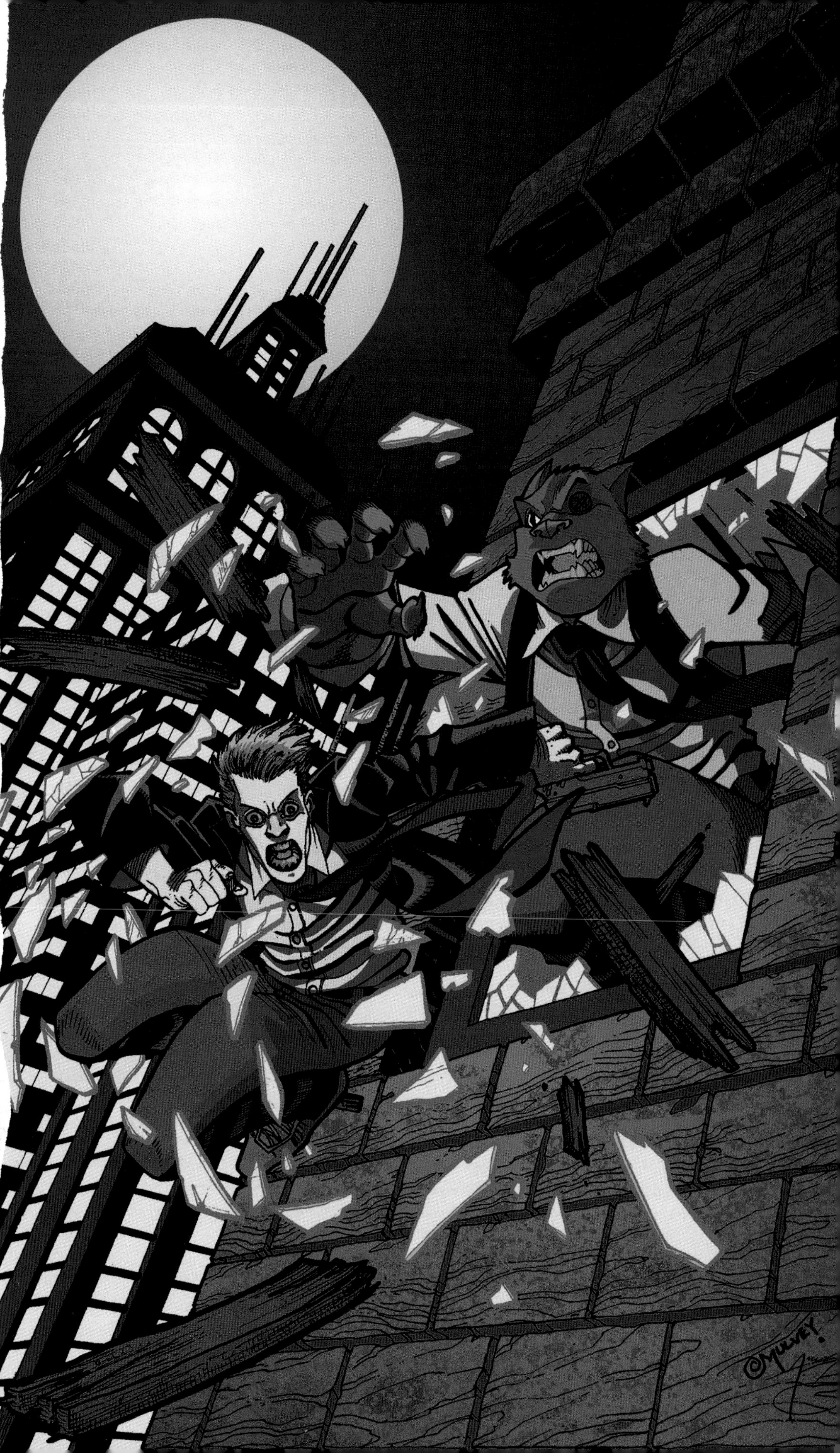
©MULVEY!

AFTERWORD
BY DAVID PEPOSE

"Why would I ever want to stop?"

Everybody's got friends. Some of them are just imaginary. But as I look at SPENCER & LOCKE, it's hard not to feel as if they were my own flesh and blood. There's plenty of ways you could describe this story — a parody, a black comedy, a hard-boiled noir drama — and you wouldn't be wrong.

But at the end of the day, I think SPENCER & LOCKE is a love letter.

A love letter to the creativity and craft of comics. To pioneers like Bill Watterson and Frank Miller — the spiritual godfathers of SPENCER & LOCKE — who have forgotten more about how to make comics than I'll ever hope to know. To the hours we spent as kids reading and loving these books, enough to take the insane leap of creating comics of our own. We stood on the shoulders of giants to create this book, and I'll always be grateful.

Yet along the way, SPENCER & LOCKE became something else entirely. It wasn't just a story about storytelling — it became a story of redemption. That underneath all the pain and the sadness and the shame, it's never too late to hope again. That if Locke can survive the demons of his past, then dammit, so can you. I'm not afraid to say there's more than a little bit of Locke inside me — that I've been prone to doubt, to self-recrimination, to replaying my own fears and failures and heartaches over and over again.

But SPENCER & LOCKE reminded me that I wasn't alone. That I didn't have to be defined by my scars. And I hope they'll remind you of that, too.

Books like this don't come out of thin air, and I'd be lying if I pretended the magic of SPENCER & LOCKE didn't come from our entire creative team. Thank you to Jorge, my artist and partner-in-crime, not just for your long hours and immense skill bringing this story to life, but also for being the first to believe; to Jasen, our colorist, who worked tirelessly to make this comic pop off the stands; to Colin, our letterer, who turned my scripts into something readable; to Maan, Joe and Ben, who drew some amazing pieces of art to show off our book; and to Dave, Bryan, Shawn, Danielle, Nicole and the rest of the Action Lab team for giving us this incredible opportunity.

And most of all, I want to thank you, our readers. For taking this journey. For believing in us. And for never, ever stopping. Because SPENCER & LOCKE may be imaginary... but they'll always be as real as you need them to be.

- David Pepose

AFTERWORD
BY JORGE SANTIAGO, JR.

Before I get started, let me thank you. If you're reading this, it means you've read the book all the way to the end, and for that I'm grateful!

When I was 16 or 17, I was brought back into comics by Ranma ½, and what began as a hobby has become a compulsion. I have to make comics — I get ill when I don't, no lie. I've been steadily piling on the pages for years because I need to, but I've always yearned for my work to make it into comic stores. As much as I've enjoyed self-publishing (and I still do!), my dream is for my book to be widely available for everyone's enjoyment!

The response to SPENCER & LOCKE has been astonishing. This is my first professionally published work, and in the time since David first pitched me this project, it has been a bevy of new and exciting experiences. You don't realize when you're doing a book alone what it's like to work with another person, let alone have them provide you a script, or color your work, or put all of the speech bubbles in place, or print it and get it into the hands of readers. When people ask how I feel, I say it feels unreal.

I need to thank a lot of people, because this work didn't happen by itself. I have to thank my Mom and Dad for giving me the bravery to strive for my dreams; my awesome friends for their unending support when I was tired and hungry; my professors who taught me the skills I needed to make the best art possible; the retailers who took a chance and gave us a platform to put our work on display; and the professionals who gave my art a thorough and honest critique so I could improve and make steps toward their level.

I need to thank our publisher Action Lab for taking a chance on our book and letting us tell the story we wanted to tell. I want to thank Jasen and Colin for adding so much atmosphere and power to my art I couldn't convey alone; without you, this book would not have been the success that it has been. And lastly, I need to thank David, who took a chance on a weirdo comic machine from Texas, and even through all the long emails on panel layouts and page design, still trusted me enough to be his co-creator. Thank you, man — you made this all happen, and I hope you know how grateful I am.

I want to thank the readers again for their love and support on the book. You all are what made this book the slice of heaven that is was, so I am indebted to you. I hope when you see our names in the future, you smile and remember a fun story with a lot of love (and gunshots) on every page!

We'll see you soon, most likely on a Wednesday. Keep that pullbox open!

- Jorge Santiago, Jr.

ABOUT THE CREATORS

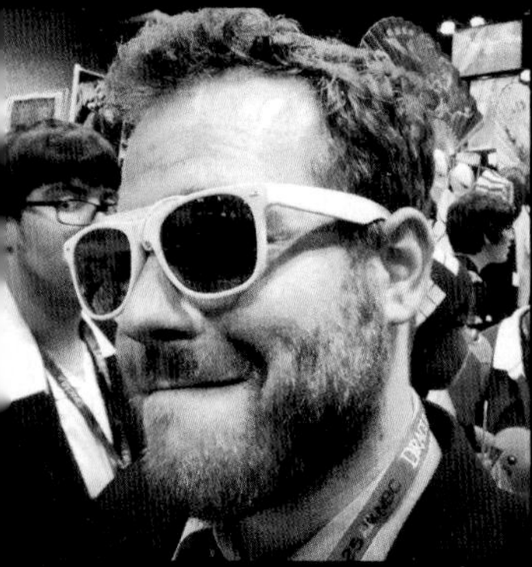

DAVID PEPOSE

David Pepose covered crime and politics at newspapers around the country before making the jump to comics, TV and film companies such as DC Comics, CBS Entertainment and Netflix. SPENCER & LOCKE is his first published comic. Follow him on Twitter at @peposed.

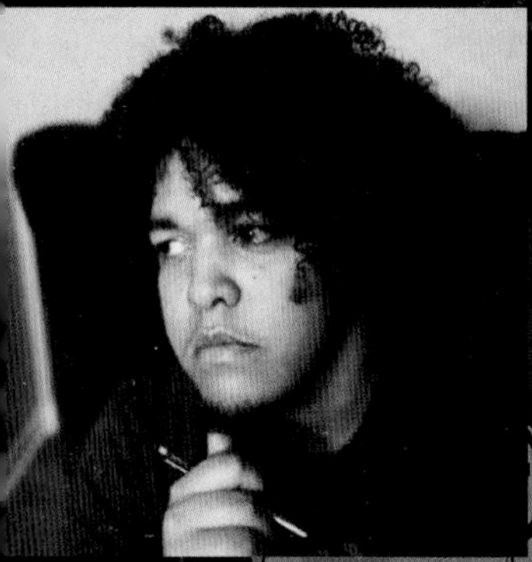

JORGE SANTIAGO, JR.

Jorge Santiago, Jr. self-published for years before getting his MFA in Sequential Art from the Savannah College of Art and Design. When not graphic designing, he is usually working on his hit webcomic, CURSE OF THE EEL. Follow him on Twitter at @jorgesantiagojr.

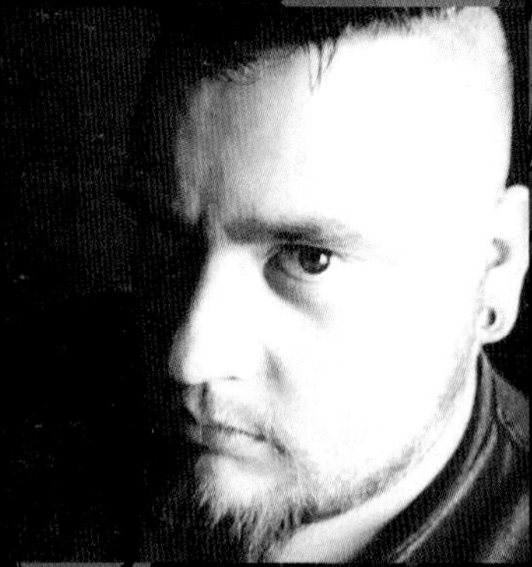

JASEN SMITH

Jasen Smith has worked as a newspaper writer, cartoonist and voice jockey before landing a job as a colorist at the popular studio Hi-Fi. He has worked on comics from publishers such as Image, DC Comics, Top Cow, Aspen and more. Follow him on Twitter at @jasen_smith.

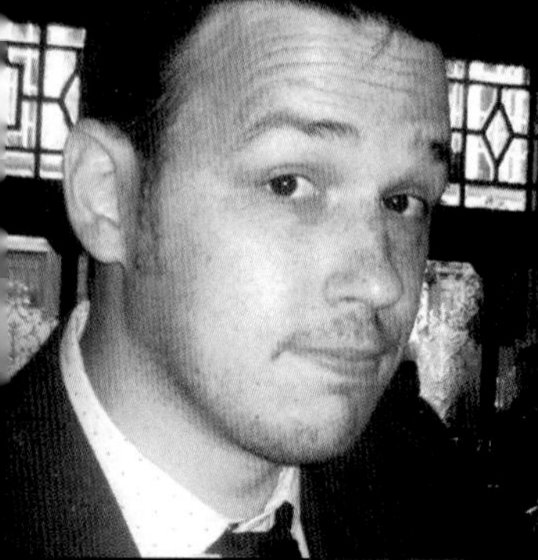

COLIN BELL

Colin Bell is known not only for his lettering work at publishers such as Image, Dark Horse and BOOM! Studios, but also for being the SICBA Award-winning writer of DUNGEON FUN and the backup strips for Titan Comics' DOCTOR WHO: THE TWELFTH DOCTOR. Follow him on Twitter at @colinbell.